Nations of the Modern World
Malaysia: Economic Expansion
and National Unity

John Gullick

Malaysia:
Economic Expansion and
National Unity

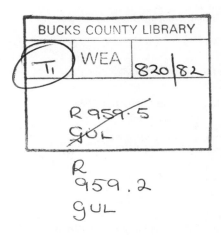

London • Ernest Benn
Boulder, Colorado • Westview Press

First published 1981 by Ernest Benn Limited
25 New Street Square, Fleet Street, London EC4A 3JA
& Sovereign Way, Tonbridge, Kent TN9 1RW
and Westview Press
5500 Central Avenue, Boulder, Colorado 80301
Frederick A. Praeger, Publisher

Distributed in Canada by
The General Publishing Company Limited, Toronto

A Nations of the Modern World Book

British Library Cataloguing in Publication Data

Gullick, John Michael
    Malaysia — (Nations of the modern world).
    1. Malaysia — History
    I. Title
    959.5   D5596

    ISBN 0-510-39043-9

Library of Congress Cataloging in Publication Data

Gullick, John
    Malaysia: economic expansion and national unity.
    (Nations of the modern world)
    Bibliography: p.
    Includes index.
    1. Malaysia. 2. Malaysia — Economic conditions. 3. Malaysia — Politics and gov-
ernment. I. Title. II. Series.
DS596.G8 1981   959.5   81-991
ISBN 0-86531-089-0 (Westview Press)   AACR2

Printed and bound in the United States of America

Contents

Contents

Illustrations

Illustrations appear between pages 158 and 159.

1. Sir Hugh Low, British Resident, Perak 1877-89

2. Tengku Abdul Rahman, Prime Minister 1957-70, in May 1977

3. Tun Abdul Razak, Prime Minister 1970-76, in May 1974

4. Datu Hussein Onn, Prime Minister since 1976, in March 1979

5. General Sir Gerald Templer, High Commissioner of the Federation of Malaya, witnessed by six representatives from Tanjong Malim, opens replies to his confidential questionnaire to each household of the town asking for information on local Communists, March 1952

6. The Emergency Special constables guard factory installations

7. Malaya's first King, the Yang di-Pertuan Agong, at the state opening of parliament in Kuala Lumpur in 1959

8. Federal elections, August 1974

9. Tapping a rubber tree

10. Cocoa seedlings in a Sabah nursery

11. Harvesting an oil palm by cutting through the stalk with a chisel

12. Rubber smallholders weighing their latex at a collecting station

13. Harvesting padi

14. Settlers' houses on a FELDA development scheme near Segamat, Johore

Illustrations

Illustration Credits

Acknowledgement for kind permission to reproduce illustrations is made to the following:

Camera Press, London: Photographs 5, 6, 7, 16, 19, 23, 24, 26, 27, and 29

The Guthrie Corporation, Malaysia: Photographs 11 and 17

The Natural Rubber Producers' Research Association: Photograph 9

The New Straits Times Press, Malaysia: Photographs 1, 2, 3, 4, 8, 10, 12, 13, 14, 15, 18, 20, 21, 22, 25, and 28

The Tourist Development Corporation of Malaysia, London: Photograph 30

Preface

In the preface to a revised edition the author has usually to do no more than invite attention to selected passages of the latest version which differ from those of the previous one. In this case, however, I have to explain why a revised edition, which covers the same range of topics, has been completely rewritten so that practically nothing of the text of the 1969 edition is repeated.

This is not to disparage the 1969 edition, which still appears to me to have been adequate for its purpose at the time when it was written. But 1969, as it turned out, was the end of an era for Malaysia. The euphoria of independence and of the successful formation of Malaysia in 1963 had passed. The British connection, preserved so harmoniously in the liquidation of the colonial regime, had begun to fade and Malaysia with the formation of ASEAN had sought to find her place in a regional Southeast Asian context. Above all, the upheaval and bloodshed of 13 May 1969 led to a suspension of the constitution and of normal political life for almost two years. It was not, as was predicted at the time, the death of a democracy. But the restored democracy of 1971 was subject to guidance and oriented towards objectives which were new. Since then Malaysia has successfully completed almost a decade of progress under new policies. It is in many respects a quite different society from that of a few years before. These themes will be developed in their place later in this book.

There are other and less unusual reasons for attempting a fresh appraisal of a country and a society which has been of absorbing interest to me since I first joined its civil service thirty-five years ago. A study of the current political, economic, and social aspects of a developing country must give special emphasis to the immediate past. In a situation of rapid change today is still the child of yesterday. But as time's winged chariot moves on, yesterday soon becomes the day before yesterday and the grandparent of today. The 1950s, which took up so much of the 1969 edition (and still more of the 1963 and 1965 editions of *Malaya* in this series), have now receded into the background and so deserve more condensed treatment — important as they still are.

A third reason for wholesale rewriting is the continuing flood of published work about Malaysia, old and new, written by scholars in many academic disciplines, historians, political scientists, economists, and sociologists. After eleven years (1945-56) as a working civil servant in Malaya I have had a quarter of a century of working association with one of the historic British businesses in Malaysia, founded in 1821. But whatever insights one's own experience may yield, the author of a general, synoptic study such as this owes an immense debt to the many specialists whose books and articles, many of them of outstanding quality, help him to develop his understanding and knowledge of the subject so that he can express his own views and conclusions on the basis of a body of knowledge in depth. This edition has a much longer Bibliography and more notes than its predecessor. I hope that I have thus acknowledged my debt — as I certainly wish to do — to so many scholars, contemporary writers, and journalists (in particular here the contributors to the invaluable *Far Eastern Economic Review*). In compiling the Bibliography I have included the books, etc., to which I have referred in collecting material and also — as an aid to the further reading of readers of this book — a number of studies of particular topics which in my opinion help to an understanding of modern Malaysia. Limited space has compelled me to omit from the list some excellent general studies of Malaysia and also the considerable corpus of autobiography, reminiscence, and the like which so often give the flavour of personal experience to one's understanding of the subject. The reader will have no difficulty in finding this sort of material if he has need of it.

It only remains to explain some points of structure and terminology. The past decade has made it clear that for this generation at least the exclusion of Singapore from Malaysia in 1965 is irreversible. I have in this edition dealt with Singapore only as an historical and marginal element of the Malaysian scene. The official term for the Malay Peninsula (and Penang island) is now — after a number of changes — 'Peninsular Malaysia' (in contrast to the Borneo states of Malaysia). I find Peninsular Malaysia cumbersome and have preferred to refer to 'Malaya' to denote the peninsula. Unless the context indicates the contrary, 'Malaya' does not include Singapore. Malaysia now publishes its statistics in metric units. I have used metric measures in Appendix 2 (Selected

Statistics), but I felt that in the main text of the book it would be anachronistic to convert what were pounds and acres at the time of recording into kilograms and hectares. A rather similar problem arises over the spelling of Malay words, including place names. In reaching an agreed Malaysian–Indonesian romanized spelling of the same words Malaysia some years ago modified the standard spelling of Malay words which had stood unaltered since it was introduced early in the colonial period. In time we shall perhaps become familiar with 'Melaka' instead of 'Malacca', 'Aceh' instead of 'Acheh' — and so on. I have generally used the new spelling of common words such as *kampung* (formerly *kampong*) because these are readily recognizable to those familiar with the old style. But for proper nouns I have retained the old spelling which is found in books published up to the 1960s.

For sixty years down to 1967 the Straits (or Malayan) dollar had a fixed parity with the pound sterling, i.e., $1 = 2s./4d. (9 dollars to the guinea was the convenient mnemonic). But this is no longer so and the British pound is divided into new metric pence. In the recent period of fluctuating exchange rates sterling has fallen to a lower value against the Malaysian *ringgit* (dollar) so that at most times the rate has been about 4 or 5 dollars to the pound. Back in the last years of the nineteenth century, before the fixed rate was established in 1906, the pound could buy as many as 10 dollars at some times. There is no way of adjusting for these fluctuations in any historical sequence of values. For that reason I have omitted the series of rubber and tin prices which appeared in the earlier edition. Wherever a dollar figure appears, this denotes the Malaysian dollar.

I have had much valuable help from my colleagues of The Guthrie Corporation Limited, in particular from its joint managing directors, Mark Gent and Ian Coates. For this I am most grateful — in particular to Mark Gent who found time in the busy working life of a chairman of a large international company to read a considerable part of the manuscript and make some valuable comments on it. If the reader finds mistakes or prejudices (I hope neither), the fault is entirely mine and the views expressed are my own.

February 1980   J. M. Gullick

1 Introduction

Malaysia is a modern state established in 1963. It is a parliamentary democracy which functions within the framework of ancient kingdoms adapted and federated to become constitutional monarchies. In its constitution and in its economic and social system Malaysia bears the mark of British colonial rule to which every part of the country was subject for a long period of years. It is one of the most prosperous among developing countries. But its wealth has been obtained by undue specialization in the past in the production of raw materials, rubber and tin, for export. To develop its export economy it imported immigrant labour which has settled in the country. Hence Malaysia is a society of distinct communities with the contrast and tensions which must result from ethnic and cultural cleavage. It is a country rich in its traditions as much as in its gross national product, complex in its contrasts.

Certain dominant themes run through this study of Malaysia as it now is. The first of these is the multi-racial character of Malaysia and, in particular, the existence of two major communities, the Malays and the Chinese, whose interests and influence must remain roughly in balance if stability and harmony are to be preserved. A second major theme is the contrast between the cities and large towns with their westernized middle class and sophisticated economy and the millions of peasants who live a simpler and more traditional life in the villages of the countryside. This second theme overlaps with the first in that the Malays are predominantly villagers and the Chinese townsmen. It also has a regional significance within Malaysia because of the great concentration of urban population and of economic development on the west-coast side of the Malay Peninsula. The east-coast side of Malaya and the Borneo territories are entirely agricultural and conscious of their backwardness.

Yet there is here a danger of oversimplification which can put the picture out of perspective. To be a Malay or a Chinese or an Iban is of much importance to the individual. It identifies the group to

1

which he belongs and marks out the others as different. But within each community there are also differences of status, economic interest, and education which by subdivision diminish the solidarity of the group. Since the upheaval of 1945-48 the major communities of Malaya have accepted the inevitability of accepting each other. It is not the existence of a multi-racial society which is usually in question but only the terms of the inter-communal bargain. Deliberate policies of evening-up and of assimilation work slowly like a leaven through the system. Whether this process will in time create a more united nation is an open question. Malaysia until now has had good government and prosperity. A regime which delivers the goods is thereby assured of a fair degree of acquiescence if not support. But the struggle for stability, tolerance, and a better standard of living is unending.

The story of a nation is a study of people working out their destiny in the physical environment of their territory. The land and the people are therefore the themes of the remainder of this chapter.

In the course of world history Malaya was first a land-bridge by which migrant peoples of the prehistoric period moved southwards from the Asian land-mass to Indonesia and Australasia. In the depths of Malaya's central jungles or along the fringe there are still some 40,000 aborigines, many of whom are descended from those earliest migrants. They live a primitive existence, remote from modern life — as they wish to be. Next came the Malays who reached Malaya and Sumatra about 2000 B.C. using the same overland route from the north.

Thereafter the Malay Peninsula became an obstacle to be crossed or circumnavigated by voyagers who approached from the east or west in ships. There were in antiquity two main routes between Europe and the Far East. The overland route across central Asia is relevant here only to the extent that many travellers avoided it because of the incessant wars which made it dangerous. The sea-route began at the Red Sea or in the Persian Gulf and went by way of western India to the region of Malaya. Here the earliest travellers crossed the narrow neck of land (the Kra isthmus of southern Thailand) at the northern end of the Malay Peninsula and took ship again in the Gulf of Siam. Later voyagers (from about 1000 A.D. onwards) braved the dangers of piracy in narrow seas and sailed on round Malaya, using either the Straits of Malacca between Sumatra and Malaya or passing west of Sumatra to enter the Straits of Sunda between Sumatra and Java. Once past the barrier of these land masses they sailed on to China or to the Spice Islands of eastern Indonesia. There was also traffic by the same routes from east to west.

Until steam replaced sail as the motive power of ships, the prevailing wind was the all-important factor. This is the region of the half-yearly monsoon winds. With the north-east monsoon, ships could sail westwards from China or Indonesia as far as Malaya and also from Malaya to India. The south-west monsoon carried them in a reverse direction. Few traders made complete journeys between India and China or vice versa. Instead they made a crossing to Malaya where they could exchange cargoes with mechants coming in the opposite direction. In this way various ports in the region of the Straits of Malacca became trade centres for the transhipment of cargoes from distant places and also for the collection of local produce and the distribution of imported goods within the Straits region. This entrepôt pattern of regional trade radiating from major sea-ports persists to this day.

The sea-borne traffic moved along the coasts of Southeast Asia. Until a hundred years ago few travellers penetrated into the interior of Malaya which was difficult of access and almost uninhabited. Mangrove swamps along the west coast were the first barrier. Then came the tangled thorns, the hungry leeches, the steamy heat and the mud of the lowland jungle belt. Beyond lay the blue mountain ranges of the central watershed. The prudent traveller, especially if laden with goods, preferred to pole a boat along the winding reaches of the rivers rather than hack his floundering way overland. So the rivers were the only practicable line of communication between coast and interior. The central ranges formed a barrier or division, not because they were difficult to climb, but because they were a watershed dividing river basins. The Malay Peninsula was thus divided into an east-coast and a west-coast zone, each approached from the river mouths by travelling up the rivers as far as the boats could go.

These geographical factors determined both the political divisions and the economic development of Malaya. Malay villages were sited along the banks of rivers because these were the only lines of communication. A Malay Ruler who established a stockade with a few brass cannon at the mouth of a river could control — and tax — all people and goods moving in and out of the inland river basin which was therefore his territory. Hence many Malay States bear the name of their principal river and have their boundaries at its watershed and their capital at the river mouth.

In the second quarter of the nineteenth century world demand for tin exceeded Malay capacity to produce it by simple methods. Immigrant groups of Chinese miners moved inland along the rivers into the empty interior in search of alluvial tin deposits in the valleys at the base of the central range, especially on the west-coast side. In time railway and road communications were built to replace the winding and silted rivers as communications between the interior and the coast. When the second wave of economic development began in the decade 1900-10 with the widespread planting of rubber, the planters naturally selected land which had been made accessible by the communications to the mines.

From this sequence of development two consequences followed. The alien economy of mine and plantation filled up the empty lands between the west coast and the watershed. It bypassed the older areas of Malay settlement but did not mingle with them. Later on the Malays took up land for rubber smallholdings in the same zone as the plantations but still apart from them. Secondly, development was concentrated on the west side of the Malay Peninsula and, because of the situation of the main tin deposits, in the centre of that strip of territory (and later to the south in Johor). As a result Malaya has two economic systems and two types of settlement. In the north-east and north-west regions are large and fairly compact areas of Malay settlement, based on rice cultivation and fishing. Here the traditional Malay way of life sets the pattern. Much of the rest of the developed area of Malaya (three-quarters is still under rain forest) is a patchwork of smaller zones of Malay and non-Malay populations and economic systems.[1] The development of oil-palm cultivation and of manufacturing industry in recent times has also occurred mainly in the west-coast area.

Agriculture is still the main prop of the Malayan economy. In the estuaries, valleys, and swamps there is fertile soil which when cleared and drained will support permanent rice cultivation and also coconut and oil-palm culture. Most of the fertile areas of this type, other than some relatively inaccessible parts, have already been brought into use. The greater part of the cultivated land — and the area to be developed as the population grows — is undulating or hilly country. Such land in its natural state grows luxuriant rain forest from which excellent hardwood timber can be extracted. But this kind of land, if it is completely cleared of its natural forest cover, quickly deteriorates by erosion and leaching of the topsoil under the heavy rain. For this reason it is suitable only for permanent tree crops and by good fortune the rubber-tree, imported from South America, and the oil-palm, imported from West Africa, have proved well suited to Malaysian conditions.

Up to a hundred inches a year fall in Malaya and even more in Borneo. The rain falls throughout the year, though especially heavily at the change of the monsoon in the second and fourth quarters. The shade temperature is in the daily range 20°-32° C at all seasons. This is the humid, monotonous, somewhat enervating climate of the wet tropics. Until malaria came under effective control in the twentieth century Malayan mortality from that disease, especially on newly opened mines and plantations, was heavy.

Northern Borneo has always been more remote from the mainstream of movement in Southeast Asia. But because it flanks the sea-route to China, the Chinese themselves and then the Malays and a succession of European powers impinged upon its coasts. As in Malaya, 'the land divides and the sea unites'[2] and so the two coasts of northern Borneo, north-west and north-east, are to this day separate zones of settlement. Like Malaya there is a sequence of coastal flats, then further inland a belt of low hills and undulations, rather steeper than in Malaya, and in the interior ranges of up to 8,000 feet with the majestic Kinabalu towering to 13,000 feet. Owing to the rapids and to the sandbars at their estuaries the rivers of northern Borneo were less useful as means of access to the interior and owing to the absence of tin deposits there was no inducement to nineteenth-century pioneers to penetrate inland. Hence when the rubber boom began, Borneo could not offer the same inducement of developed communications as Malaya, nor was the climate as well suited to rubber. Borneo remained sparsely inhabited and economically backward.

The Malaysians tend to think of each other (as communities) in stereotypes.[3] In fact there is much variety within each group. The 'Malay peasant' comprehends the rubber smallholder of central Malaya, who may be either a proprietor or a landless sharecropper, the tenant rice farmer of the north and east, and the fisherman of the east coast as well as many whose mixed economy partakes of more than one crop. The traditional picture of the people of Borneo envisages longhuts and headhunting, both institutions which are on the wane if not extinct. The Chinese are not only traders and labourers working for a wage but include peasant cultivators. Above all these are communities in which conservatism, which cherishes values and practices inherited from the past, competes with a process of change. This is a society in which roughly one adult male in three and two women in three have had no schooling at all, but (in Malaya at least) universal primary education is available to their children. Rural development, vernacular newspapers, radio and television, and political parties are vectors of new ideas and practices which are being absorbed — at differing speeds and depths — by Malaysians of one group or another. No one, the Malaysians included, can say what Malaysia will be like in twenty years time — and part of that future is being shaped in the cauldron of social change at the present time.

Later chapters deal at length with the historical processes by which the modern communities were formed. But something may here be said to introduce the way of life and the physical environment of the Malaysians. The majority of the Malays[4] live in villages (*kampung*) and earn their living as smallholders. But the old semi-subsistence economy has widened into production of rubber, copra, and palm-oil, and also rice for sale grown on *padi* land irrigated by modern engineering works. Population pressure on the land may drive the younger generation to wage labour on plantations and in the towns, to employment in the public services, especially the police and the armed forces, to taking up newly cleared land on the government's settlement schemes.

The pattern of Malay village settlement varies a good deal according to economy or topography. It may be a string of houses along an irrigation canal in a rice area or fronting the beach if it is a fishing community, or laid out according to a plan if it is a land settlement scheme, or stretched along a public road or footpath with the smallholdings running back from it. In its most traditional and attractive form a Malay village runs along the sides of a narrow valley in the centre of which, on either side of the stream, is a strip of rice-fields, vividly green in the early growing season and brown when the *padi* is ripe. The houses stand in an irregular line on the rising ground above the flood-level, surrounded by small gardens and orchards of fruit trees. Higher up the slope and behind the houses are the rubber smallholdings. Malay houses are typically wooden structures on stilts and thatched with palm leaves. The house is approached by a flight of steps and consists of three parts. The front verandah is the public part where the householder entertains his male guests; the central room contains the sleeping mats or (if the family is well-off) a double bed ornate with elaborately embroidered pillows and coverlets; the women's domain, the kitchen, is at the back. Some undersized poultry scratch a frugal living around the house and the assorted possessions stored beneath the raised floor. A hut at the back may contain the simple implements of rubber processing or there may be a small granary. There is a wide difference between the elaborate woodcarving, the concrete approach steps, and the miscellaneous knick-knacks of a rich peasant and the rickety shanty of his poor neighbour. A footpath runs its winding way from house to house down to the end of the valley where a row of mainly Chinese shops and a village police post mark the intersection with a public road. Along the path one finds the village school to which the children, neatly clad in blue and white, go to and fro; the mosque where the men gather on a Friday for prayers and afterwards a village conclave; the coffee shop to which the lads of the village and their elders resort to gossip, read the newspapers, and listen to the radio.

Malays are Muslims of the Sunni sect and are tolerant in their observances. Their women, who do not veil their faces, often own the houses and the rice-land which passes from mother to daughter. They are the guardians of the village rituals, many of them of pagan or Hindu origin, which are paraded forth at a wedding or a harvest home.

The pattern of Chinese settlement is even more varied. As a result of the resettlement of the early 1950s many rural Chinese live in compact villages which lack the aesthetic quality of Malay settlements. Each house is a rectangular structure of wood, galvanized iron, or thatched roof, subdivided into living, sleeping, and kitchen areas. In a position which usually faces the main doorway is a simple shrine to the ancestral or protective household deities of Chinese religious belief. Chinese workers on a tin-mine or a rubber estate may share a large hut in which each man has his allotted sleeping-place and the centre is a communal living-space; if they have families, they have left them behind in some village to support themselves as rubber-tappers or market-gardeners. Perhaps the most typical Chinese building is a shophouse in a village or town. Nineteenth-century town-planning has imposed on Malayan towns a universal pattern of a covered pavement, or 'five-foot way', to which the shops stand open. Above the shop a signboard in Chinese characters announces its business in auspicious terms. A general dealer in Chinese foodstuffs will have an aromatic array of articles such as dried or salted fish and preserves of all kinds; or if he is a rice-dealer, he will have sacks of rice of different grades open for use. At the back of the shop is a counter behind which the shopkeeper (colloquially 'the *towkay*') and his assistants operate the accounts system with the aid of an abacus and a paintbrush (for writing Chinese characters). Behind the shop, or above it if it has a storey above, are the living quarters of the *towkay* and his family and those of his assistants who 'live in'. After the close of business at the end of the day the *towkay* and his male staff may be seen sitting at the back of the shop at a round table, chopstick in hand sharing a common meal. In the typical Malayan Chinese success story[5] the shop assistant makes his first step towards a fortune by setting up in business, perhaps in an outlying village, with the aid of initial stock-in-trade on credit from his former employer. On his side the *towkay* recruits his staff from among his kinsmen or fellow clansmen. Thus social solidarity has an economic base.

However, all is not benevolent harmony between employers and workers. Many Chinese urban workers live in shanty areas or in overcrowded tenements and commute to work on foot or by bicycle. Out of urban overcrowding and troubled labour relations has come the unrest in the large towns which have proved a fertile ground in the past at least for the seeds of communism.

The majority of Indians in Malaysia are from the Tamil, Telugu, and Malayali linguistic areas of south India.[6] Some are traders whose mode of life in its externals is very like that of the Chinese. But most Indians work as labourers on the plantations or in government organizations such as the railways or the public works department. On a modern rubber estate the traditional 'labour lines' (long wooden huts divided into family cubicles) have been replaced by rows of neat if rather monotonous two-room cottages painted in a variety of pastel shades. A football field at the foot of the slope below the houses is the forum of athletic contest between estate teams and an open-sided cinema hall is the main centre of evening recreation. The estate provides a school (and a crèche) for the labourers' children and a hospital (on a very simple scale) for the sick. Most important of all is the temple which houses the images (strange to the European eye) of Hindu deities which emerge in gay procession at the annual festivals of Deepavali and Thaipusam. All around the residential area extend hundreds of acres of rubber which isolate it from the public roads and the towns.

In northern Borneo individual houses, grouped in village settlements, are coming to replace the traditional longhouse. With the passing of raids by headhunting parties the need for each community to have its stronghold has likewise disappeared. To a much greater extent than in Malaya the agriculture of the peoples of northern Borneo is a swidden (or shifting cultivation) system. Accordingly the villages are temporary rather than permanent sites.

The middle classes of all the Malaysian communities are mostly town-dwellers—though the bungalows, suitably graded in size and position on the rising ground, of senior and junior management are a prominent feature of a plantation or a mine. In every town there is a 'right side of the tracks'—for this is a hierarchical society—in which the winding roads pass between rows of bungalows (or two-storey dwellings), each set in its compound bright with the flowers of hibiscus, bougainvillea, or frangipani. In the centre of the towns with their multi-storey buildings, honeycomb in structure, the visitor might easily imagine himself in some other country.

This outline picture may serve as an introduction to the more detailed examination, from the aspect of historical development, of certain elements of modern Malaysia which follows. Chapters 2 and 3 deal respectively with the Malay State and with the colonial heritage as sources of the modern constitutional structure. In Chapters 4 and 5 there is an account of the process of social change which created the indigenous and immigrant communities of Malaysia. From that groundwork Chapters 6 and 7 trace the political progress of the past forty years.

Notes

1 In 1975, 23.3 million acres out of a total area of 32.5 million acres in Malaya were under forest, but half the forest area was classified as 'logged and disturbed'. TMP, para 681.

2 Fisher (1966), 662.

3 'Their ideas of each other are derived from dubious and faulty sources of information . . . the relationships, as they are undertaken by individual members, are guided by stereotypes which were formulated in colonial times, and which were learnt as part of the normal course of socialization in the communities of the respective groups.' Wilson (1967), 17. Wilson has some very interesting material on this theme.

4 'Malay' is not to be confused—as it often is by foreigners—with 'Malayan'. A Malay is a person of the Malay race. A Malayan is a person whose home is in Malaya; he may be a Malay, a Malayan Chinese, etc. In census reports for years before the formation of Malaysia in 1963 'Malaysian' or 'Other Malaysian' was used to describe Indonesians settled in Malaya.

5   On the most legendary of all Chinese millionaires, Loke Yew, see Hawkins in Gullick and Hawkins (1958), 65 and also Wright 893. Middlebrook (1951) tells the story of Yap Ah Loy, the famous founder and Capitan China of Kuala Lumpur.

6   'Indian' is used in this book to include Pakistani and also in some contexts the Ceylon Tamils.

2 The Malacca Sultanate and Its Successor States A.D. 1400-1786

Of the thirteen States which make up the modern Malaysia nine, all in the Malay Peninsula, are ruled by Malay Sultans or by other Malay royal Rulers drawn from long-established dynasties. The modern Malay community claims its political pre-eminence on the basis of the sovereignty of the Malay Rulers. In spite of the changes arising from a tight-knit federal constitution and parliamentary rule the modern Malay State and its people retain in some measure the social structure and ideology of an earlier age. For that reason as much as to provide an historical introduction it is necessary to consider the evolution of the Malay State as an element of Malaysia.

In the previous chapter it was explained that maritime trade passing to and from Southeast Asia must pass either through the Straits of Malacca or through the Sunda Straits between Sumatra and Java and that the regime of the monsoon winds made this land barrier a natural point of concentration of trade carried in sailing ships. For a long period ending with the thirteenth century the great trade centre of the Straits region was Sri Vijaya, a Buddhist kingdom whose capital was on the south-east coast of Sumatra, probably at Palembang. The decline of Sri Vijaya was due in part to changes in the pattern of Chinese foreign trade and to the rise of rival centres of power both in Thailand and in Java. Towards the end of the fourteenth century a Malay leader from the royal house of Palembang established himself for a few years at Tumasik (the modern Singapore island), but he was driven out by Thai forces and removed himself with a few followers to the neighbourhood of what was to become the port of Malacca. Throughout the centuries covered by this chapter Malay kingship was a mobile institution; a Ruler if he retained a following could readily remove himself from a devastated or inauspicious site to found a new capital elsewhere. By skilful diplomacy the founder of Malacca re-established the old trade links between China and the Straits and he was able by war and alliances to extend his influence along both coasts. In the second quarter of the fifteenth century a later Ruler of the same dynasty married the daughter of a Ruler of Pasai, a port at the northern tip of Sumatra. Pasai was the first centre of Islamic penetration of Southeast Asia and by this connection the Ruler of Malacca became a convert to Islam, taking the name Muhammed Shah, but retaining much of the court ceremonial and titles of rank of the earlier Hindu period.[1]

From these beginnings the state of Malacca flourished during the rest of the fifteenth century A.D. as the regional trade centre of Southeast Asia and as an important link in an international maritime trade route between Europe and the Far East. From China came cargoes of silk and other luxury textiles, porcelain, pearls, rhubarb, camphor, and less valuable but essential products such as salt. China imported through Malacca pepper, spices, tin, and other products of Southeast Asia or of India, using Canton as its port of entry where the trade could be strictly regulated by the imperial government of China. From Borneo, Sumatra, and the Celebes pepper and other local produce was shipped to Malacca in exchange for Indian cotton cloths. Java sent spices shipped thither from the Moluccas and also rice and other foodstuffs. On the western side Malacca's main trade link was with the port of Cambay in western India, through which came cargoes of cotton and woollen cloth and merchandise of many kinds, which had been imported to this Gujerat region from Arabia, Persia, the Levant, and Europe. There were also trade links with the ports of the Coromandel coast of southern India and of Bengal to the north.

The shipping which called at the port of Malacca was of many types and mostly foreign to Malaya. From western India the Gujerati seamen came in heavy dhows of 100–400 tons burden; the timbers of these vessels were lashed rather than riveted by metal nails to avoid the risk of disintegration by rusting, but could break up nonetheless in heavy storms. Pegu in Burma was a major centre of shipbuilding which exported ships as well as foodstuffs to Malacca. The regional trade of Southeast Asia was carried across the narrow waters in lighter but well-built junks. The Bugis of the Celebes, whose descendants were to play a prominent part in Malayan history, were already pre-eminent among local seamen.

In Malacca itself the foreign trader could rely upon finding a well-developed mercantile organization to deal with the arrival, unloading, reloading, and departure of some hundred large ships, as well as a host of smaller ones, in each year. The monsoon winds imposed on the maritime traders a strict timetable and so it was essential that they should avoid delay. On arrival the master (*nakhoda*) of each ship applied to one of the four harbourmasters (*shahbandar*) who allotted to him a space in a warehouse for the temporary accommodation of his cargo. Warehouses were often built underground to reduce the risk of fire spreading from neighbouring wooden buildings. The cargo was discharged and moved into store by elephants. Before it could be sold, customs duties must be paid; for this purpose every commodity was weighed in accordance with the port's standard measures. In addition to customs duties there were often gifts to be made, of 1 or 2 per cent of the cargo, to the great officers of state of Malacca. All these matters were regulated by predetermined scales which varied according to the port of origin of the ship. Import duties were the main source of revenue of the Rulers of Malacca. On export cargoes there was only a nominal 1 per cent shipping charge. To prevent any rigging or undue fluctuation of local prices the owner of the cargo (or the master as his agent) negotiated the sale prices on a collective basis with the principal Malacca traders. The buyers then bought the entire cargo as an entity and divided it between them.

By these means traders could resort to Malacca with fair certainty of finding a safe anchorage, an active but stable market for their cargoes with prearranged duties to pay, and the protection of a major centre of political and naval power. They could also count on finding available for purchase stocks of the commodities which they wished to procure as their return cargoes. The Rulers of Malacca profited from this well-organized system, but it left substantial profits to the merchants themselves. A successful voyage could yield a profit of from 80 to 300 per cent — though there were obviously risks to be taken too.

The political power of Malacca was built upon the revenues of its trade. At the apex of the system was the royal Ruler, descended from the founder. In normal times the executive head of the government and also the chief judge was the *bendahara,* drawn from another mighty family eminent enough to supply wives as consorts of the royal Rulers. When the throne fell vacant, the *bendahara* family was often the kingmaker which influenced the selection of a new Ruler. The other principal officers were the *laksamana,* or high admiral, and the *temenggong.* Since Malacca was a maritime power, the *laksamana* was usually the commander in time of war of the warships and their crews. The *temenggong's* function was to maintain order within the town, including the exercise of authority over its many foreign residents. He was the chief of police and also the master of ceremonies at the royal court. In the royal hall of audience the Ruler was seated on a long raised dais with his officers of state ranged alongside in due order of precedence. Young men of high family who did not yet hold a public office sat at lower levels. Behind the Ruler stood the bearer of the sword of state and other bearers of insignia. A foreign envoy or visitor or a local subject was formally presented and moved to the dais to crouch at the royal feet. He had to be appropriately dressed in sarong, scarf, and bearing a *keris* (the Malay dagger). To this day all such matters of ceremonial (*istiadat*) are of great significance on formal court occasions.

The foreign traders, many of them semi-permanent residents at Malacca, who made up the greater part of the town's population were divided into four groups; each group was placed under the authority of a *shahbandar*. Most senior of the four was the *shahbandar* for the Gujerati seamen and merchants; a second had charge of the other Indians and of the Burmese; a third of the Javanese and other Indonesians; and a fourth of the Chinese and some other groups. The main task of each *shahbandar* was the management of the markets and warehouses of his group, the settlement of disputes between them, and keeping check on the weights, measures, and coinage in use.

Malacca was essentially a trade empire in which the port town was the centre of power. It also had outlying territories where local rule was in the hands either of families established there or of junior members of the Malacca ruling class despatched from the capital to serve an apprenticeship in the hinterland. The power of Malacca lay in its ships, which were small, light craft manned by seafaring people, the Celates, or *orang laut* (seafarers), whose main settlements lay further south than Malacca in the islands of the Straits of Singapore. It was their function to hold piracy in check — it could never be entirely suppressed — and to police the narrow waters of the straits. The territorial basis of Malacca's power was a system of alliances with local rulers along both sides of the Straits and extending at its widest range to the east coast of Malaya also. These links were forged by diplomacy, dynastic marriage ties, and if necessary by warfare. By the mid-fifteenth century Malacca had become a strong centre of Islam with an assembly of

Muslim divines at the court. From Malacca, Islam spread outwards, notably towards Java.

The Malacca kingdom was as strong as the cohesion of its main elements, the Malay ruling class and the foreign merchants. It was an unfortunate coincidence that the first major impact of European expansion came at a time when dissension had weakened the Malay regime and there was disaffection among its merchants. In 1511 the Portuguese admiral d'Albuquerque took Malacca. It fell after a fierce struggle and its Rulers, exiled, battered, and humiliated, survived and moved on. For the next hundred years a tripartite struggle for control of the Straits replaced the old unified trade system of Malacca in its heyday. The contestants were the Portuguese, who had built themselves a powerful fortress at Malacca, the exiled Malacca dynasty now established on the Johor river at the extreme south of the Malay Peninsula, and the rising kingdom of Acheh at the northern end of Sumatra. The initial Portuguese victory of 1511 was due to surprise and to superiority in armaments and seamanship. But Portugal lacked the strength needed to dominate the Straits; its garrison at Malacca, although it dealt some hard blows, was generally on the defensive. Over the century and a quarter of Portuguese rule the fortress at Malacca survived twenty-five attacks or sieges — mainly by Achehnese forces. The commercial aim of the Portuguese and of the Dutch after them was to secure control of the important export trade in Indonesian spices and Southeast Asian tin and of the import into the region of Indian textiles. The Portuguese established an inefficient and expensive state trading monopoly. Their virtual crusade against 'the Moors' did much to stimulate and to strengthen Islam in Southeast Asia.

The first Dutch ships reached Java in 1595, but the Dutch did not take Malacca until 1641. In pursuing their commercial objectives they used private enterprise under state regulation in the form of the Dutch East India Company (VOC). In the area of the Straits of Malacca they were a less disruptive influence than in Java itself. The Dutch rulers of Jakarta (then 'Batavia') wished to keep open the sea-route to Java with the minimum of military effort. They were therefore prepared to accommodate and even to ally themselves with the Rulers of Johor if this would promote stability in the Straits of Malacca. For the sake of this *modus vivendi* Jakarta did not seek to enforce a local trade monopoly for the benefit of its outpost at Malacca. In these more favourable circumstances the Malay kingdom of Johor regained some of the trade and therefore the sea power which had been lost in 1511. The capital of the kingdom which had been moved more than once before was transferred from the Johor river to Riau on Bentan Island southeast of Singapore (then uninhabited) following the destruction of the old capital in 1673 by invaders from Sumatra. Here the main port of the kingdom was centrally placed among the settlements of the *orang laut* who were the main support of its Rulers. The system which had been so successful at Malacca was revived, though on a reduced scale; foreign and regional trade moved through the port under the patronage of the officers of state (*orang kaya*). Johor was under shrewd and effective Malay leadership during the final quarter of the seventeenth century.

Two major setbacks then disrupted the Johor kingdom. In all the struggles for power within the ruling élite at Malacca and then at Johor there had been in form at least a show of loyalty to the royal Ruler. In the Malay tradition he was the embodiment of supernatural majesty (*daulat*) and the symbol of the power of the state. To be disloyal (*derhaka*) was in the Malay scale of values the worst of crimes. But in 1699 the Ruler, a degenerate sadist — so at least the hostile tradition of his successors pictures him — was killed in an aristrocratic putsch. Thus ended — after almost two centuries — the royal dynasty which had founded Malacca. It was replaced by Rulers drawn from the *bendahara* family, but these parvenus did not command the same dedicated loyalty of their subjects as had been given to their predecessors.

The second disaster was a prolonged struggle for power in the first quarter of the eighteenth century between two factions, both foreign to the kingdom. In their efforts to control the spice trade of the Celebes the Dutch displaced the Bugis from their homeland. These energetic seamen were also formidable fighting men. So the vikings of Southeast Asia moved into the Straits in the power of their ships and of their corselets of chain mail. At the court of Johor they established themselves as 'underkings' (*Yam Tuan Muda*) to the enfeebled Johor Ruler; as such they were the effective governors of the state. Further north the Bugis settled along the central stretch of the west coast of Malaya, in the area of the Selangor and Klang rivers, and in time made a new State of Selangor (from 1742) with one of their leaders as the Sultan. But the Bugis intervention in Johor provoked a reaction which was exploited by a Sumatran leader, Raja Kecil, who claimed to be the posthumous son of the Johor Ruler murdered in 1699. The claim was no doubt political propaganda aimed to attract the support of the disaffected *orang laut*. During the 1720s a prolonged struggle for power swayed to and fro until in the end the Bugis emerged as victors. But in Johor itself a gradual process of intermarriage and political alliance merged the Bugis and old Malay ruling class and resolved the feuds between them. In the latter part of the eighteenth century down to 1784, when a Bugis attack on Malacca failed, the Bugis and the Dutch slogged it out in fruitless warfare. By this time both were in a decline.

There were other successor States to Malacca besides Johor. The Rulers of Perak and of Pahang in central Malaya descend from the Rulers of Malacca. Further south in Negri Sembilan, between Malacca and Selangor, a major part of the Malay population were Sumatran immigrants from the matrilineal society of Menangkabau in central Sumatra. Under the pressure of Bugis expansion this group of small territories (Negri Sembilan means 'Nine States') formed a loose federation in which their social structure was preserved — to fascinate the modern anthropologist. In the north, Kedah (then including Perlis), Kelantan, and Trengganu emerged as Malay States within the sphere of influence of their more powerful neighbour Thailand.[2]

The legacy of Malacca and Johor (and the other Malay States of this period) to the modern Malaysia is to be found in the traditions which still permeate Malay society. The Ruler of the State and his turbulent officers were the administrators and warleaders of their community. They were a class apart from their subjects, exercising unquestioned and sometimes oppressive authority over them. By a process of adaptation to be described later (Chapter 4) the modern Malay upper class has come to provide the politicians, the diplomats, and the civil servants (other than in the technical services) who govern the modern Malaysia. The Malays have specialized in government as the Chinese have in commerce. With the spread of education it has become possible for the son of a peasant to rise in the world and to become a member of the upper class — which would not have been possible two centuries ago. Although this class is now more democratic in its composition, it preserves the old ideology and values. Malay society is still very much led and directed from above.

So far as there is information available it appears that the structure of Malay village communities was then much as it is now. Population was then scanty and the villages isolated. But they were already communities in which the leadership was provided by a village headman (*ketua kampung*) drawn from one of the prominent families of the village, the other more prosperous peasants, and the officials of the mosque and other worthies such as the pilgrims (*Haji*) returned from Mecca. To these in modern times one would add the men of superior education such as the schoolmaster and the retired government servant. It is a society which holds the Sultan and the ruling class in respect and looks to them, as the acknowledged leaders, for the protection of the Malay interests. The Malays, even of the village class, who have moved to the towns are regarded as a different kind of people.[3]

This is not of course a static situation. There is a more radical and less acquiescent spirit abroad — subjects to which we shall return later.

Notes

1　In this chapter I have drawn on the detailed studies of various periods by L. Andaya, Meilink-Roelofsz (1962), Wilkinson (1935), and Wolters (1970), to all of whom I make my grateful acknowledgements — any errors are mine. In conformity with general practice I have referred to Malay Rulers of this early period as *Sultan,* although this did not become the conventional term until the nineteenth century. In earlier times a Malay Ruler was designated *Raja,* a Hindu title, or *Yang di Pertuan* (Malay for 'he who is made lord'). This latter title is now used by the paramount Ruler of the Malaysian Federation (*Yang di Pertuan Agong*) and also by the paramount Ruler of Negri Sembilan. On the linguistic development of *Sultan* see Wilkinson (1932).

2　Thailand was known as 'Siam' until 1939.

3　Although the Malays who move to the towns usually preserve family ties with the villages from which they come, and may return to them at the end of their working lives, villagers regard 'urban Malays as a subspecies of Malay culture' which rapidly loses its rural qualities: Wilson (1967), 45. See also Husin Ali (1975) especially at p. 168 and the same author (1964) at p. 140; Swift (1965) at p. 161. Although Wilson is inclined to explain this attitude as a case of equating the town Malay (*orang bandar*) with the detested Chinese, the same phenomenon appears in studies of Kelantan society where many more of the townsfolk are Malays. See, for example, Ibrahim Nik Mahmood in Roff (1974) at p. 67, and Kessler (1978) references indexed under 'relation of town and country'.

3   British Colonial Rule in Malaysia 1786–1942

On 15 July 1786 a British force led by Francis Light occupied the island of Penang. On 16 September 1963 Malaysia was formed by bringing together the Federation of Malaya, an independent state since 1957, and the remaining British colonial territories in Southeast Asia (other than Brunei and Hongkong), i.e., Singapore, Sabah (formerly British North Borneo), and Sarawak. Singapore, however, withdrew in 1965. 1786 to 1963 are thus the terminal dates of the beginning and the end of British colonial rule in all or some part of the territories now comprised in Malaysia. As will be explained, the Japanese occupation of 1942-45 was much more than an interruption; it destroyed the authority of the colonial regime and thus paved the way for the advance to a self-governing Malaysia. From 1945 onwards it was colonial rule on sufferance as a transition to independence. Accordingly this chapter deals with the period down to 1942 and the transitional period from 1945 is described in a later chapter.

Malaysia is what it is because of its peoples and their characteristics and traditions. But one cannot ignore the legacy left to them by yesterday's rulers. Colonial rule was more than a system of government, alien and transient. It was also a powerful agent of change which has left its mark on Malaysia in many places — in its constitutional and administrative structure, in its economic development and its multi-racial communities, in its educational and legal systems, and in its use, albeit diminishing, of the English language. This chapter is more particularly concerned with the evolution of the machinery of government in Malaysia.

The arrival of Francis Light at Penang in 1786 with his three small ships resulted from the interaction of British strategy with local circumstances and enterprises. The island of Penang was then an outlying and unimportant part of the mainland state of Kedah. The Sultan of Kedah had for some time past felt the need of a foreign ally who would protect him if he resisted the pressure exerted on him by the powerful and at times aggressive state of Siam to the north. Siam (the modern Thailand) was engaged in a long-drawn struggle with the kingdom of Burma for the control of the isthmus of Kra and the coastline northwards towards Mergui. The Siamese therefore needed to assert control over Kedah as a tributary state at the far end of the disputed territory. Local Siamese governors of the southern provinces were eager to extend their grip southwards.

The British East India Company had for a generation past been fighting the French for the control of the east coast of India. In 1623 the British had relinquished the territories of Southeast Asia to the Dutch as their trade sphere. But trade with China and with the spice islands of the Celebes still offered to local traders attractive opportunities of expansion. Francis Light was one of the merchant captains of country ships who for the previous twenty years had been trading with Kedah and other local centres. As far back as 1771 he had tried to interest the East India Company in acquiring an outpost on the Kedah coast. But the Company was eventually moved in 1786 to expansion eastwards, mainly by its need for a small naval base on the far side of the Bay of Bengal. Its square-rigged sailing ships could not cruise off the eastern coast of India during the period of the north-east monsoon without a base to the east to which they could retire in bad weather. Penang seemed suitable for their purpose.

The East India Company was unwilling, however, to pay the price demanded by the Sultan of Kedah: a defensive alliance against Siamese or Burmese aggression. But by diplomatic evasion Light led the Sultan to believe that he would secure what he wanted and on that basis Light was allowed to occupy Penang while the negotiations continued their protracted course.[1] The Anglo-Kedah treaty signed in 1791, after an unsuccessful attempt by the Sultan to expel the British from Penang, gave him no cause of satisfaction. A generation afterwards the Siamese drove a later Sultan of Kedah into exile in 1821 and he got no help from the British, other than a refuge in Penang itself; the Sultan was only restored to his throne in 1842 by submission to Siamese control of his state.

Long before that discreditable episode the situation in maritime Southeast Asia had been fundamentally changed by the local repercussions of the Napoleonic Wars in Europe. France overran Holland and the object of British policy in Southeast Asia was to forestall any French use of Dutch bases against British shipping. As part of this strategy Java was occupied in 1811 and Thomas Stamford Raffles became Lieutenant Governor of Java until 1816. Raffles had been in the service of the East India Company at Penang, an unflourishing backwater, since 1805. Among several able British administrators who served in Malaysia there were only two really creative minds. Raffles was one (and Hugh Low the other). Raffles's aim was to establish a British sphere of influence throughout the entire region. In this grandiose object—and also in his administration of Java—he failed. His vision extended beyond his ability as an administrator. He was also devious and uncertain in his methods—'full of trick and not so full of truth as was desirable, and he was the most nervous man I ever knew', said a contemporary who knew him well and disliked him.[2] When the war was over, Java and also Malacca, which had been occupied by the British in 1795, were restored to the Dutch and Raffles was relegated to the charge of remote, malarial Bencoolen on the west coast of Sumatra. From Bencoolen, however, Raffles continued his efforts to break the Dutch hold on Southeast Asia. In February 1819 he found the means to do so by negotiating an agreement with Tunku Hussein of Johor by which the British were conceded the right to occupy the almost uninhabited island of Singapore. It was a characteristically unprincipled manoeuvre in which Raffles accorded recognition as Sultan of Johor to the elder brother of the Ruler whom the Dutch had recognized. Thus in his last years (1819-24) Raffles established a great centre of maritime trade and of British influence in the free-trade port of Singapore, to which ships and traders of many nations resorted in ever-increasing numbers. Raffles did not live to see it, but Singapore soon became the commercial capital of Southeast Asia. In 1830 Singapore became the capital of the newly formed Straits Settlements (Singapore, Penang, and Malacca) which was a dependency of the government of India. From 1800 Penang included a strip of coast on the opposite mainland, called Province Wellesley.

The Anglo-Dutch treaty of 1824 in effect partitioned Southeast Asia into British and Dutch spheres of influence—and thus delimited the frontiers of the future states of Indonesia and Malaysia. Britain gave up Bencoolen in exchange for Malacca in order to concentrate her power on the sea-route through the Straits of Malacca by holding Penang at the north, Malacca in the centre, and Singapore to the south of the Straits. With this chain of ports went a sphere of influence over much of the Malay Peninsula. The rest of maritime Southeast Asia was relinquished to the Dutch.

The continuing threat of Siamese expansion or intervention in northern and central Malaya was with some difficulty contained by an Anglo-Siamese treaty of 1826 under which Britain recognized an ill-defined Siamese suzerainty over Kedah in the north-west and over Kelantan and Trengganu on the north-east coast of Malaya. But Siam ceased to threaten Perak.

Over the ensuing half-century down to 1874 there was little change in the formal diplomatic and constitutional position. The three Straits Settlements were enclaves of British territory. The Malay States which lay between Singapore and the boundary of the Siamese zone of influence, i.e., Johor, Pahang, Negri Sembilan, Selangor, and Perak, were in appearance independent of foreign control though in fact subject to some measure of British influence and occasional interference. The northern States of Kedah (then including Perlis), Trengganu, Kelantan, and Patani (to the north of Kelantan) were tributaries of Siam, though they were in practice allowed considerable freedom — especially in their economic relations with the Straits Settlements. As the Dutch gradually extended their hold on what became the Netherlands East Indies, the centripetal pull of two rival spheres of influence pulled Southeast Asia apart — though Singapore and to a lesser extent Penang did a flourishing trade with islands of the Dutch sphere.

In the northern end of Borneo the Sultan of Brunei was nominal overlord as far north as the point to which the Sultan of Sulu laid claim.[3] There was uncertainty and dispute as to whether the Anglo-Dutch treaty of 1824 denied Britain any right to a foothold in northern Borneo. But the position of north-western Borneo athwart the sea-route from Singapore to Hongkong (annexed by Britain in 1842) made it important. In the 1830s ships of the British navy were engaged in operations against pirates in northern Borneo. In 1839 James Brooke arrived off the Borneo coast in his own yacht, the *Royalist,* to take part. At that time the Malay Rulers of Brunei were in difficulty over a local revolt in the province of Sarawak and accepted Brooke's offer of help. Brooke became the governor and in 1846 the independent ruler of Sarawak, which, enlarged by stages at the expense of Brunei, continued as the fief of the Brooke family until ceded to Britain in 1945. Labuan was acquired as a coaling station in 1846 and became part of the Straits Settlements. The tortuous origins of the British North Borneo Company, successor to a short-lived American settlement of the 1860s, date from 1878; it was granted a British royal charter in 1881 and governed the northern extremity of Borneo on crown colony lines until it became a colony proper in 1946.

Although the formal boundaries of British rule in Malaya did not advance into the Malay States until 1874, the relationship between the Straits Settlements and the nominally independent States began to alter significantly from the middle of the century.[4] From the outset there had always been an economic dimension to the relationship. The ports of the Straits Settlements were centres of trade and the revenues of the local government depended on the volume of trade — though they adhered strictly to the principle of free trade laid down by the founder of Singapore. In its early phase the trade between the Straits ports and the Malay States consisted of the purchase of what the States had to offer and the export to them of the manufactured goods and foodstuffs which their simple economy could absorb. But the situation changed in the 1840s as the demand of Western industrialized countries for tin expanded. It was beyond the capacity of Malay tin-miners to increase output to meet this demand. Chinese merchants in the Straits ports began to import labourers from China to open new mines in the most productive areas of the western Malay States. The mining of alluvial tin takes time since a large pit has — under traditional methods — to be dug before the ore-bearing stratum is reached. Over a period of at least six months the entrepreneurs had to supply food and other necessaries to the miners before they could recover their outlay in tin. In the early days these ventures were promoted in association with the Malay chiefs who governed the districts in which the mines were situated. The capital invested in the new mines could take the form of an advance to the chief who in turn controlled the miners. But even if, as became the usual practice later, the financiers dealt direct with the miners, they depended on the goodwill of the local chief and on his ability to fend off attacks from Malay rivals, jealous of his wealth from the mines. Part of the return from a successful mine was obtained in the form of monopoly rights ('farms') for the supply of opium, spirits, and gambling facilities to the miners; these rights were generally granted by the local chief to the financiers who were backing the mines. In this way complex but very close links were formed between interests, mainly but not entirely Chinese, in the Straits Settlements and the Malay ruling class in the tin-producing areas of Lukut (then on the coast of Selangor but now part of Negri Sembilan), Larut on the Perak coast, and Kuala Lumpur on the upper reaches of the Klang river of Selangor.

Competition for territory, power, and revenue drew Malay chiefs and Chinese miners into opposed coalitions in the Malay States, each supported by merchants, who had a great deal of money at risk, in the Straits Settlements. Long before 1874 the economic nexus between the Settlements and the States was beginning to generate intolerable strains at both ends.

To these problems the Government of India, far away in Calcutta, was generally indifferent. The guiding principle of policy for the Straits Settlements was — non-intervention in the Malay States. In Singapore the Governor as much as the merchants could only fume in impotence as this principle was repeated to them. This led to pressure for the separation of the Straits Settlements from India so that it might become a crown colony. That change was accomplished in 1868, but yielded little satisfaction of local grievances since the Colonial Office was just as adamant as its predecessors in restraining any move towards political involvement in the Malay States to protect the Straits investments. From about 1868 onwards there was intermittent civil war in the main mining areas of Perak and Selangor with considerable repercussions in the Straits Settlements. There was now a local legislature in Singapore in which prominent merchants could demand that something be done — but nothing was. In 1873 the European unofficial members of the legislative council resigned in protest at what they considered to be the autocratic attitude of a very unpopular Governor over an internal matter.

At this point, towards the end of 1873, a new Governor, Sir Andrew Clarke, arrived and within a few short months Perak, Selangor, and Sungei Ujong (the mining district of Negri Sembilan) had been brought under direct British control. In taking such rapid action Clarke exceeded his instructions from the Colonial Office, which merely required him to report on possible action. But it is clear that there had been a major change of policy in London. Several historians have examined the probable causes of that volteface but without reaching complete unanimity.[5] It may be that at a time when the European powers were competing in the expansion of their colonial empires, Britain feared possible German intervention in the Malay States. But for all its apparent suddenness the decision to abandon the policy of non-intervention was, like the breaking of a dam, the result of a long build-up of intolerable pressure over a period of time.

Clarke gave priority to Perak in his policy of intervention since it was of critical importance to the commercial interests of the Straits Settlements. The agreement signed at Pangkor, an island off the Perak coast, on 20 January 1874, by Clarke and by Sultan Abdullah of Perak and other Malay chiefs, set the pattern. The key clause provided for the appointment of a British Resident 'whose advice must be asked and acted upon on all questions other than those touching Malay religion and custom'. In this formula there were the seeds of conflict; it was both ambiguous and impracticable. Hugh Low, then Resident of Perak, commented in 1878 that 'we must first create the government to be advised'.[6] The Sultan, even if he had been disposed to act on the advice given, would have been unable to do so because the traditional political structure of a Malay State at that time was not adapted to British administrative methods. Yet that traditional structure, which British advice must seek to alter, was part of the Malay custom on which British advice was excluded.[7]

More serious was the mutual lack of comprehension. The Malay Ruler contemplated that he would obtain British political support, which he needed, in dealing with his adversaries in Perak — but essentially on terms which would leave his authority unrestricted. The British intended, as another clause in the Pangkor agreement makes clear, to take into their own hands the collection of State revenues. But in doing so they would be depriving the Sultan and the major chiefs of the very foundation of their power. The inevitable conflict was sharpened by a clash of personalities. Hugh Low's private verdict on his predecessor, J.W.W. Birch, was that 'Mr Birch knew no Malay, was violent, drank and did some high-handed things'.[8] But in his hasty attempt to alter the *status quo* Birch had the support of Sir William Jervois who succeeded Clarke as governor in 1875. On the other side, Sultan Abdullah of Perak was young, inexperienced, and irresponsible. The clash between them ended with the assassination of Birch in November 1875. Jervois then took alarm and made an expensive demonstration of British military power dignified with the title of 'the Perak War'. In Selangor and in Sungei Ujong there were also minor and ineffectual episodes of Malay resistance.

From this unpromising start there was a slow recovery in which the State Councils played a key part. These were advisory bodies in each of the three protected States, including in their membership both Malay aristocrats and Chinese mining employers. The function of the Council was to give advice — in form to the Malay Ruler who presided but in fact to the British Resident whose administrative measures came before the Council. In Perak, where Hugh Low was Resident from 1877 to 1889, there was the most skilful progress towards an Anglo-Malay accommodation which set the pattern for the other States, where the Residents of the period were less talented. Low had originally come to the East as a naturalist. He had been with James Brooke in Sarawak in the early days and had spent almost thirty years in the obscurity of Labuan before being posted to Perak. He brought to his difficult task patience, tact, and above all a sympathetic insight into the problems of adjustment which British rule imposed on the former Malay Rulers of Perak. The Malay ruling class had been shaken by the events of 1875; Sultan Abdullah and other leading figures had been sent into exile. To those who remained the new regime offered dignity and affluence but little power. The British adviser ruled and the Malay Ruler advised, it was said. Even a man of Hugh Low's gifts had little doubt that for an indefinite period it was necessary to take the government of the country out of Malay hands.[9]

After a decade of uncertainty the comparative success of the protectorate regime and the prosperity which came with it induced a second wave of expansion. In the later 1880s British rule on the familiar lines was extended to the remainder of Negri Sembilan and to Pahang. With the successful consolidation of British rule in central Malaya two new issues demanded attention. First, was it possible to bring the individual States into a closer association? The business community found it irksome to deal with several State governments, each of which differed somewhat from the others in their legislation and administrative practice. This pressure led to the formation in 1896 of the Federated Malay States of Perak, Selangor, Negri Sembilan, and Pahang under the *de facto* control of Frank Swettenham as Resident General. Swettenham was a forceful and ambitious administrator who had been prominent in the Malay States since 1874. The effect of the new centralization was to deprive the State governments of their vitality. The State Councils could no longer carry questions under debate to an effective conclusion since the policy would have to be whatever might be approved in the federal capital of Kuala Lumpur for the FMS as a whole. The Malay Ruler and the other members of the Council were thus placed at a distance from a burgeoning federal bureaucracy which was largely indifferent to them. A British Resident of Negri Sembilan in 1910 wrote a letter from his Residency at

Seremban to the Malay Ruler of Sungei Ujong in which Seremban is situated; the local post office returned his letter marked 'addressee unknown'.[10]

The other issue of the turn of the century was how to enlarge 'British Malaya' by prising away from Siam the four northern States of Kedah, Perlis, Kelantan, and Trengganu. Anglo-French rivalries in and around Siam made this a delicate task which was achieved by stages.[11] The Siamese government was first persuaded to post advisers, who were British nationals, to key States to assist them in the management of their precarious finances. In 1909 Siam, without any consultation with the Rulers of the States, transfered its suzerainty over them to Britain. The State of Johor between the FMS and Singapore presented a different problem. It had always been very much within the British sphere and subject to economic penetration from Singapore, especially after the construction of a railway line in 1908 to link the FMS railway system with Singapore. But the strong personality of its Malay Rulers, Sultans Abu Bakar and after him his son Ibrahim (who reigned for sixty years from 1895), preserved the independence of Johor. In 1914, however, the Sultan agreed to accept a General Adviser and so Johor became the fifth of the Unfederated Malay States (UMS).

There were now two contrasted styles of administration in the Malay States. In the FMS the administrative structure was that of a crown colony. The government of each State, subject to overriding direction from the federal capital, was conducted in the name of the Malay Ruler. But the executive head of the government was the British Resident. The State was divided into a number of administrative districts under the charge of British District Officers. The main functions of the DO were to act as Collector of Land Revenue, as Magistrate, and as general administrator with special responsibility for the Malay population of the district. The FMS now had a well-developed land system, based on registration of title on the model of the Torrens system developed in South Australia. The system had been introduced to meet the needs of commercial plantation companies, but it also comprised the entry in a local sub-district register (EMR) of every individual smallholding. Thus the Malay peasant was given a permanent but also a marketable title to his land. Landowners paid a perpetual quit rent as a form of land revenue. In his dealings with the Malay population the DO worked through sub-district headmen (*penghulu*) drawn from prominent local families, usually of the peasant middle class rather than the old Malay aristocracy. It was a traditional office adapted to an alien administrative system.

In the UMS, however, British control was much looser. The State revenues would not have sufficed to support British staff on the scale found in the FMS. Here there was a British Adviser (not 'Resident') — except in Johor where the title was General Adviser — and one or two (in Johor rather more) less senior British administrators employed as Commissioner of Lands (for the State) or as Assistant Adviser or as District Officer of a key district. But many executive posts in the administrative hierarchy, including Chief Minister (*Mentri Besar*), State Secretary, and most District Officers, were held by Malay officials of the aristocratic class now grouped as a State Civil Service. Thus the government of the UMS retained much more of its Malay character although subject to considerable British influence.

In addition to the administrative services there were a large number of technical and professional services in the FMS, with a sprinkling of such staff in the UMS. In time all these services, except such as were recruited for the State alone, were treated as a pool so that individual officers were freely interchangeable between States of the FMS and UMS. In the Straits Settlements (SS) there was a third structure. In each Settlement the local head of the administration was the Resident Councillor (a civil servant who was also an *ex-officio* member of the SS Legislative Council) with District Officers working under his direction. The head of the SS administration was the Colonial Secretary SS on parity with the Chief Secretary FMS (the title given later to the former Resident General). There was no central co-ordination of the UMS, but in his supervisory function the Governor of the Straits Settlements also acted as High Commissioner for the Malay States and (in his dealings with the British Advisers) was assisted by a more junior secretary of the administrative cadre.

Thus step by step a curious and ramshackle constitutional structure had been erected in what is now Peninsular Malaysia and Singapore. The Governor/High Commissioner also had functions in relation to the Sultanate of Brunei and the island of Labuan. In each of the FMS and the SS there were component units subject to strong central authority and institutions. The Governor/High Commissioner had to resolve the inevitable conflicts of local interest and clashes of personality in the bureaucracy. This ultimate control, albeit from a great distance, by one man and the supply of staff from a common pool made the system workable. But its absurdity and inefficiency had become obvious long before it was cruelly exposed in 1942.

In retrospect one can see that the formation of the FMS with its strong centralizing tendency was the major error of policy which for half a century frustrated subsequent attempts to achieve the desirable and inevitable unification of Malaya as a whole. The problem worked itself out in thirty years (1909-41) of ineffectual attempts to decentralize the FMS so as to attract the UMS States to join it. In 1909 there was a reorganization of the FMS in which the Resident General took the title Chief Secretary and a Federal Council was established. In its original form the Federal Council comprised the four Malay Rulers of the FMS, the High Commissioner, the Chief Secretary, and the four British Residents and four unofficial members appointed by the High Commissioner. The purpose of the Council was to provide a forum for discussion of policy in which the Malay Rulers, and their advisers the British Residents, could express their views to the central bureaucracy. But the effect was quite otherwise. Instead of a dialogue between Malay Rulers and British administrators such as the State Councils had provided (up to 1896) the proceedings of the Federal Council were dominated by discussion between the businessmen, who were the appointed unofficial members, and the bureaucrats on a variety of commercial, fiscal, and technical matters.[12]

The four Malay Rulers, seated in lonely dignity on a raised dais, remained silent observers of these proceedings. They were unfamiliar with the matters under discussion and unable to join in a dialogue in English since they were not fluent in that language. The futility of this situation was recognized by a reorganization in 1927. The Rulers withdrew from the Council and were replaced by Malay unofficial members who were able to enliven and to vary the debates by raising matters of concern to the Malay community — though here they spoke as Malay aristocrats, which they were, and not as spokesmen of the peasant majority.

A second untoward effect of the establishment of a Federal Council was a further decline in the activity and influence of the State Councils, which now concerned themselves with such small matters as the appointment of *penghulu* and the granting of loans for the building of mosques. Control of policy was more than ever in the hands of the federal government of Kuala Lumpur.

In the interval between the two World Wars there were two more attempts, equally fruitless, at a major reorganization of the government of the Malay States. In 1925 the High Commissioner (Sir Laurence Guillemard) put forward a scheme of administrative decentralization in the FMS in which the post of Chief Secretary would disappear and control of various services would be returned to the State governments. These proposals were vehemently opposed by the Chief Secretary (Sir George Maxwell) and by the business community. In the end only minor changes were made. In 1931 the High Commissioner (Sir Cecil Clementi) again proposed a scheme of decentralization in which the all-powerful Chief Secretary FMS would be downgraded to become Federal Secretary, junior in status to the Residents of the four States. Clementi also envisaged a customs union of the whole of Malaya and a form of Pan-Malayan Union of SS, FMS, and UMS. Again there was much local opposition. The outcome (following a visit to Malaya in 1932 by Sir Samuel Wilson from the Colonial Office) was a modest amount of decentralization in the FMS including the replacement of the post of Chief Secretary by a less senior Federal Secretary. In the main it was a battle of vested interests ending with some tinkering rather than real reform. But although the advocates of decentralization could not carry the day, there was a general but inconclusive recognition that the FMS as then constituted was becoming less and less acceptable to Malay opinion.

In the course of these changes the Federal Council grew to a total membership of twenty-eight, of whom sixteen were officials headed by the High Commissioner. Of the twelve appointed unofficial members four were Malays, five Europeans, two Chinese, and one Indian.

In the Straits Settlements there was a Legislative Council of a similar character: it had a majority of official members and the unofficial members were appointed by the Governor. There were demands, more especially from the local-born Straits Chinese, for the introduction of elections to the Council. Both the government and commercial interests were opposed to such a change which appeared dangerously radical (the 'crass folly' of a few 'misguided idealists').[13] It was argued that the majority of the population of the Straits Settlements were aliens of different races who had little interest in the government of a territory in which they were only temporary sojourners. Even the Malay, Eurasian, and Straits Chinese, who were the domiciled minority groups, gave little support to demands for elections or for an unofficial majority in the Council.

There was little to show, up to 1941, as the result of much discussion. Yet perhaps discussion was a necessary means to preparing public opinion for the changes to come after the catalytic episode of the Japanese occupation of 1942-45. A logical case had been made for the two reforms of the immediate post-war period: the unification of Malaya and the institution of more representative councils through which local opinion could be communicated to the executive branch of the government. The weakness of councils in which the unofficial members were a minority appointed by the government was not that they failed to criticize. Forthright criticism was often made of government policies. But such a system is based on the selection of unofficial members by a process of behind the scenes consultation with the upper class of businessmen, lawyers, and Malay aristocrats. They were sometimes men of talent and very serious in their participation in the system. But inevitably they spoke for the class from which they were drawn. Thus Raja Chulan, one of the liveliest of the Malay members of the Federal Council, opposed the opening of English-medium secondary schools in areas of Malay settlement; it would encourage the sons of peasants to leave the land.[14]

At the level of parish-pump affairs there were lesser advisory bodies such as the Municipal Commissions of the towns of the Straits Settlements and in the FMS the 'Sanitary Boards' which served as town councils in up-country districts. Again the unofficial membership was drawn by nomination from the established leadership of the local communities.

In the next two chapters, concerned among other things with the growth of nationalism, it will be seen that the modest political activity compatible with colonial rule in this period did have its effect on later events. Tan Cheng Lock, who was to found the Malayan Chinese Association in 1949, was a lone voice advocating liberal reform in the Legislative Council of the inter-war period. Datuk Onn bin Jaafar, the first President of the United Malay National Organization founded in 1946, accepted appointment as an unofficial member of the Johor State Council in 1936 on the express understanding that he was free to speak his mind — and did so in characteristic fashion.[15]

Notes

1   Bonney (1971) gives a detailed account of Anglo-Kedah relations down to

1821 and Clodd (1948) a biography of Light. Mills (1925) and Turnbull (1972) deal fully with the history and external relations of the ss in the mid-nineteenth century.

2   Captain (later Admiral Sir George) Elliot, son of Lord Minto, Governor General of India (1807-13), cited in Wurzburg (1954) at p. 296. Raffles's rapid rise was due to Minto's confidence in him. Elliot was the captain of the warship which took them both to Java in 1811 and later mediated in Raffles's quarrel with the British military commander in Java, Gillespie.

3   Leifer (1968), Tregonning (1965), Irwin (1955), and Runciman (1960) on the emergence of the modern Sabah and Sarawak from the Sultanates of Sulu and Brunei together with the Anglo-Dutch rivalry in Borneo.

4   Khoo Kay Kim (1966) and (1972).

5   Parkinson (1960), 109; Cowan (1961), 172 and 264. McIntyre (1961), Chew (1965), J. de V. Allen (1963), Khoo Kay Kim (1966). Broadly opinions are divided as to whether commercial pressure, and, if it was this, which particular instance of it, or British fear of foreign intervention in a strategically important area was the decisive factor. There is ample evidence that both factors were present in the minds of ministers and civil servants at the Colonial Office. Khoo argues cogently that as early as 1872 the Colonial Office had been persuaded to the inevitability of a change of policy but would not permit it to be made so long as Ord, in whom they had no confidence, was Governor of the ss — 'the present Governor cannot be trusted to interfere wisely', wrote Herbert, the Permanent Under Secretary at the Colonial Office, in October 1872 (cited by Khoo at p. 67).

6   Hugh Low in a letter dated 28 May 1878 to Sir William Robinson, then Governor ss.

7   Apart from general misconceptions over the nature of the new arrangement there were discrepancies of meaning between the Malay and English texts of the Pangkor 'Engagement': Parkinson (1960) at p. 138 concludes that it was not 'a masterpiece of lucidity even in English'.

8   Isabella Bird, the Victorian lady traveller who visited Low and stayed with him in February 1879. The relevant passage in her book is based on a long letter to her sister which is preserved by her publishers (the house of John Murray). In using her letters from Malaya as material for her book she omitted this and other frank comments by Hugh Low. Passages from the letters are quoted in Gullick (1978) and (1979).

9   Apart from official papers by Low sent to the Colonial Office (CO/273) he kept a Journal (Sadka 1954). The minutes of the Perak State Council (Wilkinson ed. Burns (1971)) and also Sadka in Tregonning (ed.) 1962 give a good picture of Low's policies. On his personality see also Isabella Bird.

10   Wilkinson (1932) preface at p. iii. Wilkinson's part in the development of Malay education is described below in Chapter 12.

11   Wright and Reid (1912) Chapter XI: Goldman (1972): Kessler (1978).

12   In this passage I have aimed to follow the main lines of Emerson's (1937) exposition. See also Mills (1942).

13   *Straits Times* 14 November 1930 cited in Mills (1942) at p. 32.

14   Proceedings of the FMS Federal council 1924.

15   Roff (1967), 169.

4 The Indigenous Communities

One of the key terms of modern Malaysian society is *bumiputra,* a Malay word which means literally 'son of the soil', indigenous. In Malaya it serves to distinguish the Malays from the Chinese and Indian communities of recent immigrant origin and in Borneo it is applied to the long-settled tribes of Sabah and Sarawak. In this usage the word is modern, but the idea which it expresses goes back to the early days of British rule. A High Commissioner (Hugh Clifford) whose service in Malaya had begun in 1883 described the Malay States in 1927 as Mohamedan monarchies and declared that Britain had 'no mandate to vary the system of government which has existed in these territories since time immemorial'.[1] From this proposition it followed that non-Malays had no claim to political rights and even the Malay subjects of the Rulers could not have such rights since this would be to 'vary the system'. It was arch-conservatism expressed in such policies as the restriction on the alienation of land to Malays for the non-traditional cultivation of rubber and an education policy designed to make the son of a Malay peasant a better peasant than his father had been, but not to prepare him for any alternative occupation — themes to which we shall come in their proper place. It was an attitude expressed by the Malays themselves in great respect for tradition (*'adat*). An American wrote more harshly of an 'artificially petrified crust of old traditions'.[2]

In post-colonial times Article 153 of the Malaysian constitution requires the King, now a constitutional monarch in spite of earlier objections, to safeguard the special position of the Malays and of the natives of Borneo. It is no longer a question of safeguarding a traditional way of life against intrusive change but of recognizing the disadvantages which have followed from doing so before. The indigenous communities have fallen behind in the economic progress of the country and this weakness is to be recognized and counterbalanced by securing to them special rights in the sphere of politics, the public service, and educational opportunities.

Singapore was compelled to withdraw from Malaysia in 1965 partly because its Prime Minister, Lee Kuan Yew, advocated a gradual progression towards a 'Malaysian Malaysia' in which all communities would be on an equality. Following the bloody riots of 13 May 1969 it was made a criminal offence to question these special rights in public.[3]

Thus the concept of indigenous communities is associated with tradition and the absence of change. A Malay of 1874 who returned to his village a hundred years later might well be astonished to find his great-grandson tapping rubber, growing two annual crops of rice by the use of fertilizers and controlled irrigation, sending his children to school, taking a bus into the nearest town, reading a newspaper, and lobbying the local State assemblyman. There has been much more change than is sometimes recognized. At all events, it is the purpose of this chapter to trace the social history and in particular the political awakening of the indigenous peoples over the last century and a half.

In the first three-quarters of the nineteenth century the basis of power in the Malay States was, as it had long been, the control of economic resources. But it was a changing economic system. Up to the end of the eighteenth century the Rulers obtained their revenues mainly from the trade passing through the ports which were the centres of political power. In the ensuing half-century there was a dispersal of power. The rapidly industrializing countries of the West demanded ever-increasing quantities of tin from western Malaya. New tin mines were opened in the outlying districts where the richest deposits were situated. The district chiefs of tin-mining centres such as Larut in Perak and Lukut in Selangor became wealthier and therefore more powerful than the Sultans of those States. Immigrant Chinese miners worked the mines, but the local Malay Ruler took his share of the profits in export duties on tin, import duties on miners' supplies, and receipts from the grant of tax-collecting monopolies (farms) to Chinese headmen. The ensuing conflict within the Malay ruling class for control of these sources of wealth and power led to the strife and instability which in turn became the occasion of British intervention in the Malay States in 1874.[4]

The social structure of Malay society was little changed. Swettenham wrote that 'there was in 1874 a very broad line indeed between the ruling classes in Malaya and the rayats, the people. The people had no initiative whatever; they were there to do what their chiefs told them—no more, no less'.[5] The authority of a district chief was enforced by his control of a following of armed men and hangers-on. They looked to him for support from his revenues and augmented their livelihood by trading and minor forays and exactions. With this force stationed in a stockade at a river-mouth the chief could levy taxes on the trade entering and leaving the estuary, defend the river villages against attack, and call on his Malay subjects to render him the customary labour service (*kerah*) as he might require it for personal or public works. If oppression exceeded the accepted limits or the chief could not protect his district against raids by his rivals, his subject population melted away. The memories of these times lingered on long after they had ended—'in former days there was nothing to eat, there being a dearth of buffaloes, the planting of padi was difficult and no one could be certain that he would not have to fly on the morrow'.[6] A far-sighted chief might apply his revenues in assisting settlers to establish their villages in his district. But the more general effect of the system was to discourage the peasant cultivator from undertaking long-term improvements or achieving noticeable prosperity.

At this time much of the Malay States was uninhabited. The total Malay population of the Peninsula was perhaps 300,000, of which about 30,000 were in the agricultural districts of the Perak river valley and as many more in inland Negri Sembilan. The main centres of Malay settlement were in Province Wellesley, Kedah, and Kelantan in the north-west and north-east; here there may well have been greater stability, but very little is known of local conditions.[7] In the tin-mining districts the Chinese miners outnumbered the Malay population which was very small indeed.

The effects of the imposition of the *pax britannica* were slow to appear. From Sumatra and other parts of Indonesia and also from the northern states of the Peninsula there was a gradual influx of Malay settlers into the central area. With the opening of bridle-paths and other communications Malay settlement was no longer confined to areas accessible from the river lines. With political stability and the grant of permanent titles to land, villages took root on the sites where the settlers had made their homes. But until the introduction of rubber in the early years of this century the peasant economy lacked a firm foundation. The cultivation of rice remained a precarious source of livelihood so long as the farmer relied for his water-supply on rainfall or on irrigation from his own makeshift brushwood dams and ditches. The only major irrigation works undertaken by the colonial government in this period was at Krian on the northern coast of Perak.[8] It was a success, but it cost five times as much as had been estimated and this discouraged the government from further major schemes of irrigation until the 1930s. The peasant could supplement his subsistence agriculture by hunting, fishing in the rivers or in the sea, and by collecting for sale jungle produce such as *rattans, damar,* and *gutta percha.* With his modest cash income from these sources he bought salt, cloth, and iron utensils. He no longer had to render customary labour service to his chief, but he could not look to him for assistance in developing his land. The period up to 1905 has been well called 'the years of uncertainty'.[9]

British rule deprived the Malay aristocratic class both of its power and of the economic basis of its power. Taxes were now collected and paid into a central State treasury. There was no effective resistance, but there was a deep resentment. 'The feeling of loss of real power, possibly national dignity, of constraint and forced obedience to the law, compensated for by only a moderate salary or pension, will not at once die out in the breasts of many Rajas and of their immediate followers'.[10] The new rulers found three means of conciliating their dispossessed predecessors. Some aristocrats continued to hold traditional office in the State and were paid fixed pensions for their tenure of these much-prized sinecures. A few of the most prominent figures were recruited as members of the new State Councils described in Chapter 3. But the main solution to the problem of the frustrated and unemployed Malay aristocrat was to make him into a civil servant. Early attempts at this change were, however, a failure. In the 1880s Malay chiefs were sometimes appointed to the honorific post of 'Malay magistrate' in the districts which they had once governed so that they might advise the British District Officer who had replaced them. However, lack of education in the Western style combined with traditional attitudes to the obligations of kinship and to the customary perquisites of authority — 'nepotism' and 'bribery' in the eyes of their British colleagues — rendered the old-style Malay aristocrat unsuitable as a partner in the new regime. The second attempt consisted in educating the next generation of Malay aristocrats in the English fashion. The two young sons of the exiled Sultan Abdullah of Perak were sent to be educated in English at Malacca and one of them grew up to become the most talented and influential Malay public man of his generation, Raja Chulan — the first Malay nominated to membership of the FMS Federal Council.[11] But other experiments in particular States were unsuccessful. Finally in 1905 — in the face of much misgiving in high places — a centre of training on the lines of an English public school, the Malay College, was established at Kuala Kangsar in Perak to take pupils from all States. This 'Malay Eton', as it was sometimes called, at first took only pupils of aristocratic birth. But about 1920 a quota, later 50 per cent, of the places was allocated to the sons of Malay commoners selected by the vulgar test of merit.[12] The main function of the College was to train its pupils for appointment to the administrative branch of the government service. Aristocratic prestige even now attaches to the College; it has served to make a career in the administrative service the first choice not merely of the Malay aristocracy but also of the ablest Malays of any class. This trend towards specialization in the government service has had profound effects upon the structure of leadership in the Malay community.

Rubber became a major smallholder crop in the decade 1910–20. In spite of discouragement and restriction by the government, which would have preferred that the Malay cultivator should concentrate on the traditional, stable, but less profitable cultivation of rice, rubber rapidly became the mainstay of the peasant economy in central and southern Malaya. The economic life of the rubber-tree extends over decades and it is planted on land held under permanent title. As such it became a valuable and a saleable investment. In the period of the first rubber-planting boom about 1910 there was justified official concern lest much Malay ancestral land might be converted to rubber cultivation and then sold at the high prices offered by non-Malay entrepreneurs. The Malay Reservations Enactment of 1913 was a measure originally intended to preserve Malay land in Malay ownership. Later, however, it came to be used to reserve unalienated land in large tracts for future Malay occupation. As such it has become one of the most valuable of the special rights of the Malay community.

Economic development through rubber-planting spread to Johor (and also to Malacca in the SS). Although Johor did not accept a British 'General Adviser' until 1914, it had been very much the economic hinterland of Singapore for many years before that. It did not participate in the tin-mining boom which was the engine of development in the FMS because it has no significant tin deposits. But there was a good deal of small-scale Chinese agricultural development in the latter part of the nineteenth century. Then came rubber and railways which accelerated the tempo and drew into the State a considerable number of Javanese and other Indonesian immigrants. Johor resembles the FMS in having a considerable area of land under rubber, coconut, and oil-palm smallholdings (as well as many plantations). It differs from them in having jealously preserved its independence as a Malay State, under a strong Ruler. It was never dominated from outside by a central bureaucracy. Indeed when it joined a federation for the first time in 1948, the State government, under the leadership of Datuk Onn bin Jaafar who was then its chief minister, had some difficulty in adjusting to the new relationship.

Johor like the four northern States was part of the Unfederated Malay States (UMS) — for reasons explained in the previous chapter. It had little else in common with them. The northern States of Kedah, Perlis, Kelantan, and Trengganu had had close economic ties with the ss long before the unceremonious transfer of suzerainty from Siam to Britain in 1909 — the reigning Sultan of Kedah is reported to have said that 'my country was bought and sold like a buffalo'. These States, however, had relatively large Malay populations and few foreigners. The government of each State was in the hands of a Malay ruling class which was much more securely in control than the Malay Rulers of the FMS before 1874. They had their financial problems and the stresses arising from competition for power in the State. But there was no foreign commercial penetration nor a large alien labour force. They were essentially *Malay* States in their character. In Kedah and Kelantan in particular there had been progress towards a modern style of administration long before the transfer of 1909.[13] After the transfer much of the day-to-day administration remained in the hands of Malays, who had the solidarity of serving in a local State civil service recruited from and serving in one State. Lack of revenue imposed on the northern UMS restraint in expenditure on departmental services; the majority of the non-technical posts were filled by Malay officials and the Malay language was generally still used as the working medium of government. The influence of the British Adviser was felt in the making of policy, but he was not the executive head of the State government. There was a Malay chief minister and supporting staff. This system was taken as the model for the State governments of the former FMS when the Federation of Malaya was established in 1948. It is no accident that many of the leading politicians of independent Malaysia have been drawn from the former UMS (including Johor); it was here that during the period of colonial rule the springs of confidence in their own ability to govern continued to flow among the Malay upper class.

The position of the Malay peasant in the UMS was also different from that of the FMS. In the main he lived by the cultivation of rice rather than rubber. His standard of living, and the services provided by his government, were correspondingly more modest. There was no direct pressure of an alien economic system such as constrained the Malay community of the FMS. In the fields of religion and education there was much more native vigour. Kelantan was famous for its flourishing system of Islamic schools —

> The focus of learning in the capital at this time [about 1880] was the Masjid Kota Bharu, the central mosque, where could be found a large number of religious teachers and some hundreds of students from every corner of Kelantan. The environs of the mosque were crowded with the *pondok* (small huts of bamboo and *attap*) of students. Many teachers also taught in their own homes. . .[14]

On a smaller scale this pattern was repeated in outlying villages. There were also centres of instruction in Kedah and in Trengganu of a similar type. The officials of the village mosque and the religious teachers were active members of local élite. It was a more vigorous rural community — and less disposed to knuckle down under its own ruling class. It was further stimulated by the closer contact with centres of Islamic learning and practice in the Middle East which evolved at this time as Malays made the pilgrimage to Mecca or pursued their studies at the al-Azhar University in Cairo. At the centre of the State there was in Kelantan and other States a religious establishment in the form of *Mufti* (jurisconsult) and *Kathis* (trial judges and registrars), whose function was to administer Islamic law in the religious courts and to oversee the practice of Islam with a view to preventing heretical doctrines and beliefs creeping in. Islam requires that the faithful shall make annual contributions (*zakat* and *fitrah*) which are not public revenues over which a non-Muslim British Adviser could properly exercise control. Kelantan led the way by establishing (in 1915) a Council of Religion and Malay Custom to collect and administer these dues. With these resources the Council was able to develop schools and the publishing of books as well as to oversee the practice of religion and many social reforms. In other States such as Kedah there was less central direction, but nonetheless a great deal of activity in the fields of religion and education.[15] In his definitive study of this movement in Kelantan Roff speaks of 'the strain of insistent self-determination that ran throughout based on a clear if not always commonly shared vision of the essential elements of their own society'.[16]

Malay society in the ss lacked an aristocratic ruling class and the institutional framework of a Malay State. The intellectual leadership was provided by a small but influential group, many of whom were not pure Malays. Again the bond was Islam. The leaders were Arabs, Indian Muslims, or of mixed Malay descent (*Jawi peranakan*) — they were journalists, teachers, and businessmen. In Malay society putative descent from the Prophet is recognized by the honorific title '*Syed*' (or *Sharifah* for a woman) which confers status equal to that of a Raja of royal descent. But this group included many whose influence was derived from their theological learning or their proficiency in the written discourse on social questions. In the Malay villages of Province Wellesley and Malacca the smallholder cultivated his rice or his rubber and lived a life very like that of the Malay peasant in the FMS.

Malay opposition to the Malayan Union constitution in 1946 was a political movement based upon Malay national feeling. The origins of the sentiment and of the organization which made it effective can be traced back over three-quarters of a century before. It began with Malay resentment at British intervention in 1874, though much of that feeling had faded by 1900. The origins of Malay nationalism are to be found mainly in the social, economic, and intellectual conditions of Malaya in this century.[17] The difficulty in tracing these changes lies in the imprecise concept of 'Malay nationalism' and the fact that there were no outstanding figures and very little political content in the movement before the decade of the 1930s. It has been well said that in the early years of the twentieth century there was among a minority of Malays an 'awareness' of the presence of other major communities in Malaya and of the weaknesses of the Malay community itself. From that followed an anxious self-examination and the advocacy of various reforms. For a generation or two the Malay intelligentsia saw the salvation of their community in terms of better education and the abandonment of passive conservatism in their social values rather than in political action.[18]

It is generally accepted that three main strands can be identified in the texture of this movement. There was the intellectual debate in newspapers, books, and articles. The main contributors were the intelligentsia and journalists of the Straits Settlements in the early years; but later a number of periodicals and newspapers, some of them short-lived, provided a platform for reformers in other parts of Malaya, notably Penang and Kelantan. It is difficult to assess how much this intellectual debate contributed to the general outlook of the educated Malay in later years. In general the weakness of this reform movement was its lack of direction towards attainable and specific objectives, and its lack of a popular base among the mass of the Malay population. It was all rather woolly. But it did probably contribute to creating a general awareness of a problem affecting the Malay community as a whole.

The second element was the Islamic religious reform movement of the Malay States. This had a much wider constituency and a more definite popular base. But it foundered on the mutually frustrating opposition of two groups, the conservatives (*kaum tua*) and the reformers (*kaum muda*). Broadly the conservatives were the Islamic establishment in the Malay States to which reference has been made above. It was their function to preserve orthodoxy of doctrine and of law. But on many points the reformers challenged hallowed doctrines and practices as unfounded on true Islam. It is a feature of Malay culture that it retains elements of Hindu and pagan practices; it was sometimes difficult to separate religious from social observances (one is reminded of the midwinter feast which has become the Christmas of the Christian calendar). In these disputes the State government used its authority to support its own officials against their critics. In a society in which the authority of the Ruler is not lightly challenged this was often decisive. Although these disputes were doctrinal rather than political, the 'crack-down' on the reformers inhibited political debate.[19]

In the end the most effective expression of Malay discontent came from the civil service and the teaching profession. The latter included both teachers educated through the medium of English and their humbler brethren trained to teach in the Malay schools. In the civil service it was particularly the Malays recruited from the upper class as administrators who provided effective leadership. But they did so only in the final stages. For much of the earlier years this group remained silent — it was of course difficult for them to take part in activities which, if they escaped the censure of the British authorities, might be disapproved by the Malay Rulers.

In Chapter 3 an account has been given of the development of the central bureaucracy of the FMS responsive to pressures from commercial interests, European or Asian, rather than from the Malay ruling class. The Malays were conscious that their lost power and influence had passed to alien hands. In particular they feared the commercial strength of the Chinese. In their polite fashion the Malay Rulers had begun to protest over these tendencies as early as 1903. When the FMS was established, it became the practice (until the Federal Council was established) to hold gatherings (called *durbars*) of the Malay Rulers of the FMS at which they might exchange views with the Resident-General and the four Residents. At the second of these conferences in 1903 the senior Malay Sultan, the much-respected Sultan Idris of Perak, expressed the hope that 'the affairs of each State might be managed by its own officers'.[20] At the same meeting there had been discussion of schemes for 'the further employment of Malays in government service'.[21] It was this which led to the foundation of the Malay College referred to above. However much restrained it was, the debate recognized a problem, that in the FMS with a population of 310,000 there were only 2,636 Malays in the government service (including the rank and file of the police force) and practically none in positions of responsibility. There was some gradual progress towards remedying this imbalance. But even in 1940 only 10 per cent of the Malayan Civil Service, which manned the senior administrative posts, was Malay; moreover, even then Malay officers of the MCS were employed in district posts and not in the central bureaucracy. It is a measure of the resentment which this situation created that when Malay MCS officers took over as chief ministers of the former FMS States in 1948, they had a pact among themselves that the British Adviser (formerly British Resident) should see no working files, but be confined to his strict constitutional function of giving advice to the Ruler when required.[22] The restoration of power to the Malay upper class was, however, the product of pressure from another quarter.

The growth of Malay primary education will be described in a later chapter. By the 1920s it had created a substantial demand for trained Malay schoolteachers. In 1922 the Sultan Idris Training College was opened at Tanjong Malim (on the Perak — Selangor boundary) to replace a previous, much smaller college at Malacca.

The new College could take up to four hundred students. The intake selected by competitive examination came from the Malay peasant class of all parts of Malaya. The students were to be prepared for a life's work of teaching in village primary schools in which the range of subjects was severely practical. But the College became the focus of Malay intellectual life.[23] It brought together from all parts of Malaya young men, serious and intelligent, with a sense of vocation. It may well be that the intellectual and religious debate to which reference has been made played its part. There were other activities too which had a bearing on Malay attitudes. To provide better schoolbooks in the Malay primary schools the College developed a Malay Translation Bureau which acted as an educational publishing house. Its output ranged from Malay classical literature, in which Malays take much pride, to translations of Shakespeare and of the Sherlock Holmes stories. It was far from being a left-wing book club, but it opened a window on the world.

The other key event of the 1920s was the founding in 1926 of the Singapore Malay Association (KMS). A Malay member had been appointed for the first time to the Straits Settlements Legislative Council. The purpose of the Association was to rally communal support for the new spokesman. As such it was the first Malay association with an avowedly political purpose and it served as a model for later developments in the Malay States. The position of an unofficial nominated member of a council, however august, was one of weakness. Tan Cheng Lock, who served in the Straits Settlements Legislative Council from 1923 to 1935, retired from it (partly for family reasons) saying that 'I vowed never again to become a member of any Malayan Legislative Council under any circumstances in future but instead to work among members of the public and organize them into a strong political body'.[24] Without political parties there could be no effective political pressure.

In the FMS similar developments ensued. In 1927 the Federal Council was reconstituted and the number of nominated Malay unofficial members was increased to four (all members of ruling families in their States of origin). This ginger-group used its platform in the Council to make a public issue of the position of the Malays in the government service and in the economy generally. This was the issue on which the Malay community was becoming increasingly concerned. The Chinese were becoming a settled community in Malaya and this change threatened the Malay position.

A small but active group of the Malay intelligentsia, some graduates of the Sultan Idris Training College and others journalists, established in 1938 a radical and left-wing political movement under the name of the *Kesatuan Melayu Muda* (KMM), the Young Malay Union. The founder was Ibrahim bin Yaacob who as a student at the Sultan Idris College had gathered together a group who aspired to follow the example of the Indonesian leader, Sukarno. From 1931 to 1938 Ibrahim worked first as a village schoolmaster in his native Pahang and then as an instructor at the Police Depot in Kuala Lumpur.[25] During this time he had written a good deal for the Malay vernacular press; in 1938 he went over to full-time journalism. The KMM was opposed to colonial rule, which Malay opinion generally still accepted as something of a bulwark against Chinese domination, and it was critical of the Malay upper class for its docility. It saw the future of Malaya in a union with Indonesia. Although the KMM remained a minority group, it had considerable influence at a formative period in the growth of Malay national sentiment; its leaders were later prominent in the Malay national movement promoted by the Japanese during their occupation.

At about the same time, but probably not in direct reaction to the KMM, the English-educated upper-class élite who followed careers in the administrative and professional services took the lead in forming Malay Associations, on the model of the Singapore Malay Association, in Perak, Pahang, Selangor, and later in Negri Sembilan.[26] A first national congress of Malay Associations of the ss as well as of the Malay States was held in Kuala Lumpur in mid-1939. Its purpose was to rouse the Malay community from a state of apathy so that an effective Malay national movement might be formed to promote and protect the interests of the community.

A second national gathering of the Malay Associations was held late in 1940. By now Malay Associations had been formed in most of the Malay States and also in Sarawak and Brunei. The leadership was obliged to walk rather delicately. If the movement was to attract general support, it must be led by Malays drawn from the hereditary aristocracy of the State; the Perak Association had failed because it did not observe that principle.[27] But leaders drawn from the traditional upper class were determined to avoid any criticism of or clash with the Malay Rulers or the British colonial government. They were inherently conservative in their outlook and their public attitudes. One of the resolutions passed at the 1940 congress was a call for support of the British war effort. Among those who attended was a Malay journalist, son of a former chief minister of his native State of Johor, Onn bin Jaafar. In a fashion prophetic of his role in 1946 Onn called for a Malay effort to 'regain the political and civil rights which have slipped from them'.[28] These very moderate aspirations, however, took a much sharper tone under the impact of the events of 1942-45 and British ineptitude over the Malayan Union in 1946. The seed had been sown by 1940; the harvest was reaped after the war.

In retrospect one can see that in the period between the wars the Malay community made a transition from comparative isolation to active involvement. To preserve their traditional culture and way of life they had been encouraged to go their own way. They had been confined within the limits of areas of Malay agricultural settlement, and within the occupational bounds of peasant farming and the government service. The central government of their country and the capitalist development of rubber, tin, and trade remained in other hands. But Malay unease at the weakness of their position led to a slow awakening. Up to 1941 the moderate majority under traditional leadership was disposed to accept British hegemony as a safeguard against the economic power of the Chinese, but came to see that they must mobilize to exert pressure on their colonial rulers. The British defeat in 1942 and the imposition of the Malayan Union in 1946 demolished the assumptions on which the previous Malay attitude had been based. They must protect themselves by mobilizing their own strength; in the tentative moves of 1938-40 they had found the means to do so.

Until Malaysia was proposed in 1961 the indigenous peoples of northern Borneo had had little contact, and shared no common experience, with the peoples of Malaya. They also lacked the dominant political framework of a Malay State. There was indeed a Malay Sultanate of Brunei which at one time had ruled northern Borneo. But it had fallen into a decline by the middle of the nineteenth century. Although Brunei had a long tradition – it was in its heyday as a trade centre when Magellan's ships called there in 1521 – it is more of a foreign outpost than an indigenous element of the Borneo world. Since it is not part of Malaysia, it need not be further described here.

It has been said by a leading authority that the classification of the Borneo peoples leads to 'a sort of cultural haze'. Their divisions can only be understood in terms of tribal and cultural origins. The accidents of history, 'the tormented geography of the interior',[29] the use of inaccurate names imposed by outsiders, all confuse the picture. The main line of division, however, is between the Muslim peoples of the coast and the river estuaries, many of whom are sailors or fishermen who live in boats, and the agricultural pagan or Christian peoples who extend in scattered villages from the coast to the interior.

Many of the Muslim peoples, especially in Sarawak, are or call themselves 'Malays', but for the most part they are descendants of converts from the pagan peoples with whom they still have much in common. Of the pagan peoples the Kadazan (called Dusuns until 1963) and the more primitive Murut are the largest indigenous groups in Sabah. In Sarawak the major inland group are the Iban (also called in the past Sea Dayak though they are not a maritime people); the Land Dayak of south-west Sarawak (the First Division) are distinct from the Iban and lack their restless energy. Both Sabah and Sarawak have large immigrant Chinese communities.

Among the pagan peoples groups of families live in hamlets. In former times these groups built themselves communal longhouses for defence against headhunting raiders – but in more peaceable times they are tending to disperse into adjoining but separate dwellings. Their foodcrops include rice, often dry rice grown under a regime of shifting cultivation, tapioca, yams, sugar-cane, sweet-potatoes, on family plots forming part of an area which the hamlet as a group has cleared by common effort. The pattern of authority within these groups varies in different tribes. Some have traditional local leaders or chiefs chosen for their personal qualities from a family of high standing. But in other tribes even this form of social co-ordination is lacking. There is no indigenous political structure on a scale comparable with the Malay State.[30] In modern times rubber has become an important smallholder crop, but standards of productivity and of quality are much lower than in Malaya.

In Sarawak the pace of social change reflected the idosyncratic and autocratic rule of the second 'white Rajah', Charles Brooke, who first arrived in 1852, became the effective ruler in 1863, and so continued (though in his last years *in absentia*) until his death in 1917 at the age of 88.[31] Charles Brooke, much more than the colourful and romantic founder of the dynasty, James Brooke, set his imprint on the regime. He said of himself that 'I know the Dayak mind and feeling much better than I do my own brothers and countrymen' and expressed his policy as 'letting system and legislation wait upon occasion'.[32] It was essentially a conservative regime which yielded to change only when change imposed itself. It differed from the similar objective of British rule in the Malay States in that Brooke was prepared to dispense with rapid economic development rather than allow it to upset the traditional pattern. In some sense he had no choice over this since Sarawak did not offer the same opportunities of development.

Yet when change came, it was not entirely the product of the circumstances of the indigenous peoples but reflected the constraints imposed by Brooke rule. When the first Brooke took control, he was there as the ally and supporter of Malay chiefs from Brunei, who had moved down the coast to the Sarawak river to trade as well as to rule. Under the Brooke regime the Malay community of Sarawak provided the 'Native Officers', the junior administrators who worked with the Brookes and their small European staff in the government of the State. They were encouraged to abandon their traditional interest in local trade in order to specialize in administration or in agriculture. In extending his grip on the territory which is now Sarawak (filched by degrees from the Sultanate of Brunei), Charles Brooke made use of the fighting tradition of the Iban who formed the major community of the riverine districts of central Sarawak. The Iban have no hereditary ruling class nor any large political units; they are by tradition a restless, warlike people whose inclination was to travel abroad in the course of headhunting or trade. Charles Brooke harnessed the energies of the Iban by using them in place of a police force or military reserve. If there was a local tribal war, or headhunting, or even unauthorized immigration across the watershed from Dutch Borneo into Sarawak territory, Brooke mobilized an Iban force to deal with it. It was effective and it cost very little — the Brookes had no money with which to maintain a large police-force. But it amounted to the use of inter-tribal raiding as an instrument of government. In later years, as more settled conditions were established, the Iban were encouraged to pursue more peaceful activities such as long-range trading expeditions. Among the indigenous peoples of Sarawak the Iban continue to show a talent for innovation and adaptation — in their absorption of mission education (and conversion to Christianity), in the planting of rubber, and in their active role in Sarawak politics.

One of the most significant parts of the Brooke heritage in Sarawak is the clear-cut distinction of role between ethnic groups. 'You must be one thing or the other' was a recurring theme in

Brooke times.[33] It was at one time a criminal offence for a Chinese trader to live among Iban, and descent from parents of a mixed marriage was not recognized; the individual must identify himself with the culture of one side or the other of his parentage. Sarawak political life is a reflection of fragmentation of social structure. Brooke rule did not create the lines of cleavage, but it tended to preserve and to strengthen them. The last years of Brooke rule, under the third Rajah, Vyner Brooke, were in some measure a period of stagnation. The style of government became more conventional, but the last ruler could neither shake off the outmoded policy of his formidable father nor find a replacement for it.

In contrast to the personal eccentricity of Brooke rule in Sarawak the administrative system of the British North Borneo Company, which obtained its Royal Charter in 1881, was straightforward. The Company succeeded to some curious previous concessionaires and in its early years it suffered from mismanagement of its affairs both in Borneo and in London. But in time it settled down to a humdrum routine like that of a crown colony. Several of the governors of the late nineteenth century were drawn from the Malayan Civil Service and in later years some came from the colonial service in Africa. The indigenous peoples were administered through local headmen to whom were delegated powers to govern and to try disputes in their courts. In the 1930s an attempt was made, but with only limited success, to develop a system of 'indirect rule' on the model of the 'native administrations' which were then the fashionable instrument of government in British African colonies.

Notes

1 Proceedings of the FMS Federal Council 1927.
2 Emerson (1937), 519.
3 Constitution (Amendment) Act 1971. Suffian (1972), 195.
4 Gullick (1958) is a study of pre-colonial Malay political systems in the mining States.
5 Swettenham (1948), 141.
6 Annual Report of the British Resident Negri Sembilan 1892.
7 On population see Gullick (1958), 23. On nineteenth-century Kedah see Sharom Ahmat (1977) and, on Kelantan, Roff (1974), 1-61 and Kessler (1978), Chapters 3 and 4. On Trengganu, Robert (1977) and Sheppard (1949).
8 D. E. Short and J. C. Jackson (1971).
9 Lim Tech Ghee (1977) — a very full and well-documented account of the changing pattern of Malay agriculture during the colonial period.

10 'Straits Settlements Despatch to the Colonial Office' dated 21 October 1880 (CO/273).

11 Isabella Bird (see Chapter 3, note 8) who met them in 1879 wrote 'They are 9 and 12 with monkeylike irrepressible faces. They never cease speaking and are very playful and witty, but though a large sum is paid for their education at the house of an English schoolmaster in Malacca, they speak atrocious pidgeon English and never will speak Malay. They are never still for one instant, chattering, reading snatches from books, asking questions, turning somersaults, jumping on Mr. Maxwell's shoulders begging for dollars. .' See also p. 281 of her book to the same effect.

12 Chapter 12 for the educational aspects of these developments.

13 See sources cited in note 7 above.

14 Abdullah Al-Qari bin Haji Salleh in Roff (ed.) (1974) at p. 89 in an essay on To' Kenali, a leading Islamic teacher in Kelantan in his time.

15 Roff (1974) and Khoo Kay Kim (1974).

16 Roff, 'The Origin and Early Years of the Majlis Ugama' in Roff (1974), 149. On the political aspects of the *Majlis Ugama* see Kessler (1978).

17 No one can write on Malay nationalism without being indebted to the definitive study by Roff (1967). See also Soenarno (1960) and Khoo Kay Kim (1974). Haji Abdul Majid's autobiography (1978) is an account of the intellectual pilgrimage of a Malay schoolmaster (later an Islamic administrator).

18 This is a brief summary of the argument in Khoo Kay Kim (1974) at p. 190.

19 Khoo (1974), 193 relates how a would-be reformer in Kelantan 'incurred the wrath of the ulama' (the State Islamic authorities) and was prosecuted for writing an article which was treated as 'an attack on the administration in Kelantan.'

20 Roff (1967), 97.

21 Stevenson (1975), 174.

22 In the first month (February 1948) of the new State and Federal constitution in Negri Sembilan the British Adviser (formerly the Resident Commissioner under the Malayan Union) was sent one file from the State Secretariat. It contained the minutes of the State Social Welfare Committee 'for information'. (As a member of the State Executive Council he also received the more important documents issued in connection with its meetings.) He discovered from correspondence with other British Advisers that they had had rather similar experiences. I was Secretary to the British Adviser Negri Sembilan at the time (with absolutely nothing to do). But the outbreak of the Emergency (Chapter 6) shortly afterwards created a host of new tasks, in particular liaison with the British-led security forces, and the British Advisers absorbed themselves in that work. In time, when the point had been made that the function of the British Adviser was to advise and no longer to administer, a more relaxed and co-operative attitude evolved.

23 Roff (1967), 143. See also Chapter 12.

24 Tregonning (1979), 47.

25 Roff (1967), 173.

26 Roff (1968) gives a detailed account of the transactions of the Selangor Malay Association based on its records.

27 Roff (1968), 121.

28   Roff (1967), 247.
29   Harrisson in Wang Gangwu (ed.) (1964). The phrases cited are at p. 168 and
     p. 165.
30   King (ed.) (1978) has 10 essays which bring out the many points of contrast
     in the social and political systems of Borneo communities.
31   In this brief account of the very personal regime of Charles Brooke I have
     drawn on Pringle's fascinating study (1971) and on Ward's no less in-
     teresting reminiscences (1966).
32   Pringle (1971), 178 and 137.
33   Pringle (1971), 298.

5 The Immigrant Communities

In Malaysia just over 45 per cent of the population is officially classified as non-indigenous.[1] The proportions are about the same in Malaya and in the Borneo States, but in the latter area the indigenous element is predominantly non-Malay. The Chinese make up about one-third of the population in both parts of Malaysia. As a matter of history the non-indigenous communities are descended from immigrants of the past century and a half (with only minor exceptions), but they are themselves no longer immigrants. Mass migration ceased half a century ago and a very large proportion of the non-indigenous communities is local-born. Even in 1957 when Malaya became independent three-quarters of its Chinese population had been born in Malaya or Singapore. But in spite of a vigorous government policy of spreading the use of Malay as the national language and of breaking down the marked differentiation of occupations between communities there has been little assimilation so far. To the Malays the other communities are *bangsa asing* — the *different* people. For a Malaysian Chinese or Indian, Malaysia is his country, but he is very conscious of his cultural heritage; not only language and religion but also such practical things as what he eats and how he earns his living distinguish him from other Malaysian groups. Yet it would be an oversimplification to impute to the non-indigenous peoples a mere preservation of a heritage which their forebears brought with them when they arrived. In the process of settling in Malaysia the immigrants necessarily adapted to local conditions and needs so that there is now a Malaysian, though not a Malay, dimension to their way of life. The purpose of this chapter is to trace the social history of that adaptation.

China has been in contact with the countries of Southeast Asia for many centuries. In the period when Sri Vijaya dominated the Straits of Malacca there was trade with China. The Malay Rulers of sixteenth-century Malacca sent embassies to the imperial court at Peking as a means of strengthening their position against the threat of Siamese aggression. In the same period the Chinese admiral Cheng Ho made his celebrated voyages to Southeast Asia. There were a few Chinese among the polyglot merchant community of Malacca under Malay, Portuguese, and Dutch rule. In modern times there are Chinese families at Malacca who can trace their descent from ancestors who settled there in the eighteenth century.[2]

The main flood of Chinese migration, however, did not begin until the second quarter of the nineteenth century. The rapid growth of Penang and then of Singapore as trade centres was followed by the expansion of tin-mining in the Malay States. These factors created a demand for labour and offered an opportunity of employment and of trade which drew in tens of thousands of male Chinese of working age.[3] They came mainly from the maritime provinces of Kwangtung and Fukien in southern China. Some travelled to Malaya at their own expense, but the majority had been recruited and shipped by labour recruiters as a commodity — labour. On arrival they were sold at a profit to a Malayan Chinese employer. The employer was entitled to retain the labourer in his service for a year and in that time to deduct his initial outlay from the wages earned by the latter. At each stage there were grave abuses. There was overcrowding on the steamers; conditions were even worse on the slow sailing vessels used in the early days. The officially prescribed allowance of space below decks was 12 square feet per man, but even this was often not provided. Suicide and mutiny at sea were common. In time the conditions of the passage to the Straits were improved. On arrival the labourers were detained as virtual prisoners and were often marched off under armed guard to private centres of detention (labour depots) pending their disposal to employers. On the mine or plantation they were supplied with food and other necessaries by the employer, who habitually overcharged them so that if they were not positively in debt, the net sum due to them from their wages was very little.

Throughout the nineteenth century disease took a fearful toll. 'Hospitals terribly overcrowded', said an official report from Selangor in 1888,

> 140,000 Chinese introduced to a most trying climate and hard work where only the fittest survive; hospital staff and buildings unable to meet the demand on their resources; the government labouring to improve sanitation in the dwellings of an apathetic people who do not yet understand the value of simple precau-

tions, and regard death and disease with the views of fatalists, making for the hospitals only when they are beyond the reach of medical skill.[4]

In fact, however, the 'simple precautions' then recommended by European doctors were useless since the causes of beriberi and of malaria, two of the worst scourges, were in 1888 unknown to Western medical science. One in five of the beriberi cases admitted to government hospitals died of undiagnosed malnutrition. Clearing jungle land for a new mine or plantation can create more favourable conditions for the mosquito, whose role as the vector of malaria was not established until 1898. In consequence it was not uncommon for a quarter of the labour force to die in the first year.[5]

For clothing they had 'short jackets and short trousers mostly made of coarse nankeen and unbleached stuff . . . a bag tied round their loins for money and other little things . . . they went barefooted and mostly wore bamboo hats'.[6] Their communal accommodation on a mine or estate was a large hut, perhaps 150 feet long and 40 feet wide with a palm-thatched roof rising to 30 feet above the ground. In the dormitories each had his allotted place . . .

Four posts driven into the ground with a plank or bamboo floor on them and a mat to cover the floor form the bed of the coolie. But the bed of the coolie is his sanctuary. Here he keeps his belongings and his furniture—his box, which also serves as a pillow, occupies a corner, and his tea-pot and opium-pipe and lamp are neatly arranged on a tray in the middle, whilst over them is the universal mosquito-curtain which the coolie can never do without however poor his circumstances. Here he retires after the day's work, entertains his friends, sips his tea, and writes 'clubbed packet' letters to his family in China. . . . The cooking range with the large rice-pan permanently imbedded in it, the kitchen dresser, chopper, saucepans and other culinary apparatus are kept scrupulously clean, though so much cannot be said of the draining and outside surroundings. . . .[7]

The Chinese labourer felt isolated. The mine or plantation to which he was sent was often in the remote interior of a Malay State. He had no contact with the government nor any means of communicating with it. The first Chinese-speaking European official of the Straits Settlements government was appointed in 1871; he was William Pickering, who later in 1877 founded the Chinese Protectorate, a government agency created to supervise Chinese immigration and to hold in check the abuses of the system. But it took a long time to break the wall of silence and gain the confidence of the mute, often sullen labourer. They were uneducated men of the peasant class and they arrived in this foreign land as individuals or in small groups. They spoke a number of different dialects of Chinese which were often mutually unintelligible and they regarded a man of a different group 'almost as a foreigner'.[8] Still more alien was the European official.

The Chinese labourer brought with him, apart from the modest tangible assets, a determination to survive, a capacity for hard work and the tradition, religion, and culture of his native China. His purpose was to make money and then to return to China. In Malaya he had desperate need of support, of help if attacked, of a decent burial if he died. In this alien and often hostile environment he adapted the social organization of his native village where the dominant institution was the lineage, based on partrilineal descent and inheritance of property in the male line. The lineage was the group of kinsmen of the same clan surname, living in the same locality and speaking the same sub-dialect of Chinese. In Malaya the immigrant usually had no kinsmen at hand, but he could ally himself with men of the same dialect group (Cantonese, Hokkien, etc.) and from the same district of origin in China. This was the attraction of the clan or district association, the *kongsi,* to the immigrant. It also suited the established Chinese entrepreneur — merchant, planter, or mine headman — who employed the labourer. In this way the employers could organize and control their workforce through the bonds and discipline of the associations in which the employers played a leading part. For much of the nineteenth century the association took a more sinister form, the Chinese secret society (called either *kongsi* or *huey* in the anglicized terminology of the time). The secret society was also an importation from China where it had its origins in patriotic underground resistance to the Manchu rulers.[9] In Malaya it became a concealed government of Chinese by Chinese.

On his arrival at a port in the Straits Settlements the Chinese immigrant was admitted to membership of one of the secret societies. There was a deliberately fearsome ritual of oath-taking under drawn swords and the like. The new member undertook to observe a code of conduct including absolute secrecy about everything connected with the society, promising to give aid to a brother member in any conflict with the authorities or with another society. For a time the British administrators were content to leave the Chinese to their own devices, of which they knew very little. But the societies by their nature caused breaches of the peace and other crimes. There were gang fights between members of rival groups and extortion was used to collect contributions to society funds; a member suspected of disloyalty was likely to be murdered. In the notorious Singapore riot of 1854 more than four hundred Chinese were killed. In 1867 there were riots in Penang and Province Wellesley in which some 30,000 Chinese and also 4,000 Malays were said to have been involved. The British intervention in the mining districts of Larut in Perak and Kuala Lumpur in Selangor followed years of intermittent but savage fighting between rival groups of miners, organized and financed by a secret society leadership based on the Straits Settlements; they fought for the control of the richest tin areas. As we have already seen, Malay participation in the revenues of these enterprises led to related struggles for power between Malay factions.

There were, however, two schools of thought about secret societies, — what should be done about them. The inquiry which followed the Penang riot of 1867 and the arrival of Pickering in 1871 led to a better understanding of the societies. It could be argued that the government lacked the means of exercising direct control of the growing Chinese community. On that view it was surely better to do no more than check the abuses and crimes but to leave the societies in existence as a useful, indeed an essential, means by which the Chinese could govern themselves. This policy was followed down to 1890; in some measure it reflected the still incomplete understanding of the extent of secret society ramifications in the western Malay States.[10] In the end, however, it was concluded that nothing less than root and branch eradication of secret societies could assure peace and good order. The new system required that all societies should be registered: those which had a criminal tendency (including societies which used the traditional secret society symbols and rituals) should be proscribed. Against secret society organizers there was the much-feared sanction of banishment to China — by an extra-judicial process of inquiry since intimidation made it impossible to obtain convictions in a court of law. Drastic action and better intelligence, with the expansion of

55

the Chinese Protectorate throughout areas of Chinese settlement, were effective enough to break the power of the secret societies as an *imperium in imperio*. But the societies persisted—and do so to this day—as small criminal groups living by intimidation.[11]

Other serious social problems afflicted the immigrant Chinese community so long as it was essentially a group of adult males working in a foreign country. In the harsh conditions of the nineteenth and early twentieth centuries they took their recreation in drink, gambling, opium-smoking, and brothels. In Kuala Lumpur in 1880 one side of the main market square was filled by a huge gambling booth in which throughout the twenty-four hours of day and night wildly excited miners gambled away their earnings. One or two blocks away prostitutes plied a brisk trade in squalid windowless cubicles six feet by four. These recreations, and the supply of drink and opium, were provided by the Chinese capitalists on the basis that this was a proper adjunct to the profit-making of their enterprise. The British protectorate regime in the Malay States continued the Malay practice of granting monopolies—'the revenue farms'—so that a proportion of the profits came into the public exchequer. Again it was argued that such practices were ineradicable and that it was better to tolerate and regulate them than to proscribe them and drive them underground. But with the advent of more normal social conditions and the awakening of public opinion the pressure grew for an outright suppression of these vices. Licensed gambling houses lasted until 1912 and licensed brothels until 1930. The supply of opium was more difficult to eliminate since it had become a major source of government revenue. Up to the 1920s half the public revenue of the ss government came from opium; by the 1930s it was still about one-quarter.[12] As a first step the sale of opium was restricted in 1929 to registered smokers; in 1934 the register was closed so that no new smokers could be admitted to it; the supply of opium by government monopoly was finally discontinued as a reform following the end of the war.

There were also gradual changes in the conditions of employment of Chinese labourers. The first task of the Chinese Protectorate, established in 1877, was to supervise the arrival of Chinese immigrants, and their transit through depots in which they were virtual prisoners awaiting sale to their future employers for employment under contracts (indentures) which too often facilitated exploitation at the place of work. Essentially it was a system of employment of Chinese workers by Chinese employers.

When the labourers worked on a European estate or mine, the manager obtained his labour through a contract with a Chinese labour contractor to whom he paid an agreed rate for the work done. The contractor was the labourers' immediate employer. It was difficult to check abuses since the labourers were easily intimidated and very few Europeans could speak any dialect of Chinese. The abolition of the indenture system in 1914 was an apparent rather than a real change. Malayan employers continued to recruit labour through recruiting agents sent to China. On his arrival at his place of work in Malaya the labourer was debited in the employer's books with a sum covering the cost of his importation. He was no longer bound to work for a long period for the same employer, but if he wished to change his employment, he had to pay off the balance of his debt. In time — but very gradually — conditions improved. It was a sequence of first discovering and bringing to public notice what was happening, then of legislating to prohibit abuses, and finally of making the new law an *effective* safeguard. As the authority and experience of the Chinese Protectorate increased, it earned the trust and goodwill of the Chinese working man.

Although the mass migration of Chinese male workers continued until 1930 the Chinese community in Malaya had begun to settle and to stabilize itself long before that. The gradual progress towards a more even balance of the sexes reflected both an inclination towards permanent settlement and a more normal way of life. In 1911 the ratio of men to women in the Chinese community was 4:1. By 1947 it had improved to 10:8 partly as a result of increased female immigration during the 1930s when male immigration was virtually prohibited. Many of the women who arrived came in the first instance to work. But as they married, a Chinese family settled in Malaya was the usual result.

Apart from the sex ratio the other indicator of a more settled Chinese community was the increasing proportion of the local born. It almost trebled in a generation — from 22 per cent in 1911 to 62 per cent in 1947. Yet it was an almost unobserved change until it had become an accomplished fact. The object of the Chinese who came to Malaya was to make money and eventually to return to China with their savings. But the Chinese flair for business led some of them to invest their cash as shopkeepers, traders, miners, or estate-owners. When they had made these ties with Malaya, the achievement of their own effort, they were tempted to remain in

Malaya for the rest of their lives rather than sell out and return to a village in China from which they had been separated for most of their adult lives. Once the first generation of immigrants had settled, it was all the more likely that their children would spend their lives in Malaya. It was noted in 1931 that 'the majority of adult Malaya-born Chinese are traders and shopkeepers and not labourers and agriculturalists and they are proportionately more numerous in towns'.[13] But neither the ownership of property nor local birth extinguished the sense of remaining Chinese—reflected in a preservation of their language and culture and of ties with the part of China from which their immigrant forebears had come. The government which had begun by identifying the Chinese in Malaya as a unique and alien problem continued to deal with them on that basis. In retrospect one can see that one of the lost opportunities of the 1930s was the failure to adapt policy to a new situation. Official recognition at that time of the Chinese as a settled community would have aroused even more Malay misgivings and would probably have elicited little active support from the Chinese. But it was an alternative which was not apparently considered at all.

The gradual stabilization of the Chinese population solved some problems but created others. The Malayan economy was subject to violent upsurges and downturns of demand for labour, reflecting changes in the world market for rubber and tin. The slump which followed the 1914-18 War was the occasion of a drastic programme of repatriation of Chinese labourers. The slump of 1932-34 was even worse in its effect on employment; no less than 400,000 people were repatriated to China and India.[14] But a much larger proportion than before of the unemployed remained in Malaya, which had by this time begun to carry its own reserve of labour. With the passing of the era of pioneer immigration, relations between employer and employee began to take on a more modern aspect. In the early days of the mid-nineteenth century the labourers and their immediate 'bosses' on the mines (but not the financial entrepreneurs of the Straits Settlements who had sent them there) were engaged in a united struggle to survive in times of adversity and of danger. There had been exploitation and maltreatment, but it was relieved to some extent by a sense of common interest. By the early decades of the twentieth century Chinese society in Malaya had begun to stratify into opposed classes. At the upper level the employer, entrepreneur, or manager was usually Malayan-born; the toiling mass of labourers, skilled and unskilled, artisans, street traders, and market-gardeners (and a host of other occupations besides), was mainly immigrant Chinese. In his autobiography, a Chinese employer relates how in 1936 he got a hearing from angry strikers by explaining that although he was Malayan-born, he had spent his youth in China; it made him almost one of them.[15]

In times of unemployment the Chinese who had made their homes in Malaya reverted to the traditional peasant economy of China by growing their own food. As they were usually unable to secure official permission for the occupation of vacant land, they took themselves off to remote areas on the edge of the main jungle belt and made clearings on which to plant their crops. It was the beginning of the 'squatter' areas which were to be the central problem of the Emergency of the 1950s (Chapter 6). The squatter felt insecure since at best he might obtain from the Land Office a temporary occupation licence entitling him to occupy his land from year to year; at worst he might be evicted.

In the towns the population was increasing rapidly both in absolute numbers and as a proportion of the total population. In 1911 one-tenth of 2½ million people in Malaya lived in towns with a population of 10,000 or more; by 1931 the proportion of urban population had increased to one-seventh of 4 million. The large majority of the town-dwellers was Chinese. In the centre of the larger towns there were tall tenement buildings whose upper floors were divided into airless cubicles with a floor area of not more than a hundred square feet each. A family was fortunate to have a cubicle in which to live, eat, and sleep, sharing with up to twenty other families the use of a single cooking hearth and latrine. They were in some degree fortunate because the alternative was likely to be life in a shanty town on the outskirts in equally bad conditions of overcrowding and lack of sanitation.

Industrial relations in the modern sense were inhibited by government policy which up to 1940 was opposed to the formation of trade unions as legal organizations in case they should be infiltrated by the underground Malayan Communist Party. But in the absence of an alternative the need of working-class solidarity afforded scope for the remnants of the proscribed secret societies. An official report of 1927 stated (of conditions in Singapore) that

> the typical secret society consists of a number of pangkengs, or coolies' lodging-houses. The pangkeng is rented by a number of Chinese of the same tribe and engaged in the same kind of work.

Each subscribes $1.50 or $2.00 per mensem towards the rent. Some members sleep in the pangkeng; others sleep out, e.g. twakowmen if they are working an early tide, house-building coolies in the suburbs, and those who prefer the fresh air of the five-foot way or the all-night smoking shops — these keep their belongings there and use the place as a sort of club.[16]

In some old-established craft-trades such as shoemaking and tailoring there persisted an innocuous form of guild in which masters and men could negotiate wages and working conditions. The typical business was a small concern employing ten or fewer workers drawn from the same dialect-group as the employer and in some cases related to him or at least members of the same clan association.[17] These traditions helped to soften the asperities of working life in difficult conditions.

A distinguished Malayan Chinese historian of our day deprecates the assumption that 'all Chinese are alike' merely because from the viewpoint of non-Chinese they are a distinct and cohesive group.[18] There are many sub-categories within the community. Differences of local origin in China and of dialect-group are still very important; most Chinese, for example, find their marriage partners within their own group.[19] Another major line of cleavage is between those Chinese who have been educated at a school where the Chinese language was the medium of instruction and the minority who were educated at schools where English was the medium of instruction — some of the latter may, like Tan Cheng Lock, be unable to speak any dialect of Chinese. Although most of the English-educated are middle class the Chinese-educated span the range from rags to riches. Finally there are considerable differences of political attitude among the Malayan Chinese.

It is only in this century that political consciousness has evolved. Until then the main concern of the Chinese in Malaya — they were not yet 'Malayan Chinese' — was that the government should leave them alone to regulate their own communal affairs and to maximize the economic rewards of their busy lives. But 'certain shortcomings of their social system . . . were forced on the attention of the rulers', as we have seen, and this led to a transition from indirect to direct rule mainly through the intervention of the Chinese Protectorate in a number of Chinese social problems.[20] In the course of these limited policies of intervention machinery of consultation was evolved; Chinese Advisory Boards were established and prominent Chinese merchants were appointed to membership of the legislative bodies of the ss and FMS. These worthies were sometimes 'Straits Chinese', i.e., Chinese of local birth in the ss (and therefore British subjects). A Straits Chinese British Association was formed in 1900 on the initiative of two very talented men, Song Ong Siang and Lim Boon Keng, the one a lawyer and the other a doctor. A third, and even more outstanding figure, proved to be Tan Cheng Lock who began as a schoolmaster at the Raffles Institution in Singapore, though he soon returned to develop the family business interests in his native Malacca. He became a member of the ss Legislative Council from 1923 to 1935; after the war he was for many years president of the Malayan Chinese Association established in 1949 and the acknowledged 'grand old man' of his community. These Straits Chinese leaders were very westernized — in one speech, for example, Tan Cheng Lock quoted from Aristotle and Hegel as well as from Confucius and Gandhi.[21] This was to prove both the strength and the weakness of their position in their community. They could communicate readily — if not very effectually — with the British authorities and argue with them in terms of the British liberal tradition in politics. They were spokesmen for a community which had struck root in Malaya and demanded recognition as a domiciled community. One of Tan Cheng Lock's causes was the claim for admission of Asians born in the ss to the civil service.[22] In fighting for the cause of a *Malayan* Chinese community the Straits Chinese were ahead of their time. They were also isolated from the majority of the Chinese in Malaya at that time, for whom China was still the homeland.

Yet events in China had a profound effect upon the development of political consciousness and solidarity among the Malayan Chinese as a community. The sequence of events in China from about 1900 to the successful revolution in 1911 was a national resurgence in which the Chinese overseas were involved. From about 1906 until 1911, when he moved on at the request of an embarrassed colonial regime, Dr Sun Yat Sen and his circle found much general and financial support among the Chinese in Singapore. When the Kuo Min Tang government came to power in China, its ideology included the three principles of Sun Yat Sen, one of which required that all persons of Chinese descent should still be regarded as Chinese nationals.[23] The solid advantage of asserting metropolitan control of Chinese overseas was that they included men of wealth who might be persuaded to contribute to party funds. This led to a prolonged and confused struggle between the KMT government in China and the colonial regime in Malaya over KMT efforts to organize political support in Malaya.[24]

The KMT presence in Malaya had a number of side effects. Until 1927 the KMT in China worked in association with the Comintern. This strengthened the underground Malayan Communist Party (MCP), which was established as a separate organization in 1930 but which had in fact functioned in association with the KMT for some years before that.[25] Communism in Malaya has always been strongest when it has been able to tap the strength of Chinese national feeling. After 1927 KMT and MCP were in general opposed forces. The KMT in Malaya also had working contacts with the remnants of the secret societies. Another incidental effect of events in China was felt in Chinese education in Malaya. The national reform movement in China included a programme for the modernization of traditional education. In following this lead the Malayan Chinese perforce recruited their schoolteachers from the only available source — China. Many of these imported schoolteachers were exponents of extreme anti-Western views. Their influence extended beyond the schoolroom since the educated man is held in high esteem in Chinese society and the majority of the immigrant Chinese in Malaya had had little or no education in China.

The general effect of the KMT influence was to spread among the middle-class immigrant Chinese a sense of national solidarity in opposition to European rule. This sentiment in its original form had little or nothing to do with aspirations for self-government in Malaya. It was rather an extension into Malaya of the national struggle in China to throw back European penetration of China and to re-create an independent nation at home — of which nonetheless the overseas Chinese were part. During the controversial governorship of Sir Cecil Clementi (1930-35) the authorities in Malaya reacted by banning the formation of KMT branches in their territory.[26]

Although they were no longer working with the KMT, the MCP were able in the hard times of the 1930s to spread their organization among the Chinese working class. The renewed Japanese attack on China in 1937 evoked strong patriotic feelings among the Malayan Chinese and led to something of a reconciliation between MCP and KMT and also between KMT and colonial government. When Britain itself became involved in war in 1939, there was general support from the Malayan Chinese with the exception of the MCP. By now there was a well-organized drive for raising funds among the Malayan Chinese for war relief in China; it was extended so as to support the Allied war-effort. It was the policy of the British authorities not to mobilize the general mass of the local population, including the Chinese, in a local defence force. The role of Malaya in the war was at this time seen as economic rather than military. But the Chinese enlisted in the Volunteers, the part-time local defence force more especially in the SS where there was more encouragement given to them. For a time the MCP remained in opposition since directives from Moscow required it to foment labour trouble to embarrass the British war-effort. When Germany invaded Russia in 1941, there was a drastic change of Russian policy in British colonies. It was by then too late to achieve any major co-ordination of effort — nor was it British policy to rely on allies of such doubtful calibre. But some help was given; a force of about a thousand Chinese, many of them communists, fought in the last defence of Singapore island. Thereafter the MCP, as a well-organized underground movement, was able to take the lead in undercover Chinese resistance to the Japanese occupying forces.[27]

In the development of Chinese political attitudes over the period 1911-41 it is possible to distinguish three groups — those concerned wholly with the resurgence of China itself, those whose 'primary interest was in preserving the strength of their communal organisation overseas', and those who sought a political role in the countries of their adoption.[28] By the end of the period the first of these had ceased to be a significant force; the strength lay with the second who were in the main either born in China or educated in Chinese-medium schools in Malaya; the future lay with the aspirations of the third group which in this period were mainly the long-settled Straits Chinese educated through the medium of English. The fusion of these groups and ideas was to come in the post-war struggle for power following the traumatic experience of the Japanese occupation.

There was considerable Chinese immigration into Sabah (then British North Borneo) and Sarawak in the nineteenth and early twentieth centuries. Neither territory offered the same opportunities as Malaya to the Chinese immigrant. The government of North Borneo, in a desperate search for labour to develop its territory, even offered 'passes' which entitled a Chinese immigrant to a free passage for his wife and any relatives. In Borneo there was no obstacle to Chinese agricultural settlement such as existed in Malaya (where this activity was reserved to the Malays). Sabah attracted a considerable Hakka peasant community and also drew in some Chinese labour to meet the needs of its rubber plantations. Sabah also imported Javanese labour to work in its rubber industry. In Sarawak the Brooke regime gave positive encouragement to Chinese immigration for agricultural settlement. Many of the Chinese in Sarawak became traders whose main market and source of supply was Singapore. As there was no mining and little plantation development in Sarawak, it did not need to import labour to work for a wage.[29]

Before leaving the Chinese one should mention the small Eurasian community of Malaya. In the main they were descended from Portuguese and Dutch soldiers and settlers who took local wives and so were concentrated in the ss major towns. As an alien, but locally domiciled, group who spoke English as their native tongue they had something in common with the Straits Chinese—and were associated with them in such demands as Tan Cheng Lock's campaign for the opening of the administrative service to local recruits who were not Malays.

The Malayan connection with India is even more ancient than with China. In northern Malaya there is evidence of sites of Indian settlements of some fifteen hundred years ago. It is probable that these were occupied by traders engaged in seaborne trade which at that time crossed the narrow isthmus south of Kra between the Indian Ocean and the South China Sea. It was Muslim merchants from India who brought Islam to north Sumatra whence it spread to Malacca at the beginning of the fifteenth century. There was an Indian commercial community at Malacca and some evidence that Indian merchants were used as intermediaries in trade by Malay Rulers in the eighteenth century.[30] When Light established himself at Penang in 1786, there was an influx into the new port of Indian traders from Kedah across the water. The Indian connection was particularly important—from the Malayan end at least—during the period in which the ss were dependencies of the British government in India. The inflow of Indian labour to work on plantations began on a small scale in the mid-nineteenth century. The Indian government, which was prepared to use the Straits Settlements as a repository for convicts serving long sentences, had misgivings about the transfer of ostensibly free labour to work under onerous contracts of employment.[31] As the development of the modern plantation economy in Malaya gathered momentum, the inflow of Indian labour accelerated. In the 1870s Indian population was about 30,000 and the greater part of it was in Province Wellesley, to which labour had been imported to work on the sugar estates. Thereafter it grew to about 120,000 in 1901 and 625,000 in 1931; the main concentration in the twentieth century was on the rubber estates of west central Malaya.

Until 1910 Indian labour was generally imported under an 'indenture' system by which the labourer was bound to work for a fixed period, usually of three years, for an employer who had engaged him through recruitment agencies in India. A British administrator in India called it 'a regularly organized system of kidnapping'.[32] This system was prohibited in 1910 and thereafter until 1938 most recruitment of Indian labour for employment on Malayan plantations was under the *kangany* system. An estate in Malaya, which required labour, despatched to India a recruiter selected from the senior or long-service element of its existing labour force. The *kangany* visited his native village in India and the surrounding district (most of the labour came from the area around Madras and further south) and persuaded local peasants to accompany him back to Malaya at the expense of a central Malayan fund to which all employers of Indian labour contributed. The labourer was in principle free to move from one estate to another in Malaya — though in practice he might find it difficult to do so if for example he was indebted to the *kangany* who had recruited him for personal loans. There were a number of abuses and mortality was high. Both the Government of India, which maintained an official Agent in Malaya from 1923, and the Labour Department established in Malaya in 1911 were concerned to protect the Indian labourer from harsh or unhealthy working conditions and to promote his welfare. The Malayan governments themselves were large employers of Indian labour in such departments as the Railways and Public Works. From 1922 wages were regulated by a system of 'standard rates' fixed (as a minimum in key districts) by a central Indian Immigration Committee. But the fixed wage related to a theoretical 9-hour day and in hard times some employers paid less on the basis that the labourer was not in fact working a full 9-hour stint.

The paternalistic character of the various agencies for the protection of the Indian labourer indicates sufficiently the core of the problem. In contrast to the self-reliant and sometimes turbulent Chinese, the south Indian labourer was generally docile and rather apathetic; he was very much in the hands of his employer, good or bad. On the estate he was accommodated in labour 'lines' built to conform to government regulations. In its original form the lines were long buildings with a thatched or corrugated iron roof; they were divided lengthwise by a central partition and subdivided by side partitions (which did not reach to the roof) to provide 'back-to-back' cubicles. One of these gloomy rabbit-hutches was allotted to each family; there was overcrowding and little privacy. From the mid-1930s, however, the official housing standard changed to require that the lines should be gradually replaced by semi-detached bungalows usually of two rooms each. In connection with wages, working conditions, housing, sanitation, and the provision of education, there was a long-running war of manoeuvre between official agencies seeking to impose tolerable — but far from splendid — conditions of life for the labourer, and the plantation managers, some of whom were less progressive than others. The estate manager was aiming to keep his estate costs of production to a level acceptable to his board of directors in London and argued also that some of the things which he had to provide were more properly a service to be supplied by the government. In 1923 the FMS Federal Council was debating the subject of estate schools, which the employer had to provide. A planter who was an unofficial member spoke of painting the word 'School' on the outer wall of his smokehouse.[33] The jest is more revealing — of an attitude of mind — than the speaker perhaps intended. In time — though it took several decades up to the post-war period of the 1950s — the large estate-owners, mainly foreign companies, came to accept that self-interest and the reputation of their enterprises required that satisfactory standards should be willingly observed, as in modern times they are. The sale of a large estate for subdivision into smallholdings is now deplored and resisted because it is likely to deprive the labour force of good living conditions.

The world of the Indian estate labourer in Malaya down to 1941 was a narrow one.[34] Each day the able-bodied adults, men and women, were mustered just before dawn for a roll-call and then despatched in gangs under their *kangany* to their tasks of rubber-tapping, weeding, or estate maintenance. In spite of the norm of a 9-hour day the allotted tasks could generally be completed in 6 to 8 hours by the early afternoon. Off duty as much as at work the life of the labourer was regulated by the hierarchy of estate authority. Nearest and most immediate was the *kangany,* the gang foreman. Above him in ascending order were the conductors (supervisors), estate assistants, and at the apex the manager. Owing to the preponderance of males, which was acute until a more even balance of the sexes was achieved in the 1930s, and their life at close quarters, quarrels could disrupt the monotony of their lives. In time preventive medicine, based on scientific anti-malarial and other health measures, ensured a fair standard of protection against epidemic disease. But medical care of the sick and education of the labourers' children were often of a poor standard. In particular the teachers were not usually adequately trained and some were not qualified at all.

The main centre of social life was the Hindu temple managed by a committee, or *panchayat,* drawn from the senior Asian staff and from the *kanganies.* Hinduism is rich in the variety of its cults, rituals, and festivals. At a grosser level the labourer relieved the tedium by imbibing toddy, an alcoholic liquor which can be obtained readily and cheaply by fermentation of a liquid tapped from the coconut-palm. Since the sale of toddy was difficult to suppress, it was, like the sale of opium to the Chinese, permitted under a system of control. In this case the estate had a licensed toddy shop and part of the profits were set aside to provide estate amenities. But the evident abuses and damage to health from toddy-drinking gave a stimulus to the movement for total prohibition of the sale of toddy which began to gather momentum in the Indian community generally.

The Indian labourer did not come to Malaya to make his home there. At the end of his working life or sometimes at shorter intervals he returned to his native village in India. There was thus a considerable flow in both directions and the inflow could be regulated by the Indian Immigration Committee which issued passes to *kangany* recruiters. In 1910, for example, which was a year of high demand for labour, total immigration of Indians (of all classes) into Malaya was about 90,000 and emigration (almost entirely return to India) was 40,000. In 1932, a year of acute depression, the inflow of labourers was a mere 6,500 (out of total Indian immigration of 28,000) and repatriation and other departures totalled 85,000.[35] By regulating supply to match demand the bargaining position of the employer was considerably strengthened. Gradually, however, the familiar place of work (for many estate labourers spent their whole working lives on the same estate) became home and the place where the elderly man's children were now settled. A study of a post-war estate working population, when another generation in time had added to the gradual process of settlement, showed that just under half the heads of households had never worked on any other estate, and that most of the remainder had come to this estate after working on other estates.[36] The more enlightened estate managers were persuaded by humanity as much as self-interest to allow the elderly labourer to remain, even if he still occupied accommodation on the estate, among his kinsfolk and his friends. The law required that the estate should allocate one-sixteenth of an acre of land to each family to be used as a vegetable garden or for grazing cattle. This was the only land available for farming to most Indians since, in general, land for smallholdings could not be obtained by alienation through the land offices.[37]

By 1957, when the first post-war census was taken, the Indian population as a whole had stabilized. The ratio of men to women was about 10:7, and two-thirds of the community, with a much higher proportion among the young, was local born. Four-fifths of the Indian population are Tamil-speakers from the districts around Madras. There is also a much smaller Telugu-speaking group likewise from the Madras area. These linguistic and cultural groups form the bulk of the labouring population. Cultural lines of cleavage between different sub-groups of the Indian community are the sharper in their effect because they often correspond with differences of occupation. On the estates, for example, the clerical and supervisory staff were either Malayalis from south India or Jaffna Tamils from northern Ceylon. There was often a virtual state of war between them, but both held themselves aloof, as educated men, from the mass of Tamil labourers. In the government offices the clerical posts were filled mainly by Jaffna Tamils since they afforded a pool of educated staff which Malaya itself lacked in the early days of Indian immigration. Then as Malay education expanded, there was, from 1920 onwards, a demand from the Malays that a proportion of government clerical posts should be reserved to them. At this period Malaya offered an opportunity to professional men — doctors, lawyers, teachers, and technical staff — and thus drew in Indians from the growing surplus produced by the Indian educational system.

The Nattukottai Chettiars from the southern part of Madras state became a major element in the economic system in Malaya.

They specialize in banking and moneylending. From their villages in India young men were sent to overseas countries such as Malaya to work as the local agents of the family banking enterprise. After a period of service the young man would return to India and be replaced at his foreign post by another delegate. It has been said that the 'Chetties' were 'generally reputed to be honest and trustworthy businessmen though they would drive a hard bargain and would not let sentimental considerations enter into the transaction of business'.[38] Much of the capital which they introduced into Malaya was lent on the security of agricultural land and many of the borrowers were Malay smallholders. In the depression of the 1930s there were numerous defaults and foreclosure became an acute problem. It was estimated that loans by Chettiars to smallholders in the FMS then amounted to $125 million (say £15 million).[39] The Malay Reservations Enactment 1933 (to amend the original law of 1913) prohibited the charging or transfer of land in Malay Reservations to non-Malays. The controversy over this issue, since the Chettiars were being retrospectively deprived of their security, showed how much the Chettiar community, 'introvert and separatist in outlook',[40] was isolated from the main body of the Indian community in Malaya.

The Indian Muslim and Sikh groups were equally distinct but less isolated from the main body. Common religion drew the Indian Muslims into a closer relationship with the Malays with whom they intermarried to some extent; the Jawi Pekan or Peranakan group who are concentrated in and around Penang are nowadays Malay rather than Indian but are of this mixed descent. Indian Muslims in Malaya have generally been merchants and traders and are also to be found in the professions. The Sikhs (and Punjabi Muslims often called 'Pathans' in late nineteenth-century literature) have a strong military tradition. In the first decades of British rule the police had a large Sikh element.[41] From 1896 to 1919 the only local defence force, the Malay States Guides, was recruited from the Sikhs. The modern Sikh is a nightwatchman and often a moneylender, a lorry-driver or cattle-drover; a small number of Sikhs are merchants, policemen, or professional men such as doctors.

As with the Chinese, the Indians in Malaya first awoke to nationalism by their interest in the events occurring in their mother country, to which down to 1941 many intended ultimately to return. But there were also local issues over which Indian feeling ran strongly. To the educated minority it seemed a shameful thing that other Indians should be shipped into and out of Malaya like cattle to serve their time as labourers. At every stage in the long fight to ameliorate the status of the Indian labourer in Malaya, and eventually to prohibit the recruitment of labourers in India for shipment to Malaya, the critics in India drew support and information (whether accurate or not) from the Indian community in Malaya. But the latter did very little which was effective in Malaya itself; they did not identify sufficiently with the Tamil labourer but used him as a moral stick with which to beat the regime which thus insulted Indians. The campaign came to a head in 1937, when the Government of India sent Srinivasa Sastri, a distinguished member of the legislative council of India, to investigate and to report on the condition of Indian labourers in Malaya. His report is a fair and balanced assessment of a situation which by then had much improved from the early days.[42] He was, however, critical of the standards both of medical treatment on the estates and of estate schools. Sastri recommended that the system of recruitment of labourers in India through visits by *kanganies* should cease. In fact *kangany* recruitment had never recovered after the check of the slump of the early 1930s; but there had been a considerable inflow of non-assisted labour. The Indian government prohibited the emigration to Malaya of assisted labour in 1938 and tightened the control of other emigration. This in effect marked the end of Indian emigration on a mass scale to Malaya.

As the Indian labouring community settled down in Malaya, it lost some of its traditional submissiveness. A new generation born in Malaya was less in awe of authority, European or Indian. The nascent nationalist movement among the Indian community of the towns had a modest effect on the estates. With the ending of assisted migration of labour from India, the employers could no longer regulate the flow so as to augment the supply when there were demands for higher wages or better conditions. In some areas, more especially the ports and larger inland towns, Indian labourers were working alongside Chinese as dock labour or on public works. By this contact they absorbed a little of the Chinese resilience against economic pressure. The first signs of incipient Indian labour unrest came to a head in strikes. The strike in 1941 on estates around the town of Klang was political; the strike failed and the leaders were deported.[43] But the labourers did get a wage increase; it was a landmark which left behind both a sense of industrial power and of resentment. But the results did not appear until after the Japanese occupation period.

Unity is strength and disunity is weakness. This factor as much as any denied to the Indian community in the 1930s, as it still does, the influence which its collective talents might otherwise secure. Apart from the campaign against importation of Indian labour, the other grievances were inadequate Indian representation in the various legislative bodies in Malaya, and the trend of official policy towards local, Malay, recruitment to the government subordinate services. It was particularly galling that in selecting members of local councils the regime treated Indians and Ceylonese as a single group. The Indians did not consider that a Ceylon Tamil was their representative.

There were a number of local Indian Associations in the main towns; the first had been formed as early as 1906. The leaders were generally of the business and professional class and had no roots in or contact with the mass of the Indian labourers whose interests, as well as their own, they sought to advance. In their activities the Indian Associations were social rather than political bodies. The time had hardly arrived when overt political activity was socially approved. These bodies were also prone to relapse into apathy or to be riven by personal feuds between different cultural and linguistic sub-groups. The local worthies competed with each other in an assiduous search for the favours of Malay Rulers and of British proconsuls — but made little impression on either.[44] In addition to the associations there were Malayan Indian monthly journals published in Singapore (from 1925) and in Kuala Lumpur (from 1932).

Grievances over alleged discrimination against the Indians in recruitment to the public service were the occasion of the formation in 1936 of the Central Indian Association of Malaya (CIAM), with representation from existing Indian Chambers of Commerce and local Indian Associations. It was the first step, though very tentative, towards the formation of a representative body for the Malayan Indian community as a whole.[45] Different sub-groups of the Indian community found more scope for common action in the activities of cultural and religious bodies, very much a focus of Indian society then and now.

In a chapter concerned with immigrant communities it is necessary to take account of the considerable inflow into Malaya of settlers from Sumatra, Java, and elsewhere in Indonesia. To some extent they shared with the local Peninsular Malays a common culture; above all they were all Muslim. Within a generation, or at the most two, such groups merged with the other Malays as an homogeneous and indistinguishable community. But for a time they were recognized as a separate element, both in culture and in occupation.[46] They were officially classified as 'Other Malaysians'; they sometimes immigrated not as settlers but as gangs of contract labourers who were employed on such special tasks as felling the huge jungle trees in preparation for rubber-planting. As late as 1931 one-quarter of the total Malay and Other Malaysian population of Selangor had been born outside the State.[47] To this day the different origin of neighbouring Malay villages is remembered by the inhabitants and is sometimes reflected in their mutual attitudes. 'The people of Jenderam Hilir have virtually nothing to do with Sungei Buah' it was noted in 1964; the former were Menangkabau from Sumatra and the latter Javanese, though both were long settled.[48] But time is a great assimilator of peoples who begin with a common cultural heritage.

A small group of Arabs who settled mainly in the ports of the Straits Settlements as traders, Islamic teachers, journalists, etc., have likewise been gradually absorbed into the Malay community. As we have seen (Chapter 4), they enjoyed a considerable prestige as religious and intellectual leaders of the Malays in the early decades of the century.

All the immigrant communities were the product of rapid economic development and are still to be found in the greatest numbers in the well-developed west-coast zone of Malaya. Although they came as individuals or in small groups, which could not reproduce the larger social structure of their communities of origin, they preserved and cherished their language, religion, and culture; this served to preserve their group-identity and to prevent assimilation by contact or intermarriage with each other or with the indigenous peoples. In their distinctiveness, in being Chinese or Indian, they found the means to vitality. If they abandoned it, they would be deprived of their heritage. This is a problem to which we shall return in the context of modern education in Malaysia (Chapter 12).

It is clear in retrospect that among the immigrant communities, just as among the Malays, there was in the inter-war period an unobtrusive and hardly realized awakening of national sentiment, a kind of pre-political development. It was very slow to produce its effect in political awakening because there was no obvious or acceptable basis of inter-communal cooperation and no possibility of political action (nor much sense of the need of it) under the apparently permanent regime of the colonial power. The Japanese occupation was to alter the whole condition of the Malayan communities.

Notes

1 TMP, para 416.
2 Tan Siew Sin, formerly Malaysian Minister of Finance, and son of Tan Cheng Lock, founder of the MCA, is of the sixth generation of a family settled in Malaya. His ancestor who came from China died at Malacca, where the family has since been established, in 1801. Tregonning (1979), 25.
3 Purcell (1948), Chapters I-V.
4 Annual Report for 1888 by the British Resident Selangor (Swettenham). Blythe's monograph (1947) is still the best account of Chinese labour in Malaya. See also Blythe (1969), R. N. Jackson (1961), and Alatas (1977).
5 Mills (1942), 300 mentions a death-rate on 21 estates of one in five as the average for the year in 1908.
6 Purcell (1948), 92.
7 *Selangor Journal* (1895), IV, 29.
8 Purcell (1948), 84.
9 Blythe (1969) gives an expert and very detailed account of the complicated history of Chinese secret societies in Malaya. Blythe had spent his working life in the Chinese Protectorate and was Secretary for Chinese Affairs (i.e., senior government adviser) in the post-war period. See also Khoo Kay Kim (1972), Chapter 5 and Comber (1959).
10 Blythe (1969), 254ff. discusses the matter at length. In the 1880s it was contended that in the FMS, in distinction from the SS, there was no secret society *organization*. The immigrant Chinese, it was said, joined a society on arrival at an SS port, but there were no 'lodges', local branches, in the mining centres of the Malay States. It then followed that the Chinese mining magnates obtained their obvious influence among their community merely by personal and commercial ties. But the Chinese Protectorate, which was at that time confined to the SS, had evidence that there were lodges in the States and that the leading employers held office in them.
11 Blythe (1969) carries his account down to about 1960. In the post-war period there was a struggle for power between the MCP and the secret societies, which revived their hold to some extent. Newell (1962), 142 states that only three members of the Chinese village community in Province Wellesley which he studies c.1960 were secret society members, but that a much larger number of villagers tolerated the local society and would not betray it to the authorities—so long as the society left them in peace. Stenson and Short also deal with the activities of secret societies in the immediate post-war period.
12 Emerson (1937), 303.

13 Vlieland (1932), para 246.

14 Del Tufo (1949), para 155.

15 Choo Kia Peng—in his unpublished autobiography. He was in 1936 an appointed unofficial member of the FMS Federal Council and a prominent member of the Chinese business community.

16 Blythe (1969), 305. Not all communal lodgings of this type were secret society branches, however (309).

17 Freedman (1957), 57 illustrates the very personal character of Chinese business relationships in Singapore c.1950.

18 Wang Gungwu (1978), 5.

19 Freedman (1957), 109.

20 Purcell (1948), 147.

21 Tregonning (1979), 70.

22 The official reasons for rejecting this demand were that the Malayan Civil Service provided administrative staff for the Malay States as well as for the SS. In the Malay States the Rulers declined to accept senior administrators who were neither British nor Malay. A solution of sorts was found by the creation of a separate—but inferior—Straits Settlements Civil Service whose locally recruited members served in the SS only. The differentiation between MCS and SSCS was much resented by the latter. Tregonning (1979), 32.

23 Purcell (1948), 211-12 summarizes the Three Principles—Nationalism (all ethnic Chinese are Chinese nationals), Democracy, and Livelihood (progressive capitalism as the basis of economic welfare).

24 Purcell (1948), 213-17 gives the course of the negotiations.

25 Brimmell (1959), 93.

26 It was eventually agreed that the KMT should be a legal organization in Malaya to which individual Chinese might be admitted as members. But it was denied the opportunity of political activity through the formation of local branches.

27 On Chinese resistance to the Japanese see Purcell (1948), Chapter XIV, and Chapman (1949) and Chin Kee Onn (1946), passim. The story is continued below in Chapter 6.

28 Wang Gungwu in Cowan and Wolters (ed.) (1976).

29 For a sociological study of the Sarawak Chinese see T'ien Ju-K'ang (1953). Milne and Ratnam (1974), 8 have some interesting points of contrast between the political experiences of the Chinese in Sabah and Sarawak.

30 Both Sandhu (1969) and Arasaratnam (1970) begin with an account of relations between the two countries in the pre-colonial period. On the role of Indian merchants at the courts of Malay Rulers see Andaya (1978).

31 The Government of India was of course justified in distinguishing between Indian convicts under its control in an overseas penal settlement and Indian labourers over whom it had little control once they had left India for a foreign country. Malaya was only one of the destinations; Indian labourers also went to Mauritius, Fiji, and the West Indies in considerable numbers. The best of the studies of Indian labour in Malaya in the colonial period are Sandhu (1969), Arasaratnam (1970), and Parmer (1960). R. N. Jackson (1961) deals with both Indian and Chinese labour. McNair (1899) describes the enlightened treatment of Indian convicts in the SS in his time.

32 Geoghagan (1873) quoted by Arasaratnam (1970) at p. 13. Sandhu (1969),

Chapters 2-5 deals very fully with recruitment procedure.

33 Proceedings of the FMS Federal Council 1923 (107-8). The story is told in Arasaratnam (1970) at p. 179.

34 Jain's study (1970) both describes the historical evolution of the situation which he studied on a Malayan rubber estate in the early 1960s and the current position at that time. It is an excellent account of a working routine which has not changed a great deal over the past quarter of a century.

35 The figures (rounded) are taken from Sandhu (1969), Appendices 3 and 4.

36 Jain (1970), 28.

37 During and after the slump of 1932 a limited amount of land was allocated for settlement by unemployed Indian labourers: Sandhu (1969), 265-70. The best known of these experiments was the co-operative settlement at Chuah near Port Dickson in Negri Sembilan. Here as elsewhere success depended on the quality of leadership available among the settlers.

38 Arasaratnam (1970), 37; Sandhu (1969), 291-2.

39 Arasaratnam (1970), 94.

40 Arasaratnam (1970), 95.

41 Gullick (1978) at pp. 33 and 42 on Sikhs in the Police.

42 Sastri (1937).

43 Jain (1970), Chapters 5 and 6 deals with these events and in particular with the 1941 strike ('Nathan's trouble') at pp. 234-5. See also Stenson (1970), 49-50.

44 At this time there was a very strong prejudice among the Malay upper class against South Indians. Wilkinson in his dictionary (1932 ed.) notes that 'keling' (the Malay word for South Indian from the ancient Kalinga) 'is regarded rather as a term of abuse'.

45 Stenson (1970), 45.

46 Lim (1977) has much detail on this subject which is often given less importance than it deserves.

47 Vlieland (1932).

48 Wilson (1967), 22.

6 The Advance to Independence 1941–1961

The Japanese forces landed in north-east Malaya on 7 December 1941; the British forces surrendered at Singapore on 15 February 1942. There was a similar brief but decisive invasion of the British territories in northern Borneo.

The British defence strategy was to use the command of the sea around Malaysia, through a fleet based at Singapore, to destroy an invading force at sea or, if it landed, to sever its supply-lines. The Japanese use of Indo-China as a base for a short strike southwards to Malaya made the task of the defenders more difficult. The priority given by British strategy to other theatres such as the Middle East in a period of world war denied to Malayan defence an adequate allocation of material, especially aircraft. The *Prince of Wales,* a new battleship, and the *Repulse,* an ageing battle-cruiser, reached Singapore only five days before the invasion began; they came without the aircraft-carrier *Indomitable,* which was to provide their air-cover at sea, since she was delayed for repairs in the West Indies. Both ships were destroyed by Japanese torpedo bombers on 10 December 1941 off the east coast of Malaya. A failure of inter-service communication had denied to them even the meagre support of RAF aircraft flying from Malayan airfields.

Although the original defence plan was now in ruins, the defending land forces, British, Indian, and Australian, outnumbered the invaders by a factor of 3 or 4 to 1; they were superior in artillery but had a critical inferiority in tanks. It is possible that if these superior numbers had been concentrated for a decisive encounter with the Japanese in northern Malaya early in the campaign, they could have checked or even destroyed the invading force on land. But the defensive plan was dominated by a concern to hold the airfields of Malaya, which dictated a dispersal of forces, and if necessary to fall back in order to defend Singapore as the main base. It was a faulty plan since the British aircraft, inadequate in numbers and obsolete in type, could not command the air by flying from the airfields and the Singapore base had no purpose if there was no longer a fleet to use it. It was not possible to adopt the tactics used successfully later in Burma of standing to fight the Japanese infiltrating forces by 'all round defence'. Those tactics required that the beleaguered defenders should be supplied from the air — which was not possible in Malaya. It had been accepted by the British chiefs of staff in London that adequate Malayan air defence required a minimum of 336 aircraft; there were in fact only 158 in Malaya and these were obsolete and inferior in preformance to the Japanese planes. On the ground the devastating Japanese tank thrusts against infantry defenders might have been contained by good anti-tank measures, but the training pamphlets on this subject (based on experience in France in 1940) remained in unopened bundles at command headquarters in Singapore. It was in any case impossible to recruit civil labour, of which there was an abundance, to construct defence works because the War Office had decreed that the army in Malaya should not pay more than 45 cents per day for labour, which was about half the going rate. As is well known, Singapore was not a 'fortress' since its 15-inch guns could not be used against an attack overland from the north and its essential water-supply came from Johor across the Johor Straits. To these basic problems were added confusion, dissension, and indecision among and between military, air, and civil government leaders. There had been little attempt to mobilize local forces. The Malay Regiment, however, and also a Chinese force (Dalforce) raised at the last moment, fought with courage and distinction in the final defence of Singapore; there were also local Volunteers under European leadership who did their allotted task. The main failure in fighting performance was among the regular forces. The Indian Army units were not well led; the Australians fought well, but showed indiscipline in retreat; the British troops had not been adequately trained for fighting in Malayan conditions and some had arrived too recently to have become acclimatized. Despite the courage of individuals the campaign as a whole was a fiasco.[1]

As the defending forces retreated southwards through Malaya, the European community, official and commercial, withdrew. The evacuation of major towns, notably Penang, leaving the Asian community without a government, did grave damage to the standing of Britain as the protecting power. But the deficiencies of the civil government were not a major factor in the débâcle. When Singapore fell, most of the Malayan European community became either internees or prisoners-of-war and suffered much harsh and sometimes brutal treatment.

This was a war fought over the heads of the Malaysian peoples. In the overall war-strategy Britain had reserved to itself the task of military defence and to the Malaysians the role of producing rubber and tin, raw materials essential to the Allied war effort. The Malaysians, like the other peoples of Southeast Asia, paid a grim price for the defeat. In the first flush of their victory the Japanese aimed to harness the economic and human resources of the occupied territories to support their war effort. As the tide turned against Japan from 1943 onwards, Japanese government was dominated by short-term expedients of survival. For all the talk of the 'Co-Prosperity Sphere' they paid little regard to the interests or progress of the occupied territories.[2]

The local economy geared to the export of raw materials came to an abrupt halt. As the British forces retreated, there had been some 'scorched earth' destruction, especially in the mechanized dredging sector of the tin-mining industry. But from 1942 to 1945 the main constraint was the lack of Japanese shipping, decimated in the later years of the war by Allied submarine attack, to lift export cargoes. In 1945, for example, there were large quantities of rubber stored on estates and in warehouses. Japan was equally unable to bring in the imported rice which the Malaysian population needed as its basic foodstuff, since local production was always inadequate. The once busy economy lapsed into stagnation; the sunken dredges rusted in their mining pools and the undergrowth grew ten feet high between the rubber-trees. To relieve the food shortage town-dwellers were forcibly removed to grow food on newly cleared rural settlements, where the incidence of malaria was high. Some 60,000 of the unemployed Indian labour force on the rubber estates were drafted off to construct the infamous 'death railway' by which Japan aimed to supply her forces in Burma overland through Thailand. Only a small proportion survived to return. The Japanese 'banana currency' (the notes bore the emblem of a banana tree) depreciated rapidly; for example, the price of an egg was 3 cents in December 1941 and $35 (about £4) in August 1945.

Japanese brutality towards every section of the population was so appalling that for twenty years afterwards it was reckoned unsafe for individual Japanese to re-enter Malaya; the crews of Japanese ships which came to lift iron-ore cargoes from Trengganu were not allowed to land. But the Japanese also discriminated between the communities in such a way as to exacerbate relations between them. To the Malays there was a show of restoring the authority which the British had taken from them. But it soon became apparent that the real power was to be retained in Japanese hands. In the latter years of their occupation the Japanese gave some encouragement to the left-wing Malay nationalist movement which had emerged as the KMM just before the war (Chapter 3). The Malay leaders aspired to unite Malaya with Indonesia, where more substantial Japanese encouragement had been given, but this movement (the acronyms were PETA/KRIS) collapsed with the Japanese surrender in 1945. Its philosophy, however, was to reappear after the war in the Malay Nationalist Party (MNP). In their repression the Japanese made use of the police which was predominantly Malay; it thus became identified with the hated oppressor.

Towards the Chinese the Japanese showed vindictive animosity and much brutality. This was to pay off old scores in connection with the Malayan Chinese support of the national government of China in its resistance to Japanese invasion. In 1942 the Chinese merchant community was 'invited' to make amends by contributing $50 million to the Japanese war effort. In Perak 'the notables failed to produce their share of the "gift", they were compelled to kneel, fifteen of them, including a woman, in a corner of the Chief Police Officer's office like criminals'.[3] From this ordeal they went on to spend two or three days in prison, but were released to renew their efforts at fund-raising. The only effective resistance to the Japanese was provided by the underground MCP, which was predominantly Chinese. The small and scattered forces of the Malayan People's Anti-Japanese Army (MPAJA) took refuge in the jungle, making occasional forays to take revenge on some individual collaborator with the Japanese. The MPAJA numbered 5,000 altogether; it received weapons and other British help by airdrops and it had British liaison officers with its major units.[4] It bided its time until the Allied counter-attack should come. Many individual Chinese fled from Japanese oppression to join the MPAJA, seeking a safe refuge rather than a political conversion — but the latter followed since political education was an essential function of the organization.[5]

The Indian community, in particular the mass of the estate labourers, suffered acute hardship during the Japanese occupation period. Some, as we have seen, were drafted off to help build the railway from Thailand to Burma. Those who remained on the estates were left in the charge of and sometimes oppressed by the Indian estate junior staff who were now in charge. In visiting estates in the autumn of 1945 I myself noted the most appalling malnutrition, especially among children, which I have ever seen. For the able-bodied estate labourer the alternative to the railway in Thailand was enlistment in the Indian National Army (INA) for military service in Burma. The INA was mainly recruited from the Indian Army units which had surrendered at Singapore with the rest of the defending forces. There was some resentment against Britain among the Indian officers, which the Japanese exploited to raise a new Indian National Army for the liberation of India from British rule. To the volunteers were added many more who were coerced into joining the INA. But despite these pressures and persuasions the majority of the Indian prisoners-of-war refused to join the INA. Units of the INA fought in Burma under Japanese command and shared in the ultimate Japanese defeat. As a parallel to the military effort there was a political movement in Malaya — the Indian Independence League (IIL). From 1943 leadership of both INA and IIL was provided by the dynamic Subhas Chandra Bose. There were the same enforced financial contributions by the Indian merchant community as had been extracted from the Chinese. But there was a genuine response among the Malayan Indian community to the national call of the INA/IIL in spite of the coercion and the sense of being mere tools of Japanese imperialism. The appeal to free India from British rule aroused a local nationalism among the Malayan Indians.

In the remote Borneo territories there was a similar degree of hardship, oppression, and deprivation, though the shape of it reflected local conditions in those parts.

The Japanese occupation period drew to its close in an atmosphere of disillusion and uncertainty. When the atomic bombs were dropped on Japan in August 1945, a British force was already embarking at the ports of eastern India and Ceylon for the invasion of Malaya. The Japanese surrender spared Malaya and Borneo the devastation of what would probably have been a bitterly fought campaign.

The British returned to Malaya speaking of its 'liberation' from Japanese rule. The Malayan peoples accorded them a generous reception, reflecting the general rejoicing at the end of Japanese rule, but politely persisted in referring to the British presence as a 'reoccupation' of Malaya. The British thought that they noted signs of 'loyalty'; the Malayans welcomed the British as an improvement in terms of foreign rule, but could no longer see in what respect loyalty was now owing. One must here distinguish between genuine friendliness to the individual, and a happy recollection of the general decency of previous British rule, and on the other side the prospects for the future. For the first seven months (September 1945 to March 1946) Malaya and Borneo were under military government—the British Military Administration (BMA). This interim expedient was inevitable but unfortunate in its effects. There had been no local victory of British arms to burnish the British image tarnished by the defeat of 1942. Almost all the British personnel of the pre-war civil government had been captured by the Japanese, had suffered hardship, and were in 1945 shipped home to recuperate their health. The BMA staff was a scratch collection of army personnel, most of whom were new to the country.[6] The task of the BMA, in which it was moderately successful, was to restore the bare minimum of government services; both the schools and the land offices, for example, remained closed. In some parts of Malaya a minority of the BMA staff, and some other members of the occupying military forces, made use of the abandoned property of absent or missing owners with little regard for their rights, and there was some corruption. For these reasons, and because it was a period of hardship in Malaya, the reputation of the BMA in Malayan annals is low. It was not an auspicious start for the restored British regime.

The sudden end of the war in Southeast Asia was followed by desperate efforts to restore a semblance of peacetime systems of importing foodstuffs and other supplies and exporting raw materials. But it took time and in the interval there was genuine hardship and much discontent among those who suffered from it. In addition to shortages of everything there was disorder. The Japanese collapsed in August 1945 and the BMA established itself gradually in September. During the interregnum the MPAJA emerged from the jungle, took control of some country towns, and paid off old scores against those, often Malay police and officials, whom they regarded as willing collaborators with the Japanese.[7] There were serious clashes and even bloodshed between Malays and Chinese in some localities. The BMA had some measure of influence with the MPAJA through British liaison officers and was able to induce its demobilization and the handing-over of some of its arms. But considerable quantities of arms supplied during the war remained in jungle caches against the time when they might be needed. The political wing of the communist movement challenged the BMA by calling one-day strikes (*hartal*) in which all shops and places of work were closed. The authority of the BMA was only gradually established over a period of months.

During the three and a half years of the Japanese occupation the Colonial Office in London had been cut off from all channels of communication and, as it turned out, was out of touch with local circumstances and opinions. It decided nonetheless that the existing interruption of the pre-war constitutional system in Malaya afforded a timely opportunity of effecting the reforms which had been proposed but rejected during the period before the war. A new constitution was therefore to take immediate effect when civil government was restored on 1 April 1946. Whatever tactical advantages this approach yielded, it was a disastrous error of strategy.[8]

The short-lived Malayan Union, introduced in April 1946, sentenced to death within three months, and abrogated in 1948, was based on two main principles. First, all nine Malay States of the Peninsula were to be grouped with the Settlements of Penang and Malacca (parts of the former Straits Settlements) in a unitary Malayan Union which would for the time being be a British colony and no longer (as regards the States) a protectorate. Secondly, all persons who had made Malaya their home were to become citizens with equal political rights as the territory progressed towards self-government. Local birth or long residence in Malaya would thus place most of the Chinese and Indians in Malaya on an equality with the Malays. The old distinction between indigenous and non-indigenous peoples was to be swept away.

In order that the new system might take effect as soon as civil government was restored, the British government sent Sir Harold MacMichael to Malaya in the autumn of 1945 with the task of negotiating with each Malay Ruler a new treaty under which he would in effect cede sovereignty in his State to the British Crown. The Rulers were denied the opportunity of consultation between themselves and of consultation with the members of their State Councils (which in some cases was enjoined by the existing State constitutions). A uniform treaty for every State was put before the Ruler in his capital and he was told that it could not be altered, since it had to be uniform in all States, and that the British government expected him to show his friendly feelings towards Britain by signing it. The significance of this last point was that two Rulers who had come to their thrones during the Japanese occupation had been deposed. With varying degrees of reluctance or incomprehension the Rulers signed the treaty. In the meantime, however, strong opposition to the treaty had found expression among the Malay community by the merger of the various pre-war Malay Associations in individual States. The United Malays National Organization (UMNO) which was to be — and still is — the most powerful political party in Malaysia was born at a rally of local Malay associations and bodies held in Kuala Lumpur in March 1946. Its founder and first president was Datuk Onn bin Jaafar who had come to the fore in his native Johor during the troubles of the last few months. Onn, journalist, administrator, and State Councillor, was a vehement and effective speaker who could find the words to express the total opposition of the Malay community to the drastic changes which the Malayan Union embodied. When the new constitution took effect on 1 April 1946, the Malay Rulers made their public protest by refusing to attend the formal installation of the new Governor of the Malayan Union, Sir Edward Gent, who as a Colonial Office official had been one of the main architects of the new constitution. After a short interval of agitated consultation, the British government accepted that the new constitution would have to be replaced by some more acceptable substitute, and entered into discussions to that end with the Malay Rulers and with the leaders of UMNO. These exclusively bilateral negotiations produced a new constitution, the Federation of Malaya.[9]

In the new design both sides secured most of their essential requirements. The unity of Malaya under a strong central government, which had been an objective of the abortive Malayan Union scheme of the British government, was preserved. The power to legislate on important subjects and the control of public finance were reserved to the central federal government headed on the executive side by a British High Commissioner. On the other hand, the Malay Rulers regained sovereignty in their States. This was a necessary basis of the whole Malay community's claim to a special position — that Malay Rulers should be their sovereigns and thus remain the symbolic expression of Malaya as a *Malay* country. In Malacca and Penang, however, which had been British territory for a century and a half, the British Crown retained its sovereignty. On the vexed question of qualifications for citizenship, which would determine the electoral balance later, there was a compromise. The new citizenship qualifications were designed to admit all Malays and a proportion of the non-Malay population. In a typical case a Chinese or an Indian would qualify if he himself had been born in Malaya of parents both of whom had been born and resident in the country for fifteen years. Over the ensuing decade, however, the rules were gradually widened in their effect until 1956 when, with the coming of independence, the simple principle of *ius soli*: citizenship for all born in the country, was introduced (but not with retrospective effect). Citizenship and nationality, over which there had been much argument in the late 1940s, is no longer a major political issue.

When the new constitution was announced in 1947, it was merely a set of proposals agreed between Britain and the Malay representatives. It was then offered for comment to the non-Malay communities — though very much as a *fait accompli*. In 1946 the non-Malay communities had failed to put up a fight to retain the Malayan Union, which was much more favourable to them. By 1947, however, they were alert to the new situation and resentful of the restoration of Malay constitutional privileges. A number of nascent political movements (they were not yet organized as political parties) came together briefly as the Pan-Malayan Council of Joint Action (PMCJA), in which the Malayan Democratic Union (MDU), a group of Chinese, Indian, and Eurasian intellectuals with left-wing socialist views, played a leading part. But the PMCJA was a house divided against itself; the moderates headed by Tan Cheng Lock had little in common with the MDU, with its communist connections, except dislike of the new constitution. The left-wing Malay element differed from the non-Malay groups over the treatment of Malay rights in the constitution. The opposition was ineffectual. The new Federation of Malaya was introduced without difficulty on 1 February 1948.

Almost immediately there was an armed insurrection, known to Malayan history as 'the Emergency', which was a serious threat to the new regime until the mid 1950s (the formal state of emergency was not ended until 1960). The Emergency was a struggle for control of Malaya between the Anglo-Malay dyarchy, which had been established in 1948, and the Malayan Communist Party (MCP) and its supporters. Its origins can be traced back to the pre-war period. As we have seen, the MCP had established itself by penetration of the Malayan labour movement in the hard times of the 1930s and by its leadership of the resistance to the Japanese. The end of the war and of the Japanese occupation was followed by an upsurge of labour militancy. The British had refused to recognize the Japanese banana currency which was in circulation in 1945, and the post-war level of wages did not restore the pre-war purchasing power of the labourer. There was a shortage of the essential foodstuffs, i.e., rice, and of other commodities. The MCP turned these discontents to its own purposes by the establishment of a politically dominated trade-union movement.[10] In this movement young Chinese and Indian leaders who had gained confidence and convictions in the MPAJA and the INA played an important part. For a time the more conservative forces were at a loss. The British did not find it easy to re-establish their authority—the more so as in the era of post-war reform they were committed to a more liberal approach to individual liberty and to industrial relations. The traditional mercantile leadership of the Chinese and Indian communities was preoccupied in rebuilding its business empire and was disinclined to 'put its head above the parapet' in case either the British or the MCP should mark them down as opponents.

Gradually over the period 1946-47 the balance swung against the left wing. It was as much a question of ideology as of force, though there was a good deal of physical intimidation and of financial extortion. The MCP influence derived from two sources—its stake in the PMCJA secured through its penetration of the MDU, and its dominance of the trade unions organized as 'General Labour Unions' which enabled it to call strikes at will in any industry and in almost any major urban centre. It was a power which reached its peak early in 1946 with an attempt to call a one-day national strike on 15 February, the anniversary of the British surrender at Singapore in 1942. But this demonstration proved a fiasco in face of firm government counter-measures. It was not the end of the struggle, which continued until early 1948. In this period the MCP came to rely increasingly on its control of the trade unions since political opposition had crumbled. On the other side, the government gradually tightened its control by administrative and legal constraints on the trade union movement. The employers also were able to reassert their authority at the place of work, such as the estates and mines. The worst of the immediate post-war hardships passed, and militancy declined as the living conditions of the working man became somewhat easier. It has been cogently argued that this was a 'conflict between one form of authoritarianism and another'.[11] The essential popular base of MCP power was eroded both by government measures and by the MCP abuse of its control of organized labour for political purposes. It had never been able to attract Malay support and its hold on the Chinese and Indian communities, from which the trade unions drew their members, was weakening. The MCP was losing a war of attrition in industrial relations and politics; it turned in the first half of 1948 to open military action — the Emergency.

In this campaign the military strength of the MCP, organized as the Malayan People's Liberation Army (MRLA) but usually known as the 'three stars' (*tiga bintang* in Malay, i.e., the cap badge representing the three major Malayan communities), was much less than the security forces mobilized against it. But the main strength of the movement was its hold on certain elements of Malayan Chinese society, which willingly or under the threat of violence, gave it support in the long-drawn struggle. In their struggle to survive (it was hardly active resistance) during the Japanese occupation period, the communist-led MPAJA had relied heavily on the aid — in food and in information — of the squatters. In Malaya the term 'squatter' should be reserved for a peasant, usually Chinese, in unauthorized occupation of his land, but in the literature the term is also extended to all Chinese small farmers of the same type as squatters proper. As has been explained (Chapter 5), the squatter community had its origin during the periods of unemployment of the 1930s when labourers, to whom the government would not alienate land under legal title since they were aliens in Malaya, took themselves off to grow their own food in remote places where the land office was unlikely to find and evict them. 'Conceived in sin and nurtured in stealth the position of the squatters was neither stable nor secure'.[12] They were the Ishmaels of Malaya against whom every man's hand was raised. It was natural therefore that they should be in sympathy with the political rebels, who could sometimes protect them, the men who had fled to the jungle. The number of squatters fluctuated since they were a reserve of labour, part of which was drawn back into employment when it was available. In addition to squatter settlements in remote places there were villages near the towns; the able-bodied males went into the towns to work leaving their families, for whom there was no housing in the towns, to live and support themselves on the land. Some of these squatter areas within reach of towns became a valuable source of food produced in excess of their own needs for sale to the town markets. It was estimated that there were about 300,000 squatters in 1948 when the Emergency began and that they occupied some 70,000 acres of land.[13]

The other main support of the insurgents during the Emergency came from the younger generation of Chinese who had been educated in Chinese-medium schools and for whom Malayan society, based on a system of Malay special rights and English-language educational qualifications for employment, offered little opportunity. 'They could not become lawyers, doctors, engineers, architects, or anything but at best a business merchant and at worst a waiter in a coffee shop or a manual labourer'.[14] For them the new China of Mao Tse Tung, which had thrown off Western domination, offered a model for a new society in Malaya and also a lesson in tactics: to establish a military base at the periphery and from there move in to take control of the centre. Much of the MCP leadership came from this group.

With this core of firm support the MCP needed to attract to its ranks, by persuasion or intimidation, the general body of Malayan Chinese, disgruntled by both the manner and the substance of the Anglo-Malay negotiations for a new constitution over the period 1946-48. Although the majority of the Malayan Chinese bourgeoisie were not ideologically in sympathy with the new China of Mao Tse Tung, they were proud of its strength and success and foresaw the possibility at least that a rejuvenated government of China might intervene actively in Southeast Asia. They had good reason to fear that if they gave open support to the government's campaign against the MCP, reprisals would be taken against them or members of their families. Tan Cheng Lock himself narrowly escaped death from a bomb attack.

The same factors which gave the MCP a broad base among the Malayan Chinese alienated them from the other communities, especially from the Malays, to whom communism was essentially a Chinese phenomenon and an expression of Chinese nationalism. No slogans about a Malayan People's Liberation Army could attract any significant degree of support from the non-Chinese communities.[15]

The long-drawn struggle of the Emergency began in June 1948 with attacks on the rubber and tin industries, which were the basic elements of the Malayan economy. Both industries had made a satisfactory and indeed rapid recovery since 1945 to full production. The rubber-trees had even benefited from an interruption of three years (1942-45) in the process of tapping bark to extract latex. In 1947 Malayan output of rubber had reached 645,000 tons as compared with 547,000 in 1940. The more highly mechanized tin-mines had only gradually re-equipped themselves in the period of post-war scarcity; in 1948 tin output was 45,000 tons as compared with 81,000 tons in 1940. The main areas of production of both rubber and tin were generally remote from the towns and so especially vulnerable to attack. The communist strategy was to halt the output of rubber and tin by hit-and-run raids on estates and mines with the killing of key personnel. The ultimate object, which was never attained, was to seize permanent control of 'liberated areas' to be used thereafter as bases for further advances towards the towns. In these operations full use was made of the veterans of the wartime MPAJA operating from their familiar jungle terrain and equipped with the balance of the weapons supplied by the Allies during the war and cached in secret places in the jungle. For supplies and information the guerrillas relied on the squatter settlements along the jungle fringe and on the labourers working on estates and mines. This scattered and widespread workforce served as a screen through which the security forces could never penetrate without advance information of their movements reaching the communist forces. If any member of these groups showed any inclination to withhold his support, it was easy enough to terrorize him into a more accommodating frame of mind. In addition to the managers, mainly European, who were the prime target of attack, a larger number of Chinese and other workers and squatters were killed with great brutality as a horrific example to the rest. In some respects, however, this was a self-defeating strategy since it alienated those whose support it was essential to retain. In 1951 the MCP leadership modified its methods in the hope of securing more general political support by greater restraint and selectivity in the choice of victims. Throughout the campaign the civilian support movement, the Min Yuen, was an essential element of communist survival and effective action.

After an uncertain and ineffectual beginning the government evolved military, administrative, and political counter-measures which gradually wore down the numerically inferior guerrillas. At the height of the campaign some 40,000 regular soldiers, including several battalions of the Malay Regiment, were deployed with the support on occasion of artillery, aircraft, and naval vessels. In addition there was a police force of about 70,000 and quarter of a million 'home guards' in the villages. This paramilitary effort was backed by the administrative and technical services of the government, for which the Emergency was the highest priority. These powerful resources were employed for several years against armed bands which in 1948 numbered some 4,000 to 5,000, increasing to a maximum of 8,000 a year or two later.

It was a grim game of 'hide and seek' in which the numerically superior pursuers hunted down guerrillas whose refuge was the jungle. For several years the terrorists retained the local initiative in areas of their own choice and did great damage. The tasks of the security forces were to protect life and property against these attacks and then to eliminate the attackers wherever they might be. The first of these tasks called for an elaborate and costly defensive system of barbed-wire fences, floodlighting, wireless communications, armoured vehicles, and other equipment manned by armed and trained men. There were numerous possible targets of attack and some of them were human beings who had to go about their essential work. Hence the defensive system could never guarantee the safety of anyone or anything. The all-pervasive nature of the risk was demonstrated by the death of the British High Commissioner, Sir Henry Gurney, in a roadside ambush in October 1951. The most exposed members of the community were the managers of estates and mines and their staffs. They had been singled out as the prime targets of communist attack and the nature of their work obliged them to live in siege conditions threatened continuously by guerrilla attack. Their bungalows, surrounded by barbed-wire, lit at night by floodlights, patrolled by armed sentries, were small and by no means impregnable fortresses. In their daily rounds they travelled in vehicles protected with armour plate, escorted by bodyguards, moving unannounced to their destinations and returning always by a different route. Like front-line troops they had to be brought out at intervals for a period of rest in the security of a large town. The strain was appalling. About one in ten of the planters was murdered in the course of the Emergency.

The estate labourer and the squatter was no less exposed and much less protected. But if he co-operated when required, he might hope to escape attack.

Direct military action against the attackers was immensely laborious in relation to the results achieved. The gangs did not stand and fight. They had no strongpoints and no territory to defend. They made use of their own mobility and the cover afforded by the jungle to escape contact with their pursuers. In due course they reappeared elsewhere to take the local initiative against undefended or weakly held targets. British, Malay, and other Commonwealth troops spent many hours plodding along jungle paths. In places the jungle is so thick that a man may pass within two or three feet of another in hiding and miss him. It was difficult to achieve surprise and contacts were fleeting. It was reckoned that each soldier must put in a thousand hours of 'jungle-bashing' for each brief moment of contact with his quarry. It was found that the most effective tactics were to lie in ambush for terrorists emerging from the jungle to obtain supplies. For this purpose it was necessary to have good sources of information and to break the links between the jungle gangs and their supporters outside. Thus the resettlement of Chinese squatters in 'New Villages' became the most decisive measure of the campaign. It was also to have considerable economic and social consequences since it brought the squatter community into contact with and under the control of the administration as never before.

In the first year of the Emergency campaign (1948-49) the government policy was to round up squatter settlements suspected of assisting the guerillas and to repatriate them to China (or India if they were Indian). Some 25,000 people were deported in this way. This method plainly could not be extended to the removal of, say, 300,000 people; in any case the authorities in China would not have accepted them.[16] The hardship which resulted from these measures caused much concern and resentment among the Malayan Chinese community as a whole. It was an ineffectual policy since the able-bodied men were often absent when the rounding-up occurred and only women, children, and old people were caught. From 1950 there was a new policy of resettlement of squatters (often referred to as 'the Briggs Plan').[17] The object of the policy was to bring the scattered squatter groups within the perimeter of compact settlements, New Villages, where they could be protected (each village had a protective ring of barbed-wire and usually a police-station) and prevented, if that was still their inclination, from communicating with or passing supplies to the guerrillas. There was a parallel 'regroupment' of labourers on estates and elsewhere into larger and more central 'labour lines' where protection and control could be achieved. A total of 573,000 people (of whom 300,000 were squatters) were moved into New Villages over the decade 1950-60 and about 650,000 labourers were 'regrouped'.[18] Most of the movement to new habitations took place in the three years 1950-53. The resettlement of squatters in particular was an urgent operation carried through in haste as a military necessity. The sites of New Villages were sometimes chosen with more regard to their defensibility than to agricultural and economic considerations. But ten years later in 1962 about nine-tenths of the New Villages survived and were regarded as permanent settlements.[19] In addition to police protection the typical New Village had a school, a dispensary, and perhaps a community hall. The population of a New Village was between 100 and 1,000 persons in most cases, although some of the larger ones had populations of 5,000 to 10,000 or even more. In these government-administered settlements the Chinese agriculturalist might hope to be granted a lease to his land. In those areas where there was alternative employment, however, many of the inhabitants gave up farming in sometimes adverse conditions and went back to work for a wage as labourers. Some villages prospered and others went downhill. An incidental effect of resettlement was to increase the urban element in the Malayan Chinese population as a whole to almost three-quarters.[20] Thus the Malayan Chinese squatter, described in 1950 as 'industrious, close-fisted, lacking in civic sense and, just now, deeply bewildered'.[21] was dragged willy-nilly in from no man's land (in a double sense).

There was an elaborate administrative system (in key areas) of food-rationing and control of the movement of foodstuffs and other essential supplies. Peasants and estate labourers, for example, were not allowed to take a midday meal with them into the fields. Identity cards were issued as a check on the movement of MCP supporters. These measures, which caused inconvenience if not hardship, were not totally effective.[22] But they sufficed to deprive the guerrillas of their previously uninhibited freedom of movement and tactical initiative in making attacks. The security forces were thus able to pin them down to a greater extent and to exert maximum pressure in a selected area on a particular gang (the MRLA was organized into State 'regiments' but operated in smaller groups). Short of food, on the run, subject to random bombardment by artillery of the jungle in which they were hidden, casualties mounted and nerves cracked. 'Voice aircraft' circled overhead emanating propaganda by loudspeaker, often the voice of a captured comrade calling on the others to surrender. For those who surrendered there was the opportunity of entering a 'rehabilitation camp' and learning a trade before returning to ordinary working life. Gradually the gangs were eliminated and the areas which they had dominated were officially declared 'white' and freed from the more irksome restrictions on the population.

Throughout the Emergency campaign and especially in the later stages from about 1954 onwards there was a political dimension. It was recognized that this was 'a battle for the hearts and minds of the people'.[23] The reasons have been given for the hesitations of the Malayan Chinese middle class in determining their attitude. When the Emergency began in mid-1948, moderate Chinese leaders, notably Tan Cheng Lock, were at a loss. Their PMCJA attack on the new constitution had failed. But they were drawn into a new political forum, the Communities Liaison Committee, promoted by Malcolm Macdonald (then British Commissioner General for Southeast Asia in Singapore) as a means to building bridges between the Malay leaders of UMNO who had won their battle for a new constitution and the Chinese and other non-Malay leaders who resented the manner of their defeat. The object of the Committee was to work out in private discussion policy initiatives which might improve inter-communal relations. At the same time the Chinese leaders established a Malayan Chinese Association (MCA) to represent the interest of their community. Until 1952, when the first municipal elections led to declared political activity by the parties, the MCA was much engaged in the resettlement of squatters in New Villages, to which it contributed substantial funds to provide services and amenities.[24] Tan Cheng Lock, as the elder statesman of his community, became president of the MCA. It was very much a businessman's pressure-group rather than a mass party. But it did provide a means by which moderate Chinese activists could participate in the evolving political process. Thus it came to be co-founder with UMNO of the Alliance coalition which was to take Malaya to independence.

Malaya is a country in which the political leaders, though not always their followers, are inclined to search for consensus. From 1946 to 1950 the president of UMNO was Datuk Onn bin Jaafar, who had come to the fore in 1946 as the vehement exponent of Malay opposition to the Malayan Union constitution. In spite of the fire in his belly Onn could recognize that the Malays would have to pay the price of political accommodation with the other communities if they were to advance towards self-government which he ardently wished to achieve. When he found that the Malays would not agree to enlarge UMNO to admit non-Malay members, Onn founded a new, non-communal party – the Independence of Malaya Party (IMP) – to which he hoped to attract leaders from all communities. In this he had the initial support of Tan Cheng Lock. But when it became apparent that the Malays would not follow Onn into IMP, Chinese support for it waned. Onn himself lost the presidency of UMNO in promoting IMP, and was succeeded in UMNO by Tunku Abdul Rahman, a relatively unknown Malay barrister in the government legal service and a brother of the Sultan of Kedah. In time Abdul Rahman was to prove the main architect of the intercommunal accommodation. But in 1950, when he succeeded Onn, he insisted that there could be no dual membership of UMNO and of IMP, as Onn proposed. The Malays must choose – and they chose UMNO. The first test of the popular appeal of the non-communal IMP came early in 1952 when the first elections were held for membership of the Kuala Lumpur municipal council. UMNO and MCA then formed a limited and local alliance to oppose and defeat IMP – and they won nine seats against IMP's two. Thus the Alliance was formed which was to rule Malaya for twenty years or more. It was a setback from which the IMP never recovered. The pattern of Malayan politics – compromise between communal parties – had been set.

Before coming to the development of Malayan politics in the 1950s, the constitutional framework must be described as it was down to the coming of independence in 1957. Under the Federation of Malaya constitution established in 1948 there was a central legislature, the Federal Council, with a total membership of 76, all of whom were *ex-officio* or officially nominated members. In making the choice of nominated members from the local and business communities the High Commissioner selected those who had been recommended to him by various associations and bodies. In addition to the communal bodies representation was given to economic and social interests such as the rubber-producers, large and small, and the trade unions. It was not in any way a democratic assembly, but in practice it was fairly representative of the middle and upper classes and of the interests which dominated the economy.

The government was unlikely to be defeated on essential points in such an assembly – though on occasion it was compelled to make a diplomatic retreat. In addition to its obvious function of providing a forum for public discussion, the Federal Council gave to the nascent political parties the opportunity of practising parliamentary manoeuvres against each other and to their leaders some practice in the function of ministers. This latter aspect was promoted through the 'Member system' introduced in 1951. In his executive function the British High Commissioner was advised by an Executive Council to which prominent local leaders as well as British officials were appointed to form a kind of cabinet. In 1951 there was a reorganization by which government departments were grouped to form quasi-ministerial portfolios, such as Finance or Natural Resources. These portfolios were allocated to members of the Executive Council, some of whom were Malayans. Datuk Onn, for example, became Member for Home Affairs. The individual Member was in practice in executive control of his group of departments and spoke for them in the Executive and also in the Federal Council. But there was no government with collective responsibility; each Member dealt with the High Commissioner (or his deputy the Chief Secretary) as questions of policy or administration might require. Several of the key portfolios, such as Defence and Economic Affairs, were as before entrusted to British career officials. In practice, nonetheless, prominent Malayans did have the duty and the power to direct the work of government departments as if they had been ministers.

In any system of government the allocation of money for public expenditure is all-important. In the 1950s Malaya was hard-pressed by the heavy cost of the Emergency campaign. Its revenues fluctuated with the world prices of its exports, rubber and tin. After the hectic 'Korean boom' of 1951 there was a relapse and then a slow recovery. The executive branch of the government had to make its proposals for expenditure to the Federal Council in the form of an annual budget and supplementary estimates. These were examined by a standing committee on finance of which the British Financial Secretary was chairman, but the members were drawn from the nominated unofficials of the Federal Council. The working civil servants, of whom I was one at the time, well knew that if departmental proposals failed to stand up to scrutiny, sometimes searching and expert, by the committee they would have to be withdrawn. The committee was the most effective means available to nominated unofficial members of the Council of exercising control over the bureaucrats. As such it was useful experience for those of them who were to be ministers later on.

In each Malay State the structure reproduced the pattern of the pre-war UMS: the principal executive was a Malay chief minister (*mentri besar*). The Malay Ruler had a British Adviser and also a

State Executive Council; there was an appointed State Council as the local legislature. In practice the State governments had lost most of their powers to the federal government and had little influence on the shaping of policy. But it was a cumbersome system since every federal proposal for legislation had to be referred to each State government for its comments before it could be introduced into the Federal Council. It was a procedure which imposed months of delay on even the most ordinary of proposals. As compared with the pre-war situation the most significant change was that the routine administration had passed from British to Malay hands in the former FMS. The British Advisers tended to concern themselves particularly with the local Emergency operations and with the necessary liaison between the State governments and the military commanders. In the former Settlements of Penang and Malacca, which were still British territory, the executive head of the administration was a Resident Commissioner responsible to the High Commissioner in Kuala Lumpur. From 1952 (following the death of Sir Henry Gurney) to 1954, control of the civil government and of the military forces used in the Emergency operations was combined in the person of Sir Gerald Templer, a British general (later field marshal) who was appointed High Commissioner as well as General Officer Commanding. Templer exploited the cyclonic impact of his forceful personality in the conduct of the Emergency campaign; the civil functions of the High Commissioner were discharged by his deputy, Sir Donald MacGillivray, who succeeded him as High Commissioner in 1954 and became the last holder of the post.

By 1954 the crisis of the Emergency had passed and the tempo of Malayan politics had quickened under the stimulus of elections to municipal councils, the first Malayan experience of the ballot box, and by the sharper edge of competition for power which must assuredly devolve to local political leaders in the next few years. The main competitors were the Alliance and Party Negara. The Alliance of UMNO and MCA, born of opposition to Datuk Onn's IMP in 1952, had become an effective movement throughout Malaya though some observers doubted its ability to hold together under the stresses of communal tensions. The Indian community, fissiparous as always, had a number of representative bodies. But the Malayan Indian Congress (MIC), which was the strongest, joined forces with UMNO and MCA as a member of the Alliance. After the collapse of IMP Datuk Onn had formed Party Negara which professed to be another non-communal party, but in fact made its appeal mainly to the Malay electorate. It included some prominent Indian figures among its leaders and was at the time considered to be rather more solid than the Alliance. The Alliance and Party Negara now began to manoeuvre for position. The strategy of the Alliance was to press for elections to State and Federal Councils as a step towards early independence for the Federation of Malaya. The Alliance also demanded that the reconstituted Federal Council should have a decisive majority of elected members so that the party which won the elections would have real power. Party Negara professed to seek independence but at a staider rate. In the end the colonial regime conceded most of the Alliance demands and the first elections to State and Federal Councils were held in 1955. In the first federal, i.e., national, elections held in July 1955 the Alliance swept the board, winning 51 of the 52 seats to be filled by election (in a Council with a total membership of 98). The first government chosen by popular election took office in 1955 under a regime of internal self-government with various subjects such as defence reserved to Britain. But the new Alliance government was soon able to negotiate with Britain for complete independence, to take effect in August 1957. Tunku Abdul Rahman, who had become president of UMNO in 1951, had shown considerable skill as a politician and he had won the confidence of the Chinese as well as of the Malays. The Alliance programme of rapid advance towards independence caught the mood of the electorate, predominantly Malay at this stage. The special strength of UMNO was its ability to mobilize the active support of the Malay middle class and rural leaders in the villages. MCA and MIC had a less secure electoral base, but were not at this stage troubled by effective opponents among their own communities. The new Alliance government was nationalist (in a moderate fashion), but not radical. The Malay ministers were mostly of aristocratic birth and the Chinese and Indians were well-to-do if not extremely rich. Some of them had been nominated members of the Federal Council until the change to elections in 1955 and so they had experience of the work of government. In essentials it was a government which based its authority on the tradition of Malay aristocratic leadership and Chinese and Indian plutocratic leadership, aided in each case by the novel sense of national destiny and independence.

Before the country could become independent it was necessary to decide the form of its constitution and to strike a balance between the claims of indigenous (Malay) and non-indigenous communities. For this purpose a commission of distinguished constitutional experts headed by Lord Reid was appointed. The report[25] of the commission substantially adopted the recommendations made to it by the Alliance parties jointly. But on some points there were significant changes; the commission would not accept the recommendation that Islam should be the state religion of Malaysia.[26] The commission proposed that there should be a limited right to speak in a Chinese or Indian language in the legislature and that the special rights accorded to the Malays should be reconsidered after an interval of fifteen years. It was political dynamite to modify the delicate compromises worked out within the Alliance on these points. In the subsequent discussion of the commission's report the Alliance as the government of Malaya reverted to its original standpoint.

The main features of the new constitution were:

1 The rulers of the Malay States would choose one of themselves to be Paramount Ruler (*Yang di-Pertuan Agong*) and sovereign of the Federation of Malaya for a period of five years; thereafter another of the college of Rulers would fill this office for a like term.

2 The Paramount Ruler of the Federation and each ruler in his State would be a constitutional sovereign acting on the advice of his ministers chosen from the majority party in a fully elected legislature.

3 The federal parliament would comprise a Senate (partly nominated) with limited powers and a House of Representatives all of whose members would be elected by electors on a common roll for a period not exceeding five years. These are in Malay called *Dewan Negara* and *Dewan Ra'ayat*.

4 Legislative and executive powers would as before be divided between the federal and State governments. The federal government would be headed by a cabinet of ministers under a Prime Minister chosen from the majority party in the House of Representatives. Each State government would be headed by a chief minister who would be chosen from and supported by the majority group in each elected State assembly.

5 The settlements of Penang and Malacca would cease to be British territory and would become constituent states of the Federation. In each of these states a Governor would be ap-

pointed by the Paramount Ruler to discharge functions similar to those of the Ruler of a Malay State and under similar conditions of constitutional procedure.

6 The citizenship qualifications, which had been considerable modified from the original rigour of the 1948 constitution, were to be further relaxed. All children born in the Federation after independence would be citizens, i.e., *ius soli* was recognized but not retrospectively. The concept of Malayan nationality was developed and refined.

7 Malay would be the national language, but for the next ten years English would be a second official language.

8 Islam would be the state religion, but freedom of worship was guaranteed to all creeds.

9 The Paramount Ruler was required to safeguard the special position of the Malays in respect of such matters as recruitment to the public service, award of government scholarships, Malay land reservations, and the grant of permits for certain types of business activity. But in the discharge of his responsibility he is to act on the advice of his cabinet (in which the non-Malay communities by convention but not by constitutional right are always represented) and he is required to safeguard the legitimate interests of the non-Malay communities. This principle is embodied in the constitution as Article 153, which has been a major issue of Malaysian politics, as will be explained later.

All this was hammered out and passed into law. The foundations of the Malaysian constitution were laid by the compromises of 1956, for when Malaya was enlarged to become Malaysia, the existing constitution was adapted to accommodate the new member states of the Federation. On 31 August 1957 the independence of Malaya was proclaimed amid general rejoicing.

It had been agreed that the Federal Council partially elected in 1955 should continue until 1959 when the first elections under the new constitution were held. In these elections the Alliance government was returned to office, with the support of a fully elected parliament, but it suffered from internal dissension and lost some ground to the opposition parties. This was the first stage in the evolution of politics in Malaysia, and so the 1959 election is deferred for analysis in Chapter 8.

The proposal for an enlarged Federation which became Malaysia in 1963 was first put forward by the Prime Minister of Malaya, Tunku Abdul Rahman, in 1961. For almost twenty years (1951 to 1969) the Tunku was to be the accepted national leader as well as Prime Minister (from 1955). Although born of royal blood, he was almost unknown in 1951 — he then occupied a modest office in the Attorney General's chambers as a government legal officer and he lived in an equally modest 'government quarter'. One of those natural leaders who have matured and developed personal authority in the exercise of responsibility, he had the relaxed, human, and yet very unassuming self-confidence of a man born to high estate. To the poise and charm of the aristocrat he added a remarkable sense of what his electorate, more especially the Malay element in it, was feeling. As will be explained in Chapter 8, the crisis of 1969 overwhelmed and destroyed him. But it did not detract from the achievement of his public service to his country up to that time.

Before coming to the events which led to the foundation of Malaysia, it is necessary to describe the parallel evolution of Singapore, Sabah, and Sarawak down to 1961 when they became drawn into the scheme for creating Malaysia.

Until 1942 Singapore had been the acknowledged political and commercial capital of Malaya. But in 1945 it was excluded from the unified Malayan Union and left to stand as a crown colony on its own. There were three reasons for this decision of the British government of that time. First, three-quarters of the population of Singapore are Chinese. Malaya without Singapore had a bare majority of Malays over all other communities together. But if Singapore had been included in the new country, the Malay proportion of the total population would have been about 43 per cent. At a time when the Malays were to be asked to make other concessions, it was felt to be too much to make them a minority. Secondly, the traditional entrepôt trade of Singapore with neighbouring territories of Southeast Asia, had since 1819 been founded on a regime of free trade. By contrast the Malay States had derived a considerable part of their revenues from import duties. Lastly, Singapore had been a major naval base and in 1945 it was still contemplated that Britain might wish to retain this base long after Malaya had become independent.

As a crown colony Singapore moved by stages towards an increasing measure of self-government. The decisive change came in 1955, when the first elections were held on a franchise widened to admit to the roll Chinese and others who were not British subjects, since they had been born elsewhere, but who had been long resident in Singapore. These elections produced a Labour Front government headed by a mercurial lawyer, David Marshall. But a system under which the powers of government were shared between elected ministers and British officials worked badly; there was also much local unrest and disorder. The elections of 1959, however, produced a strong government of the People's Action Party (PAP) led by Lee Kuan Yew who has been Prime Minister of Singapore since that time. In the period from 1959 to 1963, however, the government was still a dyarchy under which powers were shared. The PAP itself had come to power with the support of the Communist Party which at one stage attempted a 'take-over'. Past disputes about responsibility for law and order had been resolved by establishing an internal security council in which Malaya as well as Britain and the PAP leadership participated. A split in the PAP in 1961 left only the rump of the party in precarious control of the legislature. The outlook for Singapore in terms both of stability and prosperity, if it remained as an isolated unit, was uncertain. If Singapore became independent and a centre both of communist activity and of Chinese nationalism, the repercussions in Malaya could be serious.

In contrast with Singapore the three territories in Borneo under British control, the Sultanate of Brunei, British North Borneo (now Sabah), and Sarawak, were backward in their political and economic development. The British North Borneo Company relinquished Sabah in 1946 to the British Crown and it was governed as a conventional crown colony. It had about 200,000 acres under rubber, divided into estates and smallholdings in equal proportions. But hardwood timber became in value Sabah's largest export. The fifteen years from 1946 to 1961 were an undramatic story of steady expansion of basic services such as education and health. Of its population of just over 400,000 in 1960 a quarter were Chinese and three-eighths were Dusun (now called Kadazan); the remainder included Murut, Bajau, and Brunei Malay. There was no perceptible political activity and the first elections ever held, in December 1962, were to choose members of Town Boards, i.e., local small-town municipal councils, and district councils. Sarawak also became a crown colony in 1946 and so remained until 1963. Here there was some tension over the transition from the idiosyncratic Brooke regime to more conventional administration. In 1949 the British Governor of Sarawak was assassinated, but this was an isolated outrage and not the symbol of a revolt. Under the Brookes there had been some nominated advisory councils; Sarawak therefore moved more rapidly than Sabah in the direction of representative government. The constitution promulgated in 1957 provided for indirect elections to a territorial legislative council (the Council Negri) through local elected councils. But the first elections were held only in 1963 when it had already been decided that Sarawak would join Malaysia. The principal exports were rubber and pepper. It is unnecessary to pursue the history of Brunei as a British protectorate since it did not enter Malaysia with the other territories.

To the politicians in Kuala Lumpur who knew nothing of the Borneo territories and their peoples it seemed that there was a trio of territories which shared the experience with Malaya of British colonial rule; and these were peoples who followed a traditional way of life and who lived by agriculture. As such they would, it seemed, add their weight as indigenes to hold the balance against the Chinese of Singapore.

Notes

1 In this summary of the campaign I have drawn on L. Allen (1977) — a masterly account.

2 Purcell (1948), 249–62 and Chin Kee Onn (1946) describe the Chinese experience. On the Japanese side see Itagaki (1962), Akashi (1970), and Yuen Choy Leng (1978).

3 Purcell (1948), 253; p.255 on the price of eggs.

4 Chapman (1949), who played a leading part, gives the classic account.

5 Chin Kee Onn (1946), Chapter xv. Limited space prevents me from repeating in this edition an account of the courageous resistance movement in the towns. See 1969 edition, 97.

6 The detachment sent to Negri Sembilan in mid-September 1945, for example, was commanded by James Calder, who had served in the Malayan Civil Service before the war. I had spent a few months in the Uganda Administrative Service before being called up in 1940, but had served in other military government organizations. The other officers (about 10) included some medical and public-works specialists with pre-war experience of Malaya. Several were quite new to the work and to the country.

7 Chin Kee Onn (1946), Chapter xv and Jain (1970), 297–311 describe how some of these rancorous hatreds developed. In Batu Kikir village in Negri Sembillan a group of MPAJA Chinese taunted the Malays in a most pro-vocative fashion ('You will eat pork if we tell you to') and the Malays ran amok and slaughtered about 40 Chinese. In Rembau an MPAJA party tied the Malay District Officer (a future chief minister of the State) down to his desk and discussed cutting his throat. On 23 September 1945 I paid a first visit to the remote village of Titi, an MPAJA stronghold, where the

MPAJA flag was flying over the police station, and we got some very black looks (my companion was the Malay District Officer). These episodes were the product of abnormal experiences, but they have left their mark.

8 The Colonial Office in association with the War Office established a Malayan Planning Unit (MPU) to prepare for the transition, during the period of military government, from the pre-war constitutional position to the Malayan Union. I had some contact with the MPU and noted how determined they were to effect their reforms before local opposition to them could find expression.

9 J. de V. Allen (1967) for an account of the birth and rapid demise of the Malayan Union.

10 Stenson (1970), passim on this period.

11 Stenson (1970), 233. There were divided counsels and upheavals among the MCP leadership at this time. See Short (1975), Chapter 2, Hanrahan (1971), Chapter IV, Brimmell (1959), 203-11.

12 The best systematic account of the origins of the squatter community and of their resettlement in New Villages in the early 1950s is Sandhu (1964). Han Suyin's novel (1956) gives a vivid and imaginative picture of the character, attitude, and living conditions of the squatters. See also Short (1975) for much detailed information. The quotation is from Sandhu, 145.

13 Proceedings of the Federal Legislative Council 1950-51, B 102, cited by Sandhu (1964), 150.

14 Han Suyin (1956), 259.

15 In Pahang, however, there was some Malay support for the MPAJA arising from local circumstances. See Short (1975), 208-9.

16 The communist government in China showed itself surprisingly willing to turn a blind eye if repatriation was effected inconspicuously. A British official from Malaya was stationed at Amoy in Fukien Province in the guise of a 'British consul'. He organized the dispersal to their villages in China of each arriving shipload of repatriates. See also Short (1975), 191 and 201. But it was not a humane solution, nor could it have been a large-scale one.

17 At this stage General Sir Harold Briggs was Director of Operations, responsible for the co-ordination of government measures in the Emergency campaign. It was generally believed that in shaping the resettlement policy the creative mind, as in several other reforms, was that of Sir Henry Gurney, High Commissioner 1948-51: see Short (1975), Chapter 9.

18 Sandhu (1964), 159 and 164. The labour force was regrouped in the estate described by Jain (1970). Swift (1965), 4 makes the point that resettlement ended the residential intermingling, such as it was, of rural Malays and Chinese.

19 *Sari Berita* (31 May 1962). Sandhu (1964), 162. TMP, paras 504-5 gives data on the state of New Villages in the mid-1970s. The larger ones and those near towns have flourished. Poverty and unemployment are found in the small and remote settlements.

20 Sandhu (1964), 171. The generally accepted criterion (see Smith (1952), 5) of a town in Malayan population statistics is a settlement of at least 1,000 people. This is a rather low limit and in some analyses a settlement is urban if it has at least 3,000 or even 10,000 inhabitants.

21 Federal Council Paper No 14 of 1950 (the Newboult 'Squatter Report') on which much official planning was based.

22 Han Suyin (1956) gives a very clear account of the hard and sometimes dangerous situation of Chinese living in a New Village or in regrouped labour lines on an estate or mine. They were caught between the pressure and rough treatment of the predominantly Malay security forces and the threats and demands of local guerrilla bands lying up in the nearby belt of jungle.

23 This phrase, rather hackneyed by over-use, was apparently invented by Gurney; Sandhu (1964), 157.

24 On Tan Cheng Lock's part see Tregonning (1979), 60 and Soh (1960), 50. Much has been written about the politics of this period including Means (1970), 120, Ratnam (1965), 152, and more generally Vasil (1971), and Milne (1967).

25 Report of the Federation of Malaya Constitutional Commission 1957 ('the Reid Report'). Ratnam (1965), 58 makes a detailed comparison of the differences between the Alliance proposals and the recommendations of the Reid Commission.

26 In private conversation Lord Reid expressed much misgiving about possible loss of individual liberty if Islam was recognized as the state religion. But Islam in Southeast Asia is a very tolerant creed.

7 The Making of Malaysia

On 27 May 1961 Tunku Abdul Rahman, the genial but slightly erratic Prime Minister of Malaya, had a routine engagement to speak to a lunchtime meeting in Singapore of the Foreign Correspondents' Association of Southeast Asia. In the course of an otherwise unsurprising *tour d'horizon* of Southeast Asian affairs, the Tunku said:

> Malaya today as a nation realizes that she cannot stand alone and in isolation. Outside of international politics the national one must be broad-based. Sooner or later she should have an understanding with Britain and the peoples of Singapore, Borneo, Brunei and Sarawak. It is premature for me to say how this closer understanding can be brought about but it is inevitable that we should look ahead to this objective and think of a plan whereby these territories can be brought closer together in a political and economic cooperation. [1]

With these words the Malaysia project, usually referred to at the time as 'the Merger', was born. The project came to fruition in September 1963 when Singapore, Sabah, and Sarawak joined Malaya to form Malaysia. But Brunei refused to join and Singapore was expelled from Malaysia after two turbulent years (1963-65). Malaya's neighbours, Indonesia and the Philippines, pushed their opposition to the project to the edge of war. Indonesian 'Confrontation' of Malaysia lasted until 1966. Yet the reception accorded to the proposal made in May 1961 was on the whole constructive. The partners in the proposed new state recognized its potential advantages but also its disadvantages to them.

In the Federation of Malaya the Malay community feared that if they were reunited,[2] Singapore would again dominate Malaya as it had done under the pre-war system. Singapore's 625,000 voters, mainly Chinese, would tip the balance of combined electoral strength against the Malays and so undo all which had been achieved in 1948 to re-establish Malay supremacy. Singapore was a centre of left-wing turbulence where communists were allowed a degree of latitude which Malaya, with its recent memories of the long-drawn Emergency of 1948-60, regarded as folly. Singapore was still the greatest centre of commerce in the Southeast Asia region and might well regain its pre-eminence as the acknowledged business capital of the united territories to the detriment of Kuala Lumpur.

These Malay fears were widespread and were exploited by the leading Malay nationalist party, the Pan-Malayan Islamic Party (PMIP), which opposed the merger proposal and put forward its own scheme for a wider association of Malaya with the other 'Malay' territories (in the linguistic and cultural sense) of the region: Indonesia and the Philippines. To that concept, as proposed by President Sukarno of Indonesia, we will come later. In the face of the manifest difficulties of reunion with Singapore and the political risk of alienating their own electorate, the Alliance ministers had for several years before publicly poured cold water on Singapore's overtures for an association of any kind. But by 1961 it was becoming clear that continued exclusion of Singapore might give rise to even greater difficulties than reunion. In 1963 Singapore was due to achieve another instalment of progress towards complete independence. It was likely that at that stage the seven-man Internal Security Council of Singapore, in which Malaya held the balance between Britain and the local PAP government, would be disbanded. Increasing dissension in the PAP indicated that at the next general election the PAP government might fall and be replaced by a more extreme left-wing party. The PAP government professed socialism but practised comparative moderation. An independent Singapore might well seek allies in communist China, unstable Indonesia, and other countries hostile to Malaya. Even if these foreign entanglements were avoided, Singapore in isolation would be a bastion of Chinese nationalism opposed to the predominantly Malay Federation of Malaya. This communal polarization would create an explosive situation both within the multi-communal Federation and externally between the two states. A few months later Tunku Abdul Rahman argued in his parliament that merger was preferable to 'a situation in which an independent Singapore would go one way and the Federation another'.[3]

In Singapore the proposal for merger triggered off a split in the ruling PAP party which had been developing for some time. The disorder of 1955-59 had convinced Lee Kuan Yew, the very intelligent and articulate leader of the PAP, that in order to achieve power he would have to reach an accommodation with the underground leadership of the MCP so that the PAP would have communist support in its election campaign.[4] Once in power the PAP proved to contain both moderates such as Lee Kuan Yew himself, who could see that if Singapore was to prosper as a regional commercial centre, it must have stability and restraint, and others who were ideologically committed to shaking off the last constraints of colonial rule and subordination to the mixed Internal Security Council. In a by-election held in April 1961 a member of the more extreme wing of the PAP achieved a decisive 3:1 majority over a candidate from the moderate side of the party. The extreme wing of the PAP, represented by about half its members of the legislative assembly, was utterly opposed to the proposed merger. If Singapore were subject to the overriding control of a federal government in Kuala Lumpur, their programme and their political activities would be frustrated. The Singapore electorate could be alarmed by predictions of Malay interference with Chinese education in Singapore and with the trade-union movement.

The same factors were seen by the moderates as something of an advantage if satisfactory safeguards could be obtained. More decisive to them were the prospective economic advantages of merger to Singapore. At this stage it seemed to the leaders of Singapore that continued exclusion from the natural economic hinterland of Malaya would prevent Singapore from achieving the growth which it must have in order to provide jobs for its rapidly increasing population. Lee Kuan Yew was too good a strategist to lose the initiative. He responded to the proposals of Tunku Abdul Rahman by initiating negotiations to settle the terms of Singapore's entry into the Federation and was able to put them before his parliament and his electorate by August 1961. It was a skilful bargain. First, Singapore would have much more local autonomy than was accorded to a Malay State over such matters as labour and education policy which were sensitive issues in Singapore. It was not possible, however, to work out in detail the financial arrangements at this stage; much of the subsequent bickering was over the amount of Singapore's fiscal contribution. Secondly, Singapore would continue to treat all its communities on a basis of equality in such matters as recruitment to the civil service. The

Malays, some 14 per cent of the population, would not have 'special rights'. Thirdly, Singapore would be as before a free port outside the federal customs barrier for purposes of entrepôt trade with neighbouring territories. Fourth, internal security in Singapore would continue to be subject to federal control. Last, in consideration of her special degree of administrative autonomy, Singapore would return only fifteen members to the federal parliament as compared with the twenty-four to which she would have been entitled on a simple basis of population ratio. A second justification for this scaling-down of representation was that only two-thirds of Singapore's electorate would qualify for the vote if the stricter rules in force in Malaya had been extended to Singapore.[5] By this means Malay fears were relieved that Singapore's representatives would swing the balance of power in the federal parliament. The miscalculation was in underestimating the impact on Malayan Chinese opinion of the forceful leadership of even a few PAP spokesmen in the enlarged Federation.

The dispute within the PAP over objectives and policy came to a head in July 1961, when thirteen PAP members of the legislature broke away to form a new party, the Barisan Socialis. Of the defectors it was said that 'some were opportunists, others were weaklings, but all knew that they depended on the support which the Malayan Communist Party could muster for them'.[6] For a year the two factions slogged it out. Lee Kuan Yew, somewhat to the alarm of his allies in Kuala Lumpur, put the issue to the test of a referendum in Singapore held in September 1962. It produced a decisive majority for the agreed merger terms. The Barisan Socialis, defeated in the Singapore elections of 1963, withdrew from participation in the legislature altogether. Singapore then became, as it remains, a one-party state in practice though not in principle.

The Borneo territories being less politically sophisticated required a different approach. Leaders of the Borneo communities were invited over to Malaya to view the progress of its rural development programme as evidence of what the Federation could do for them. A Malaysia Solidarity Consultative Committee, with representatives of all five territories of the proposed Federation, was established to discuss the terms on which the Borneo territories should join the Federation.[7] The Borneo spokesmen, at first hesitant, were gradually converted to acceptance of the terms agreed. The British government, however, as the administering power insisted that there must be an assessment at grass-roots level in

Borneo of the state of local opinion. A mixed commission of British and Malayan representatives conducted hearings in Borneo and reported that about one-third of the population was definitely in favour of merger and that the remainder ranged from qualified acceptance to diehard opposition.[8] The report adopted the proposals of the Solidarity Committee for safeguards on freedom of religion, parliamentary representation, language policy in government and in the schools, immigration to Borneo from elsewhere in the Federation, citizenship and franchise rules, and recruitment to the civil and armed forces. One fundamental point, however, divided the British and Malayan members of the commission. The former recommended that in view of the admitted unpreparedness of the peoples of Borneo their accession to the new Federation should be postponed for some years. The Malayan members considered that the opportunity of merger should be taken while it existed and was generally acceptable. As Malayan willingness to reunite with Singapore was in fact conditional upon absorbing the Borneo territories as a counterweight, postponement of the latter must delay Singapore's accession also; with delay opposition to the entire scheme would probably harden. As a compromise it was eventually agreed that in consideration of immediate merger the Borneo territories should for a transitional period have wider powers of local administration.

The minority report of the Malayan members of the Cobbold commission recognized that the rural population in Borneo

feel that they are being rushed into some adventure, of whose outcome they are uncertain. Fear is the dominating factor among them—fear of Malay domination, fear of Muslim subjugation because of the proposal that Islam should be the official religion of the Federation of Malaysia, fear of being swamped by people from Malaya and Singapore who would deprive them of the land and opportunities in government and other enterprises and fear of the threat to their language and cultures and so on. . .[9]

It was then argued that a firm lead by the British administration could dispel these fears. The other factor which was recognized was the 'great expectations. . .engendered among the rural populations. . . Malaysia will be judged by whether or not it delivers the goods in the form of rural improvements, schools, and medical and social services. . .[10] Subsequent events have confirmed the shrewdness of this assessment. In the end the Sultan of Brunei found the terms proposed unacceptable and decided that his state should not join Malaysia.[11] The opposition of Indonesia and of the Philippines to the merger project led, as will be related, to a further assessment of Borneo opinion by an investigation team sent by the United Nations.

The first reaction of Indonesia to the Malaysia merger project was a tepid welcome. 'We do not show any objection towards the Malayan policy of merger. On the contrary we wish the Malayan Government well if it can succeed in this plan'.[12] At this stage Indonesia was still preoccupied with its claim to West Irian. But by the end of 1961 the Indonesian Communist Party (PKI), an essential support of the regime of President Sukarno, had decided that the Malaysia project was a manifestation of that abomination neo-colonialism. The Sukarno government swung over to this line with the effortless ease of those who, like Tweedledum, can make a word mean what you want it to mean. Apart from the need to placate his PKI supporters, Sukarno also needed a new foreign adventure (following the cession of West Irian) which would give to his armed forces, the other key supporter of his shaky authority, the opportunity of showing their strength; incidentally it would distract attention from the deteriorating economic situation in Indonesia. Two other factors may have played a part in shaping Indonesian policy. During the period of the Japanese occupation of Southeast Asia (1942-45), Sukarno had found Malay nationalist support for a scheme to create a 'Great Indonesia' which would absorb the Malay States. Secondly, Indonesia's boundaries are an inheritance from the period of Dutch rule based on Java. The constant fear of the Javanese who dominate the government of Indonesia is that wealthy 'outer islands' such as Sumatra may break away to join with Malaya. A brief military revolt in Sumatra in 1957 had exacerbated these fears of Malayan pretensions. The Malaysia project was the first post-war attempt to redraw the boundaries of the Southeast Asian states. In Indonesian eyes this was a sinister move. Hence the Indonesian policy was to revive the scheme for a Great Indonesia ("*Indonesia Raya*") and in doing so to isolate Malaya from its British allies who might support it in a territorial struggle with Indonesia.

Philippine opposition to the Malaysia project likewise reflected internal pressures on the regime and fears of a change in the post-war boundaries of the region. The ostensible grounds of the Philippines' dispute with Malaya were a claim to North Borneo as part of the former territories of the Sultans of Sulu.[13] The Philippine government also feared that Sabah under Malayan rule might become a centre of communist disaffection and of straightforward smuggling on its southern frontier. Both Indonesian and Philippine governments regarded with some concern the relatively tolerant treatment by the Malayan government of its large Chinese minority community. Both felt that their countries had liberated themselves from colonial rule, and should demonstrate the purity of their independence by striking down anything in their region which could be regarded as neo-colonialism. Malaya, with its British bases and its association with Britain in seeking to absorb the Borneo territories, was to that extent suspect.

From the start the Philippines was a half-hearted ally and Indonesia made the running. From early 1962 until September 1963, when Malaysia came into existence, their strategy was first to criticize the proposal to transfer the peoples of northern Borneo to Malayan rule allegedly without their consent and second to put forward an alternative scheme in which Indonesia (as dominant partner by reason of its size), the Philippines, and Malaya would be grouped in a loose association called 'Maphilindo' (from the first syllable of the name of each country). To this end there were successive conferences of foreign ministers and then of heads of state at Manila in June and August 1963. The terms agreed were wrecked by disagreement before the ink of the signatures was dry. But they merit analysis of the ideas which they expressed since these continue to play their part in the political ideology of Southeast Asia.

The key proposition is that

the three countries share a primary responsibility for the maintenance and security of the area from subversion in any form or manifestation in order to preserve their respective national identities and to ensure the peaceful development of their respective countries and of their region in accordance with the ideals and aspirations of their peoples.[14]

This Monroe Doctrine for Southeast Asia goes a step further with the second proposition that

foreign bases — temporary in nature — should not be allowed to be used directly or indirectly to subvert the national independence of any of the three countries. . . . the three countries will abstain from the use of arrangements of collective defence to serve the particular interest of any of the big powers.[15]

On the vexed question of the proposed merger of the Borneo territories with Malaya and Singapore it was agreed to invite the UN Secretary-General to ascertain the wishes of the peoples of those territories.

In the discussion of the issues between Malaya and Indonesia President Sukarno believed that he had obtained Malayan agreement to a rapid termination of its defence treaty with Britain (no foreign bases), and an indefinite postponement of the merger scheme while a United Nations investigation took its presumably leisurely way through Borneo. On both points he was — to his considerable chagrin — disappointed. On his return Tunku Abdul Rahman told his parliament that there would be a continuation of the arrangements over bases 'until the day comes when we are assured that we can sleep in peace and sleep in our beds without any disturbance'.[16] The Greek Kalends can be expressed in many forms of words — of which these were one. The UN Secretary-General despatched his team of investigators to Borneo within a few days of the end of the conference in Manila, and it had completed its task within a month. Tunku Abdul Rahman was so confident of the verdict which it would give that he fixed the date for the establishment of Malaysia at 16 September 1963 even before the result had been announced by the United Nations.[17]

Accordingly Malaysia was established on 16 September 1963. Neither the Philippines nor Indonesia would recognize the new state and there was a rupture of diplomatic relations. Singapore's participation in Malaysia proved short-lived and ended in 1965 (Chapters 8, 10).

Notes

1   Cited as Document 1 in Gullick (1967), which reproduces the text of the key passages in the diplomatic and political documents of these negotiations. It is said that Tunku Abdul Rahman had not discussed this initiative with his cabinet before he made it. It is not known whether he had sounded the British government on its views, but — on an informal basis — he may well have done so.

2   From 1824 until 1942 Singapore had been the administrative capital of

British rule in what is now Malaysia. The ultimate decisions were taken by the Governor ss and High Commissioner for the Malay States (the same individual). After Singapore was hived off in 1945, the governments of Singapore and Malaya had a few 'Pan-Malayan' departments such as broadcasting and postal services which served both countries. In many other matters such as trade, economic policy, and internal security there was formal and regular consultation under the general direction of a Commissioner General (Malcolm Macdonald), who co-ordinated diplomatic and defence policy with colonial government policy. But he could not resolve administrative disputes by knocking bureaucratic heads together like a pre-war Governor, nor were his occasional interventions in Malayan affairs well received. He was considered to be too much in sympathy with Chinese rather than Malay points of view.

3   Speech to the Malayan parliament on 16 October 1961 (Document 3 in Gullick (1967)); a very clear statement of the reasons why it was now judged to be in the Malayan interest to bring Singapore into a 'merger'.

4   Lee Kuan Yew's broadcasts published as *"The Battle for Merger"* (c. 1962) give a frank account of his dealings with the MCP leadership.

5   Singapore Command Paper No. 33 of 1961 sets out the terms in detail. It was debated and approved in the Singapore Legislative Assembly in the latter part of 1961.

6   Dr Goh Keng Swee, then Singapore Minister of Finance, quoted in *Malaya* (September 1961).

7   The Committee's Report is printed as Appendix 6 to the Report of the Cobbold Committee (see below, note 8); see also Document 8 in Gullick (1967).

8   Report of the Commission of Inquiry North Borneo and Sarawak 1962 (HMSO Cmnd Paper 1794) cited hereafter as 'Cobbold Report' after its chairman (a former Governor of the Bank of England). Extracts in Gullick (1967).

9   Cobbold Report, para 178.

10 Cobbold Report, para 221.

11 In Brunei, unlike Sabah and Sarawak, there was an established political institution, the Sultanate, and some attendant tensions between the Sultan and his subjects which led to a brief and quickly suppressed revolt in December 1962. The Brunei Malays could not forget that in previous centuries Sarawak and much of Sabah had been within the Brunei sphere of influence as dependencies. In entering a Malaysia in which Sabah and Sarawak were separate from and equal with Brunei, the Sultanate would formally recognize that its ancient pretensions could never be restored. Among more particular issues the Sultan and the Malayan government could not agree over the long-term control of the oil revenues which were Brunei's principal asset, nor over the Sultan's personal precedence as a member of the Malayan Conference of Rulers.

12 Dr Subandrio, Foreign Minister of Indonesia, in a statement to the *New York Times* of 13 November 1961. He made a similar statement to the General Assembly of the United Nations on 20 November 1961.

13 The British North Borneo Company, to which a British royal charter was granted in November 1881, was successor to grants of territory made by the Sultans of Brunei and of Sulu to previous concessionaires. The Sulu grant

was expressed to be in perpetuity. In 1962, however, the government of the Philippines argued that the Sulu grant was either a terminable lease or that it was invalid since the Sultan had no power to grant territory in perpetuity to a foreigner. Both Spain (in 1885) and the United States (in 1930), as rulers of the Philippines, had recognized the validity of the grant in perpetuity. To some extent the 1962 claim reflected a personal interest, not to say obsession, of President Macapagal of the Philippines. Leifer (1968) is a definitive study both of the history and of the political circumstances of the claim.

14 Manila Accord para 3. The Manila Accord was produced by the Foreign Ministers' Conference held in June 1963. The Manila Declaration and the Joint Statement were the work of the meeting of heads of governments in August. Documents 18, 19, and 20 in Gullick (1967).

15 Joint Statement para 12.

16 Malayan Parliamentary Report, 14 August 1963. Document 21 in Gullick (1967).

17 The date for the establishment of Malaysia had been fixed for 31 August 1963, the anniversary date of Malayan independence in 1957. This was the position when Tunku Abdul Rahman at the second Manila Conference in early August 1963 agreed to a UN investigation in the Borneo territories. He had presumably obtained assurances from the Secretary-General that, as in fact was done, the investigation would be most speedily concluded. Even so, the necessary time allowed for the investigation entailed a postponement of the date for inaugurating Malaysia. This delay was very unpopular in Malaya and Singapore. Lee Kuan Yew ignored the postponement and declared Singapore independent on 31 August — which caused some irritation. The UN Mission arrived in Borneo on 16 August and completed its task by 5 September; the UN Secretary-General announced its findings, which were favourable to Malaysia, on 13 September. Meanwhile Tunku Abdul Rahman sought to placate his domestic critics by fixing 16 September as the new date for the inauguration of Malaysia. His action in doing so before the UN had given its verdict was criticized by the Secretary-General. Owing to procedural wrangles the Indonesian and Philippine observers did not join the UN Mission in Borneo until 1 September when most of its work was done. See Documents 22 to 24 in Gullick (1967).

8 Politics and Government

Political Events from 1957

A strong local government, the Alliance of UMNO, MCA, and MIC, had been in power since 1955 and so the transition to independence in 1957 was made very smoothly. The federal constitution of the independent Malaya was an adaptation of the system worked out in 1948. In the inter-communal negotiations of 1956 the Malays had made concessions to the other communities over citizenship and the franchise in exchange for an entrenchment in the constitution of Malay 'special rights'. It was a bargain struck on both sides on the basis of payment deferred. The consequence of enlarging the franchise qualifications to admit more non-Malays must be a demand for proportionately larger non-Malay representation in parliament. The entrenchment of Malay privileges implied that the 'national identity' must be founded on the basis of Malay institutions and culture. The Chinese community had not really accepted the Malay assumption that special rights were to be a permanent feature of the new society. They preferred to regard it as a transitional safeguard for the Malays while they prepared themselves to take a fuller part in the 'modern' sector of the economy. The majority of Chinese and Indians now regarded Malaya rather than China or India as their country, but in the new Malaya they intended to preserve their cultural and linguistic identity. Yet this attitude was at variance with the Malay assumption that national identity was a Malay matrix to which others must assimilate themselves. Here was the seed of conflict over the education system and the use of languages.

In their search for compromise, which they genuinely desired and knew to be the price to be paid for stability, the leaders of the communal parties in the Alliance had only limited room for manoeuvre, since the broad mass of the communities which they represented was much less committed than they to the inevitability of making concessions to secure concessions. The political leaders of each party must appear to be successful in protecting the essential interests of their community. If they appeared to be worsted, the temperature of inter-communal relations could rise swiftly to boiling-point and the leaders would lose control of the led. Outside the Alliance were other political parties which offered the alternative of extremism. The Pan-Malayan Islamic Party (PMIP) argued that Malaya was a Malay country and an Islamic state in which none but Muslims should hold public office. Datuk Onn's Party Negara (PN), although it had not won a single seat in the 1955 elections, made its appeal to Malay national feeling. At the other end of the spectrum was the Socialist Front (SF), an unstable coalition of the Labour Party and the Party Ra'ayat, a left-wing Malay party formed in 1957 to oppose the Alliance. The Labour Party purported to be a non-communal socialist party, but in fact it made its electoral appeal to those Chinese and Indians who were critical of MCA/MIC subordination to UMNO leadership in the Alliance. There was also a People's Progressive Party (PPP) and a Malayan Party of broadly the same type. Hence either wing of the Alliance, Malay or non-Malay, could lose ground to the extremist element of its own community if it seemed to be conceding too much.

The preparations for the federal elections of 1959 brought these problems to a head. These elections were the first held to choose a fully elected lower house of parliament; they were held on the new electoral roll based on the wider franchise qualifications. The period of euphoria which followed independence in 1957 had passed. In local government and State assembly elections held in the period 1957-59, the Alliance had lost ground, especially in the urban areas where the non-Malay opposition parties were strongest. At the beginning of 1959 Tunku Abdul Rahman temporarily resigned the office of Prime Minister, in order to devote himself to tuning up the UMNO machine in Malay rural areas where it might be vulnerable to PMIP or PN attack. He could not afford at that moment to be seen to yield to Chinese demands. Yet the MCA did demand that the number of constituencies 'allocated' to it to fight for the Alliance should be 40 out of a total of 104 as compared with 15 out of 52 in 1955. To justify this demand the MCA argued that 36 per cent of the electorate was now Chinese and that in 41 constituencies Chinese electors outnumbered any other group. It was a faulty argument since in many constituencies an MCA candidate could not win unless he could secure the votes of Malay voters given to him as the Alliance candidate to offset Chinese votes lost to the opposition. A simple communal head-count was not a true measure of the position. Apart from the constituency question, there were also unacceptable MCA demands for inclusion in the Alliance manifesto of assurances concerning Chinese education policy. The UMNO leaders felt that they would lose ground to PMIP if they gave way. The MCA president, Dr Lim Chong Eu, was also under heavy pressure from a section of his own party. He wrote a letter to Tunku Abdul Rahman referring to the fears in his party of 'Malay communalism'. The letter was leaked to the press with a report that if it proved impossible to arrive at a 'fair' settlement (35 constituencies for the MCA was indicated as the irreducible minimum), the MCA might withdraw from the Alliance and contest the election on its own. Tunku Abdul Rahman insisted publicly that the letter must be withdrawn and that those in the MCA who had been responsible for the crisis should be expelled. After a heated and divisive debate the MCA accepted these demands—and an allocation of 31 constituencies. The MCA president and the group which had inspired his disastrous ultimatum resigned from the MCA, which suffered a severe setback in morale and in electoral support; it won only 19 seats. The Alliance as a whole did not do well. It secured another decisive majority, 74 out of 104 seats in the lower house, but its share of the total votes cast dropped to 51.8 per cent as compared with 81.7 in 1955. UMNO lost seats to the PMIP in predominantly Malay areas; in the State assembly elections the PMIP was able in the north-east to obtain outright control of the States of Kelantan and Trengganu. In urban constituencies the Alliance emerged the strongest single group, but obtained less than half the votes cast. Its strength in parliament reflected the weighting given to rural constituencies in the demarcation of constituencies.[1] But with moderate good sense when the dust had settled, concessions were made to the MCA. A ministry of rural development was established under the control of the energetic deputy prime minister, Tun Abdul Razak, to give momentum to the programme of general improvement and economic aid in predominantly Malay areas. At this stage also the decline of the MCP as a threat to the regime was marked by officially ending the state of Emergency declared in 1948.[2] By now the remaining communist forces were reduced to a few hundreds operating from bases astride the inaccessible Thai–Malayan border. The situation in Singapore (Chapter 7) presented a more serious threat to national security; this factor led Tunku Abdul Rahman to seek a solution in a merger of Singapore and the Borneo territories with Malaya to form an enlarged Malaysia. For five years (1961-65) the politics of

Malaya were dominated by this development and its aftermath.

The lower house of the Malayan parliament was enlarged to admit 40 members, chosen by the conservative process of indirect election, from Sabah and Sarawak. In numbers they far outweighed the mere 15 members elected from Singapore constituencies. But the forceful, articulate, and well-organized PAP group from Singapore had an effect on Malaysian politics out of proportion to their numbers. Here too a bargain had been struck on the basis of payment deferred. In the first rosy dawn of the Malaysia project Tunku Abdul Rahman and Lee Kuan Yew of Singapore had established an amicable relationship which permitted them to combine hill-station golf with their political negotiations. But in the later stages the atmosphere was soured by disagreements over financial matters between Lee Kuan Yew and the prickly Malayan Minister of Finance, Tan Siew Sin, who had become president of the MCA. The MCA, as the established representative of Chinese interests in the Alliance, feared and resented the advent of a rival party, brash in style and well to the left of the conservative MCA in its ideology. Tunku Abdul Rahman does not appear to have foreseen this inevitable rivalry; he had assumed that if the PAP were left in full control of the government of Singapore, they would be content with that. The PAP, however, aspired to replace the MCA, shaken and demoralized by its setbacks in 1959, as the party which could deliver the Malayan Chinese vote in support of the Alliance. Lee Kuan Yew's initial stance was that 'we are not members of the Alliance and we seek no posts in the Alliance cabinet'.[3] But it was a case of 'I took my harp to a party but nobody asked me to play'. If Lee Kuan Yew had been prepared to bide his time, he might have had his opportunity. But in fact he showed a most unfortunate lack of patience. This provoked Tunku Abdul Rahman, a man loyal to his allies, into public statements repudiating the support of the PAP and affirming his commitment to the MCA as his Chinese associates in the Alliance.

At a late stage the PAP decided to make a 'token participation' in the 1964 federal elections in Malaya, the first held since Malaysia had been established.[4] The object was to demonstrate that PAP could attract a substantial vote in urban areas. Inevitably this became a trial of strength, with much recrimination on both sides, between PAP and MCA. It was a clear-cut victory for the MCA which increased its strength to 27 (as compared with 19 in 1959). The PAP lacked effective organization and fought a half-hearted campaign in which it won only one seat in the eleven parliamentary constituencies in which it put up a candidate. It all served to widen the split between the PAP and the Alliance as a whole. The 1964 elections were a triumph for the Alliance which increased its share of the vote to 57 per cent and its parliamentary strength to 89 out of 104 Malayan seats. At this time Indonesian Confrontation (Chapter 11) had raised patriotic feeling in favour of the Alliance, which exploited its advantage by imputing to the opposition parties the reproach of ties with Indonesia or with the Indonesian Communist Party (PKI). The PMIP and the Chinese opposition parties lost ground. The SF, torn apart by the essential conflict of objectives between its Malay wing (Party Ra'ayat) and its socialist and non-Malay partner (the Labour Party), broke up in 1965. The defeat of both PAP and SF in 1964 signalled the failure of attempts to build an alternative coalition to the Alliance; taking up Chinese grievances to attract votes from that quarter outraged Malay feeling.

This, however, was not the end of the struggle. With characteristic energy Lee Kuan Yew organized a new coalition of opposition parties (other than PMIP) under the style of 'the Malaysia Solidarity Consultative Convention' and with the slogan of 'a Malaysian Malaysia'. The manifesto of the new organization began 'A Malaysian Malaysia means that the nation and the state is not identified with the supremacy, well-being and interests of any one community or race'.[5] In Malay ears these words were a declaration of open war on Malay rights as established by the constitutional provisions of 1948-56. Lee Kuan Yew became a Malay bogeyman; relations were further embittered by attempts to carry the war into his home base of Singapore which led to disturbances there. Unfortunately the crisis of mid-1965 occurred at a time when Tunku Abdul Rahman, still the respected father-figure of the nation, was abroad for a long period.[6] The Tunku's strength was his instinctive understanding of the surge of feeling in his Malay electorate; on his return to Malaya in August he concluded that he no longer had 'complete control',[7] and he decided that to restore stability and good feeling Singapore must leave Malaysia altogether. This momentous change was planned and executed in the space of three days. The Singapore leaders were much distressed at the decision, but when their own counter-proposals for a continuing but looser association were rejected as inadequate, they bowed to it. The manner in which these major changes in the balance of communal influence were effected caused discontent in Borneo also. The leaders of the Alliance there had not even been consulted over the expulsion of Singapore, although some of them had the status of ministers in the federal government whose decision it was. The change upset the tripartite balance of Malaya, Singapore, and the Borneo territories on which Malaysia had been founded. The Borneo territories, conscious of their relative economic weakness and backwardness, had now to hold their own alone in association with Malaya, the sole centre of power in Malaysia.

The history of political relations between the Alliance leaders in Malaya and the political parties in Sabah and Sarawak in the formative period of Malaysia in the later 1960s is an unhappy one.[8] The Malay leaders in Kuala Lumpur liked to regard themselves as experts in the delicate operation of a federal system such as they had had in Malaya since 1948. But in fact they relied on retaining control of the State governments so that there was no party conflict between the federal and the State regimes; there were UMNO ministers at both ends of the system. In 1959, however, the Alliance lost control of Kelantan and Trengganu to the PMIP. There was then a state of deadlock, in which the federal government demonstrated its strength by cutting off the flow of public money to finance development in States over which it had no control. In dealing with the tiresome governments of Sabah and Sarawak the bludgeon used was political rather than economic. Opposition from Borneo was treated as ingratitude or disloyalty to be suppressed with a strong hand. It was unnecessary to exert financial pressure. The unstable coalitions of essentially tribal political parties which had emerged in Sabah and Sarawak were easily fragmented. The leader of the Alliance coalition in Sabah protested at the failure to consult him over the expulsion of Singapore from Malaysia. Tunku Abdul Rahman, anxious and incensed at idle talk of Sabah following Singapore into the wilderness, visited Sabah soon afterwards. This intervention led to the resignation of the chief minister, and the control of Sabah passed for some years into the hands of a chief minister who was both an autocrat and inclined to treat his state's resources as his personal patrimony. In Sarawak the chief minister, leader of an Iban communal party, objected to pressure from Kuala Lumpur for the early introduction of Malay as the national language of Sarawak (an issue on which safeguards had been obtained in the pre-Malaysia negotiations). The federal government, on the pretext of communist activity among the Chinese of

Sarawak, suspended the constitution and broke the local coalition in order to remove the offending chief minister from his office.

It took the Alliance much longer to regain total control in the north-east of Malaya. The PMIP government of Trengganu, elected in 1959, was unstable from the outset. It split in 1961 and some of its State assembly members joined the Alliance which thus regained control. In Kelantan, however, the PMIP was stronger and more united, and UMNO had much less hold on the Malay electorate than elsewhere owing to local factors. In spite of public indications that the cornucopia of federal development finance would not begin to flow in Kelantan until there was a State government with which the federal government could co-operate, the PMIP retained its position as the ruling party until 1978, when it fell as a result of its own internal divisions and the increased strength of UMNO as a party. Kelantan is something of a case study of UMNO problems in retaining a hold on the rural Malay electorate — to which we will return later in this chapter.

Confrontation with Indonesia ended in 1966, and with it went the external threat which made some Malayan Chinese more ready to support the Alliance as the lesser of two evils. Under the arrangements made in 1957, English was to be a second 'official' language (with Malay as both an official and the sole national language) for ten years. That period ended in 1967. In practice English continues to this day as an important medium of communication; almost all official documents and reports are printed in both languages — the Malaysian taxpayer, for example, makes a return of his income on a bilingual form. But in the work of government, and above all in education, there was during the 1960s steady progress towards establishing Malay as the main medium of communication and instruction. A member of parliament or a university lecturer, for example, is expected to say what he has to say in the national language. It is perhaps not so much the imposition of Malay as the subordination of the other languages which is resented.

The Labour Party, now unimpeded by any links with a left-wing Malay party, had in the mid-1960s become the centre of Chinese resistance to Alliance policies. In its origins the party had been led by socialist intellectuals, many of them Indian, drawn from the professional classes. But after the débâcle of the 1964 election, the leadership of the party had passed increasingly to Chinese, educated in Chinese-medium schools, and committed to the aggressive preservation of Chinese culture and education.[9] The underground MCP, ever looking for an opening for re-entering political life, had discerned in the Labour Party a suitable instrument for its purposes and had begun to infiltrate it. The main local base of the Labour Party was now Penang, where for a time it had controlled the municipal council. The spark which set fire to this tinder was the Malaysian government's treatment of the devaluation of the pound sterling in November 1967. For reasons explained in Chapter 9, the old 'Straits dollar' of the colonial period no longer had parity of value with the new Malaysian dollar currency. But many Chinese had hoarded the old currency in the misplaced belief that it was a safer store of value than the new Malaysian dollar. Their acute sense of grievance when their hoards were devalued with the pound sterling (against the Malaysian dollar) was exploited by the Labour Party, and this triggered off serious but brief riots in Penang in November 1967. In retrospect one can see that this affair was a forewarning of the more serious upheaval of May 1969 — but it did not seem so at the time.

The next federal and State assembly elections were held in May 1969. The circumstances were much less favourable to the Alliance than in 1964. Some loss of seats to the opposition was inevitable and duly happened. In the important state of Selangor, in which the federal capital Kuala Lumpur is situated, the results of the elections to the State assembly suggested that many Chinese no longer supported the Alliance, and that control of the State government might be wrested from it. The jubilant opposition parties and their supporters celebrated their gains in a manner calculated to give offence to the Malay community. There was serious communal violence in and around Kuala Lumpur, in which several hundred people, predominantly Chinese, were killed.[10] The federal constitution was suspended and for eighteen months Malaysia was governed by a National Operations Council (NOC). In this débâcle Tunku Abdul Rahman lost both his confidence and will to govern, and also his former personal authority as the leader of his party and of the nation. He made way for the deputy prime minister, Tun Abdul Razak, who led the NOC and took the leading part in the reconstruction which followed.[11] The majority of NOC members were Malay political leaders, civil servants, and police and armed force commanders, but it did include the presidents of MCA and MIC. As part of the suspension of constitutional government, the elections to the federal parliament, due to be held in Sabah and

Sarawak for the first time, were postponed.

The period of autocratic rule by the NOC was much more than an interruption in the normal process of government. The interim regime had to consider what had brought the heart of the country to the verge of anarchy, so that when constitutional government was restored, there could be no repetition of the mistakes of the past. To the credit of Tun Razak and the NOC a solution was sought in terms of moderation and restraint. There was no repression and UMNO demands for a more drastic assertion of Malay dominance were resisted. Measures were taken to restore public confidence, badly shaken, in the ability and will of the police and the armed forces to maintain public order and assure civil liberty. When constitutional government was restored in February 1971, new ground rules and objectives had been laid down.

First, a state ideology (*rukunegara*) was proclaimed. It consisted of five statements of belief concerning the future of Malaysian society—that there must be national unity, democracy, justice, etc.—and of five principles—belief in God, loyalty to the Malaysian sovereign and to the country, support of the constitution, good behaviour, and morality.

Secondly, inter-communal strife in the open political arena had become too dangerous. The evil contents of Pandora's box must be bundled back into it and the lid firmly shut. In the aftermath of the May Thirteenth Incident (the official title) there had been much bitter Malay recrimination against the other communities. It had been contained, but the price was a ban on any future public opposition to, or criticism of, Malay special rights and other sensitive issues. The constitution was amended and it became a criminal offence to breach this rule. As a development of the same principle, the Alliance coalition was enlarged and reorganized as the 'National Front' (NF), with a wider span across the spectrum of political parties. Tun Abdul Razak had made it a condition of the restoration of constitutional government that the postponed elections in Sabah and Sarawak should yield sufficient support to give the government a two-thirds majority in the federal parliament, which it needed to amend the constitution. This was duly achieved; the Alliance made a clean sweep in Sabah and obtained sufficient support in Sarawak (including control of its troublesome state assembly). With normal government restored and the constitution amended, Abdul Razak was able to bring into his NF coalition even his main Malay opponents, the PMIP (now renamed *Partai Islam Se-Malaysia*—PAS as it is hereafter called). In effect Malaysia abandoned – for the time being at least – the Western style of parliamentary democracy with one government in office and an alternative government in opposition. (The latter had never really existed in any credible form in Malaysia.) Instead of polarizing the alternatives the aim must be to attract the support of all moderate parties.

The third element of the 1971 programme was a much more purposive direction of the economy with two main objectives. First, the major concentrations of poverty – much of it among the Malays – must be eliminated. Secondly, it was necessary to break down the compartmented structure of the economy in which each community had an almost exclusive economic function. In the current development plan the point is expressed as

socio-political stability could not be maintained for long in situations where, for example, a Malay farmer coming to town, even with an increased income, felt somewhat alienated, somewhat an ousider, simply because he saw so few Malays in the shops, restaurants and factories of the town. And so might the Chinese and Indians when going into a Malay-dominated agricultural area.[12]

A New Economic Policy (NEP) was promulgated, by which over twenty years (1971-90) the Malay community must be enabled to own and control at least 30 per cent of the modern sector of the economy, i.e., little and big business. The Second Malaysia Plan (1971-75) prescribed the first stage of the NEP programme and has been followed by another, Third, Malaysia Plan (1976-80); these are matters to which the next two chapters are mainly devoted.

The build-up of the wider NF coalition was a delicate matter of inter-party negotiation which preoccupied the restored parliament for a year or more. By January 1973, however, 122 out of the 144 members of the lower house were NF supporters. The accommodation within the coalition of rivals for the Malay vote, UMNO and PAS, and of rivals for the Chinese vote, MCA and *Gerakan Rakyat Malaysia* (GRM), was somewhat fragile, but survived until PAS withdrew in 1978. The main continuing opposition party was the Democratic Action Party (DAP), the Malaysian heir to the Singapore PAP, which could not take part itself in Malaysian politics after Singapore's withdrawal in 1965. In Sarawak the Iban SNAP, ousted from power in 1966, was the main opposition. The federal elections of 1974 were held in the long shadow of the eruption of May 1969. The electorate showed its preference in a subdued campaign for a broad-based government of moderation. The NF gained ground and its opponents in parliament were reduced to a mere ten members. In January 1976 the death of Tun Abdul Razak deprived the coalition of its founder. He was succeeded by the present Prime Minister, Datuk Hussein bin Onn, son of the founder of UMNO, who in his quiet way has established his authority both in his party and among the disparate elements of his administration. Datuk Hussein appointed as his deputy prime minister Dr Mahathir bin Mohamed, who had been a leading critic of Tunku Abdul Rahman in 1969, and is the author of a controversial book, *The Malay Dilemma,* which is still banned in Malaysia under the 1971 ban on communal controversy. The other rising star of the UMNO firmament is Tunku Razaleigh bin Hamzah, the Minister of Finance, who made his way to the top as chairman of the state corporation PERNAS established to extend Malay participation in business. It is striking—and can hardly be a coincidence—that almost all the leaders of UMNO at national level have been drawn from the former UMS; Datuk Onn and his son Datuk Hussein are from Johor, Tunku Abdul Rahman and Dr Mahathir from Kedah, and Tunku Razaleigh from Kelantan. But Razak was from Pahang (FMS).

In the latest federal elections held in July 1978 the NF lost ground slightly from the very high level reached in 1974. But with 131 seats out of 154 its position is secure. It faces a divided opposition, DAP 16, PAS 5, and two others.

The Political System

The political parties have their origins in and draw their vitality from inter-communal conflict. The Malays came together to form UMNO as a bulwark against the threat to Malay privileges represented in 1946 by the Malayan Union. PAS even more than UMNO is committed to achieving a Malay hegemony over the other communities. Chinese reaction to the Anglo-Malay deal at the expense of the other communities in 1947, and then the drastic measures taken to deal with Chinese squatters in the early period of the Emergency, led to the foundation of the MCA to protect Chinese interests. The Alliance coalition was itself formed as a tactical combination inspired by the fear that the charismatic but distrusted

Datuk Onn with his IMP would otherwise carry all before him in 1952. In reaching an accommodation with UMNO, the MCA has had to make concessions on matters of concern to the Chinese community. This has inevitably opened a gap into which the other parties, bourgeois or left-wing, which compete for the Chinese vote have been able to infiltrate. Whatever the radical or socialist element in their ideology, these parties attract support by exploiting the genuine and deep-seated anxiety of the Chinese community over the future of their schools, and of their general position in a constitution which gives to the Malays special rights without time-limit or even possiblity of open criticism. The Indian community is too small to have any decisive influence, but the MIC is its answer to the communal situation. The kaleidoscope of Borneo political coalitions is a struggle between tribal leaders for a share of the fruits of office.

In communities such as the Malays among whom tradition is still a strong force even in a changing social structure, the effect of this single alignment of both political and communal loyalty is to strengthen the authority of the traditional élite. The Malay upper class is now a group of Western-educated civil servants, officers of the armed forces and of the police, technocrats, and professional men such as lawyers and doctors; the political leaders emerge from this group. The present Prime Minister was first a soldier and later a lawyer; his deputy was originally a doctor of medicine; both Tunku Abdul Rahman and Tun Abdul Razak were members of the English bar. It is no longer a group of hereditary aristocrats, though it includes some of them: of the three Prime Ministers since 1957 Abdul Rahman was the son of a Sultan, Razak was one of the four hereditary major chiefs of Pahang, and Hussein is the son, grandson, and great-grandson of former chief ministers of Johor. Those who lack these aristocratic connections are usually of middle-class professional or landowning families. There is no major figure among Malay politicians who was born in poverty. The occasional parvenu does not feel at ease in these exalted circles.[13] The strength of UMNO is, however, that it comprehends so many Malays active in politics at State and local level. These are men of a different type. They are drawn from the class of smallholders, more especially those who are relatively well-to-do by reason of owning more land than most, together with the small businessmen and middle grades of the civil service, particularly the teachers in Malay schools. Such a man is likely to have begun his education in a Malay vernacular school, but may have progressed to secondary education which in the time of his youth was only available through the medium of English. He then made his way in his own walk of life and achieved some success in it as a base from which to enter politics. He is bilingual to the extent that he has a good command of English, but his horizon is more narrowly Malay than that of his betters in the hierarchy. Until now this important middle leadership has been content to occupy the middle ranks. But there are signs that men of this type, always influential in the party, are rising — and aspiring to rise — to greater heights.[14] The nature of village leadership — in politics among other things — is dealt with later (Chapter 13).

The more radical PAS finds its leadership mainly in the group just described of the successful Malays of the lower-middle class. As this group has not so far produced any leaders of the authority and charisma required for the stage of national politics, the gap has been filled by a handful of those who combine extreme Malay nationalism, some pretensions to the status of intellectuals or writers, and ability as public speakers. As national parties UMNO and PAS contend for the support of this group. At village level the strength of PAS, apart from its advocacy of exclusive Malay control of government, is that it has the support of the majority of influential Islamic teachers and community leaders, and that it espouses the interests of the Malay peasant against his betters and his grievances against the 'system' as a whole.

Among the Chinese also the identification of party and community interest likewise strengthens the authority of the traditional leaders. In this case there is of course no traditional political structure. The immigrant Chinese built their structure of leadership on an economic base. Through the machinery of trade associations, clan and district societies, and committees for community causes such as schools and hospitals for the urban Chinese, the men of great wealth — and often of great if conspicuous generosity — became the accepted leaders of the community. The general body of the Chinese *patronat*, owners of small businesses of many kinds, traders and landowners and miners, followed the leadership of the millionaires. This is the class represented by the MCA which despite periodic efforts to give it a new and more political image is still more communal than political. Its critics call it 'the *towkays*' party' (*towkay* is the general Chinese term for a businessman or employer). As has been explained, the fortunes of

127

the MCA have fluctuated with its apparent success or failure in promoting Chinese communal interests by its policy of co-operation with UMNO. It competes for influence with the Chinese, who supported the Labour Party or more recently DAP because they were disenchanted with the fruits of Sino-Malay co-operation. This group is particularly associated with the Chinese schools in which the medium of instruction was Chinese, i.e., the Kuo Yu dialect which is the standard form for all groups in the schools. The Chinese man or woman who has been educated in these schools often has only a modest knowledge of either English or Malay and possesses no qualifications which are recognized in recruitment to the public service or entry to a university. His opportunities of a career are restricted to employment or entrepreneurship in Chinese business against which the regime discriminates in the course of promoting Malay interests. The professions, the public service, and public life are virtually closed to him. His education has given him an intense but narrow pride in the undoubted excellence of Chinese language and culture. This too is a case of a lower-middle class seeking a role for itself. The most promising avenue is to develop an influence among the poorer Chinese in their manifold occupations, the manual worker, the artisan, the street-trader, the trishaw rider (the trishaw is a combination of a rickshaw and a bicycle and plies for hire in the towns), the squatter growing his vegetables for the market, the unemployed in the remoter New Villages where poverty is a real problem among the Chinese. The grievances of the Chinese working class are mainly economic, but the remedy lies — so it is argued — in fairer shares. The resentment is not so much against the Chinese bourgeoisie as adversaries in the class struggle, as against the regime which is dominated by another community. The underground MCP as much as the legitimate parties, muzzled from open discussion of these matters, finds its support among these groups and from these issues.

In spite of their talents the Indian upper class has never been able to establish an effective political organization. There are wide differences of language and culture between the classes (Chapter 5). In the post-war period the leadership of the Indian working class has passed to the trade unions which have established a *modus vivendi* with the political regime. Trade unions, and their membership, are concerned mainly with economic questions of wage rates, etc. They do not take up political, or even communal, issues — on the contrary their object is to widen the membership by increasing the

Malay and Chinese element in it. Hence the MIC as the established political leadership lacks an effective base.

The foregoing description may illustrate how much the inherent conflicts of economic and social interest within the communities are shut into a communal and monolithic opposition of one group against another. Reform when it comes is the fruit of inter-communal bargaining rather than direct response to social pressures. It is doubtful whether it can do enough to respond to the real needs of a changing society.

The more immediate problem is the risk that the conservative and moderate national leadership of the major parties may lose its control over the rank of file when some communal grievance, channelled through the party system, breaks it apart. The events of 1959, 1965, 1967, and 1969 are examples of how easily this can happen or almost happen. The solution devised in 1971, a ban on public discussion of the issue of inter-communal rights, has proved durable. It is, however, an abrogation of the normal safety-valve of politics. It has been reinforced by other means. The government information services operate as a mouthpiece for the ruling NF coalition. There is no censorship of the press, but every newspaper has to obtain an annual licence to publish. In the 1978 federal election, 'rallies', large-scale political meetings, were banned on the grounds that too many members of the police would have to be diverted from more important tasks to ensure the maintenance of order at these volatile occasions; it was of course a sequence of rallies and processions which touched off the riots of May 1969. Since open discussion is not permitted, it is difficult to judge how far the opposition objects; the DAP has been in trouble on occasion for exceeding the permitted limits. But it would be wrong to underrate the strong preference in all communties for settling disputes by compromise.[15] When an issue appears likely to explode, the parties draw back from it — by instinct as much as by compliance with the present law. But even with legal sanctions there is the risk that a genuine grievance may get out of hand.

Since the privacy of inter-communal negotiation is essential, it follows that public proceedings in the federal parliament will often lack the excitement of a real event. It is not here — on the floor of the house — that the great issues are thrashed out. Hence the backbench member recognizes that his main role is not debate. The outcome is predictable when the NF has a decisive majority and can, it has been said, 'rely on its usual parliamentary tactic of bulldozing the motion aside with a speech by a minister and a couple of backbenchers to complete the rout'.[16] The more important work of a member is done outside parliament in providing a channel of communication: he brings the needs and demands of his constituents up to Kuala Lumpur when parliament meets, in the hope of persuading a minister or a senior civil servant to allocate government money to them. In his constituency he is expected to expound and to justify government policy and on occasion to act as a conciliator in the settlement of local disputes.[17] Essentially he is a go-between rather than a policy-maker. Policy is made within the party machines of the ruling coalition. Malay ministers are much more concerned with the pressures on them at the meetings of the General Assembly of UMNO. The Assembly elects a Supreme Executive Council which includes the national party leaders, who are also the senior ministers of the NF government. The rise and decline of individual reputations and influence are made visible to the outsider by the success or failure of politicians in securing election to such key party posts as deputy president or head of an important party organization such as the Youth Section (for which there is no age limit — the incumbent is usually a senior politician of mature years). Within the MCA the nomenclature is different but the power structure is much the same. In both the major parties there is an unending struggle for leadership and influence between the well-established if sometimes undynamic 'old guard' of party veterans, and the younger men who wish to alter party policy or to project a 'new image'. These are the unavoidable problems of any party which holds office continuously over a generation or more. Within the coalition the national leaders of each party hammer out compromises through central organizations of consultation behind closed doors.

UMNO also has party structures at the intermediate levels — State Liaison Committees, divisions covering a federal parliamentary constituency or sometimes more than one, and branches which in principle cover the same area as a polling district though there may be more than one branch in a district. The national party leaders have their power base in the State of their origin; they must retain the support of key State leaders, and their stock rises and falls with the success or failure of the party in their State. For example, the energetic Tunku Razaleigh, the Minister of Finance, rebuilt the UMNO organization in his native Kelantan and achieved much prestige by the victory of UMNO in the State assembly elections of

1978, ousting PAS which had been in control since 1959. The strength of UMNO depends on the vitality of its branch leadership — a subject to be considered in the context of social structure (Chapter 13).

The different balance of power in the MCA is reflected in its party structure. It has a less secure popular base than UMNO and so local branches are less important. The Chinese business community, on which the MCA so much depends, has its centres of influence in the larger towns, some of which are State capitals and others district headquarters.

The following brief picture of parliamentary election campaigns is derived from an excellent and very detailed study of the elections of 1964.[18] It serves to show how the essential process of wooing the voter has been adapted to different local conditions. In the rural Malay Pasir Puteh constituency in Kelantan, UMNO and PMIP (now PAS) candidates competed for the support of an electorate of whom 97 per cent were Malay. The PMIP candidate, defending a seat which he had won in 1959, had once been a teacher, but for many years past he had been an active politician and he was then national vice-president of his party. His UMNO opponent was an older man who had long service also as a teacher in the State education department. In the campaign the weight of the UMNO organization, which made systematic use of 2,500 workers in this constituency alone, was matched against the PMIP hold on the loyalties of the majority of Islamic religious teachers and village headmen. This group are particularly influential in Kelantan which has a strong and distinguished tradition of Islamic learning and activity. The PMIP represented themselves as the defenders of Malay rights against the rising tide of Chinese economic domination in other States; only in Kelantan was the State government in exclusively Malay, PMIP, hands. It was argued that it was contrary to Islamic doctrine to share power (as the Alliance did) with infidels — there is in fact no doctrine to that effect. The UMNO attack was a criticism of the poor record of the PMIP State government of Kelantan, which had been in power since 1959; in particular it was attacked for its failure to open up new land on a scale sufficient to relieve local land hunger. To this was added the promise of federal money for development in Kelantan if an UMNO administration was returned to power in the State (as well as in Malaysia as a whole — which was a foregone conclusion). Thus local issues were introduced into a struggle for a seat in the federal parliament. But they are issues of a national character. In the event the PMIP candidate retained his seat, but with a narrow majority only; PMIP also held on to control of the State government, but again with a reduced margin.

The Batu constituency on the outskirts of Kuala Lumpur was a complete contrast — very mixed in its electoral composition, but mainly Chinese. Within its boundaries was the largest New Village in Malaya, Malay areas where the men were mainly employed in urban jobs, Indian estate workers, middle-class residential areas, and Chinese squatters living on the periphery of the town. But in this case also the incumbent member who was defending his seat was from the opposition — the Socialist Front. He was a Chinese doctor with a practice in the constituency, a man of great talent and many public activities, including association with trade-union movement and with the methodist church. His MCA opponent was a young Chinese journalist, son of a prominent figure in the Selangor MCA leadership. There was also a PAP candidate in this constituency, but he fought an ill-prepared and half-hearted campaign; he too was a local Chinese doctor. There was a complete contrast in campaign style between the SF and MCA candidates. MCA canvassing was done by sending round local men of influence in a relatively large group. It was a planned demonstration that the local business 'top brass' was committed to the party cause rather than the candidate, who was inconspicuous. In this way it was hoped 'to influence the uncommitted voters through men of influence and power in the area'. There was no serious attempt at political discussion or persuasion of electors when encountered by the canvassers. There was, however, much talk of past and prospective government financial aid to meet local needs such as the provision of schools, low-cost housing, and other services. The SF candidate toured the constituency with a much smaller retinue and the emphasis was on informal and unstudied chat with members of each household — 'At another place a woman might just have finished boiling sweet potatoes. The girl [a canvasser] would sit with the woman and help her peel them. . . all the campaigning was done in a completely relaxed way'. The SF candidate had the advantage that many of the electors were known to him as patients in his practice. He made a sustained effort to bridge the communal gap by wooing the Malay voters whom he alone of the three candidates could address in Malay. But he had to be circumspect about making unsolicited calls at Malay houses in the absence at work of the men. Both the candidates also held 'rallies', election meetings, but these were not of major importance. In Malay areas especially, a traditional form of meeting, the *ceramah,* is the preferred method of putting across the party case to electors. A *ceramah* is by origin a social occasion of not more than a couple of hundred people, often many fewer, assembled either in the open or in a small hall; when a case has been stated, questions 'from the floor' come more readily. When it is adapted for party use, the customary light refreshments are provided from party funds. In the Batu constituency there was again an intermingling of local and national issues; the SF candidate made much of the prospect that his party might gain control of the State assembly. In the event he retained his seat by a narrow majority, but possibly would have done better if his PAP opponent had not siphoned off part of the Chinese vote.

In Sabah and Sarawak there have been numerous changes of party alliances as individual groups move into or out of a coalition. The aim of the federal government is to construct in each State an administration which supports the National Front and which is amenable to federal influence, if not control. For preference the local ruling coalition should be constructed around a Malay or at least a Muslim party group. The inducement to enter the coalition is that this affords a share of the fruits of office and the dispensation of public money. Apart from fragmentation due to linguistic, cultural, and religious differences, the electorate is scattered over the country in remote and small settlements. One of the larger items of party political campaign expenditure is the cost of fuel for the outboard motors which drive the boats along the rivers.[19] By various means the ruling federal coalition has been able not only to keep in power local State governments which support it, but to secure the election to the federal parliament of up to 40 members from Sabah and Sarawak, who make a useful addition to the eighty or ninety government supporters elected from Malayan constituencies.

The Underlying Problems

A former Prime Minister defined the perennial problems as 'the three C's', communalism, communism, and corruption.[20] Sufficient has been said of the all-pervasive effect on Malaysian life of communal tensions. The general moderation of Malaysian attitudes, as much as the strait-jacket on public discussion of these issues imposed in 1971, suffices to contain the pressure at most times. Malaysia is unlikely to grow out of the problem within the foreseeable future. The government hopes to eradicate it gradually by eliminating poverty, more especially the mass poverty of certain communal groups such as Malay rice-farmers, the Chinese in the more remote New Villages, etc.; by breaking down communal specialization in economic activity so that not all rice-farmers are Malays, and not all shopkeepers are Chinese or Indian; and by building a national identity around the use of the Malay language in all schools and in all walks of life. To these programmes we shall come in subsequent chapters.

In the political sphere there must be two doubts about continuing restraint of communal extremism. On the Malay side UMNO seemed, on the results of the 1978 federal and State elections, to have scotched the threat of PAS as the mouthpiece of the demand for a 'Malaysia for the Malays'. PAS expresses a point of view which is widely held, but it lacks credibility. It has no coherent programme of action and a poor record of administration during its long tenure of power in Kelantan. But if economic recession should set back the programme of Malay rural improvement, PAS could recover lost ground—and not only in Kelantan. The success of UMNO in demonstrating to the Malay community its ascendancy in the NF coalition is also an indication to the Chinese community that the MCA is the weaker partner. The MCA has always been more of a pressure-group than a mass party. The 1978 elections showed that its electoral base was eroding; the number of its seats in the federal parliament was reduced from 20 to 17 (as compared with the high-tide mark of 27 in 1964). In part this was due to a pointless conflict with the other mainly Chinese bourgeois party (Gerakan), which is also a member of the NF coalition.[21] The most significant advance made in the 1978 elections was by the opposition Democratic Action Party (DAP) which has a social democrat platform, but derives its main support from the Chinese electorate. The DAP has to tread delicately between championing the interests of the Chinese and overstepping the restriction on criticism of Malay rights. But it is the DAP which finds expression for Chinese grievances over such matters as positive discrimination in favour of Malays in higher education and in business licensing. The Malay politicians of moderate views, including the Prime Minister, have a similar problem in finding a middle course between driving the Chinese electorate into the arms of the opposition and satisfying their own supporters. The skill and good sense with which these matters are handled is not the least of Malaysia's political assets.[22]

The main threat of a communist takeover was defeated in the Emergency campaign of the 1950s. The MCP divided into separate groups and, largely confined—as a military force—to the Thai–Malay border region, bides its time. It still has the choice between two strategies—military uprising, and penetration of legitimate bodies such as political parties and trade unions. The threat of military action is contained by the combined efforts of Thai and Malaysian armed forces, which since 1977 have co-operated more effectually than in the past. But if Thailand and Malaysia were obliged by some other threat to their security to divert their forces to other tasks, the MCP guerrillas might again take the initiative. During the late 1960s the MCP had some success in penetrating the Labour Party and thereby precipitating the Penang riots of 1967. It can no longer count on more than token support from the government of China. It is indeed aware that if it is to revive its political influence, it must break out of the limits of being—in non-Chinese eyes—a Chinese movement. As a result of a *cause célèbre* in the mid 1970s there was a real fear that a small but influential group of Malays, including a prominent journalist, had been converted to the communist faith. But this risk—so far as it exists—is confined to the élite. The MCP has never been able to secure support from the Malay peasantry by exploiting their economic grievances. There is also an area of communist activity in southern Sarawak along the border with Indonesia. But this is adequately contained by the Indonesian and Malaysian forces. Since 1965 Indonesia has been firmly anti-communist (Chapter 11). The main risk of a communist revival is probably economic recession causing hardship among the poor of all communities. The government strategy of providing fair shares for all (Chapter 9) could not progress if the tempo of economic growth were seriously impeded.

Corruption by its nature is surreptitious and therefore difficult to measure. Wherever there is restriction on business activity, delay in granting necessary permissions, and the like, individuals will offer rewards to politicians or bureaucrats to obtain a decision or a speedy answer in their favour. In all countries (it was so occasionally in colonial Malaya) there will be found some members of the civil service who succumb to these temptations. In Malaysia corruption in political life and in administration is probably a less acute problem than in many other Asian countries. It is nonetheless serious enough to have led the Malaysian government some years ago to establish a special agency to uncover and prosecute cases of corruption. In 1976 the chief minister of an UMNO State government was convicted on charges of corruption and sentenced to imprisonment. It was a bad case, but it is unlikely that it was a unique one.[23]

Apart from the particular question of corruption something may here be said of the general efficiency of the civil service in Malaysia. At independence in 1957 there was a major upheaval. The Alliance, under pressure from its supporters among the middle ranks of the public services, decided that true independence required that all senior civil servants must be Malayan: that the British civil servants, who then filled about two-thirds of the Division I posts, must be replaced as soon as practicable. This programme was carried through in a reasonable way over a period of about five years. The vacant posts were filled by recruiting Malayans from the universities, but mainly by promoting to higher posts civil servants who had until then filled the middle grades. (Some of them were given the opportunity to improve their qualifications by taking courses at foreign universities.) A certain number of expert advisers were engaged for limited periods to advise on policy in various fields. For a time the general efficiency of the service suffered from these numerous changes of personnel, and in particular from the promotion to senior posts of men in middle life who had become habituated to routine rather than innovation. As a new generation of young and well-qualified recruits entered the service, the general standard of energy and ability rose correspondingly. There was a systematic attempt in the 1960s to train the new bureaucrats for the many specialist tasks which awaited them.[24] There is still dead wood — what bureaucracy is without it? — but at the top level there are able and well-trained technocrats. The most serious deficiency in probably at the level of executive action to implement policies; here there are insufficient trained junior staff of the required calibre.[25] The problem has been made worse by two factors. As each programme or need is perceived, a new agency is created to deal with it. The bureaucracy proliferates and in so doing it wastes scarce manpower. Secondly, the policy of preferring Malays in recruitment means that the full pool of national human talent is not used. In principle a serving member of the civil service, whatever his race, should be selected for promotion or for posting to a position of responsibility strictly on his merits. But in practice the non-Malay civil servants find it difficult to secure advancement to which they are entitled. At the apex of the political system it is realized, however, that the effectiveness of government, upon which its ultimate survival depends, is prejudiced if it is served by inadequate administrators. In filling junior ministerial posts and making appointments to the numerous parastatal agencies there has been a welcome but necessarily unobtrusive choice of 'young well-educated technocrats with clean records'.[26] The future lies with them.

Notes

1 The Constitution (Amendment) Act 1962 provides that rural constituencies may be 'weighted', but their registered electorate may not be less than one-half that of an urban constituency. This incorporates in the constitution what had been the practice since constituencies were first delimited in 1954. In this Chapter I have drawn on the considerable number of published studies of Malaysian politics since 1945 including Means (1970), Ratnam and Milne (1967), Milne and Ratnam (1974), Milne (1967), Ratnam (1965), Vasil (1971), Simandjuntak (1969), Musolf and Springer (1979), and Bedlington (1978).

2 When the Alliance first came to power in 1955, it was committed to seeking a political settlement with the leaders of the proscribed MCP, on the basis that colonial rule was about to end and so the declared objectives of the MCP had been achieved. This led to a meeting under flag of truce at Baling in north Kedah between the chief ministers of Malaya and Singapore (Tunku Abdul Rahman and David Marshall) on one side, and an MCP delegation headed by Ch'in Peng, the MCP Secretary General. The MCP was offered an amnesty to all of its individual members against whom there were no specific charges of criminal violence. The MCP demanded, however, that their party should be recognized as a legal organization so that it could re-enter Malayan political life as a party. The talks broke down on this point. The amnesty did serve to induce the surrender of a considerable number of guerrillas. The Alliance thereafter took a firm anti-communist line. The position of the MCP is described later in this chapter.

3 *Straits Budget,* (22 August 1962), 11.

4 There could not be a simultaneous general election throughout Malaysia. Singapore had recently held its national elections in September 1963. Preparations for the first elections in Sabah and Sarawak would inevitably take time, and it was planned to hold the elections in 1968-69, but, as will be related, these were postponed.

5 *Straits Times* (10 May 1965).

6 He had gone to London to attend a Commonwealth Prime Ministers' Conference and his return had been delayed by illness.

7 This admission was made in a personal letter to the deputy prime minister of Singapore which the Tunku wrote in confidence, though in the stress of the moment he forgot to say so (or even to date his letter). Its immediate publication caused much embarrassment. Document 32 in Gullick (1967).

8 See Milne and Ratnam (1974) passim; Means (1970), Chapter 20; and also

Bedlington (1978) (who spent seven years in Sabah). Sabah and Sarawak did not lack leaders of ability, but they entered the Malaysian political scene without any experience or tradition of concerted action and the Alliance has been able to play off one against another. See below at note 19.

9 Vasil (1971), Chapter III describes them as 'Chinese chauvinists'.

10 The exact course of events before and during the riots is disputed. Slimming, who entitled his book *Death of a Democracy* (1969), was wrong in his political judgement of the consequences, but not necessarily in his account of the riots themselves. Tunku Abdul Rahman (1969) has given his own account as a personal apologia and vindication which offers a fairly alarming picture of the situation at the time. The official attitude is that this was only an 'incident' — witness the title of Goh Cheng Teik's book *The May Thirteenth Incident* (1971). The official Malaysian version is entitled *The May 13th Tragedy*. It is beyond doubt that many people, mainly Chinese, were killed, that there was a loss of control by the authorities for several days, and that the non-Malay population lacked confidence in the willingness of the army and police, predominantly Malay, to act effectively against those who attacked them.

11 Since his retirement Tunku Abdul Rahman has lived as a private citizen in Penang, maintaining a tetchy and aloof relationship with his successors. The present deputy prime minister, Dr Mahathir bin Mohamed, was expelled from UMNO because as an unknown backbencher at the time he demanded the Tunku's resignation. The events of 1969-70 marked the end of an era and the entry on the political stage of 'new men' of more marked if not extreme views on Malay 'rights'. Mahathir's book *The Malay Dilemma* (1970) is still officially proscribed in Malaysia under the rules which forbid public discussion of controversial communal questions.

12 TMP, para 25.

13 The outstanding self-made Malay leader in UMNO was Abdul Aziz bin Ishak. Son of a junior government official (an inspector of fisheries) he began his career in Malay journalism. He built up a position of influence in Selangor where many of the Malay population are sons or grandsons of Indonesian immigrants and the traditional hierarchy of rank is less securely established. He became Minister of Agriculture in 1955, and was a vice-president of UMNO from 1958 to 1962. He advocated more drastic measures for Malay economic advancement than were acceptable to the UMNO leadership in those early days, and resigned from office in 1963 rather than accept a transfer to the less politically important Health Ministry. In opposition he joined a group which became implicated in negotiations with the Indonesian government during the period of Confrontation in 1964-65 (Chapter 11), and was arrested by the Malaysian government on security grounds (see Means (1970), 340-1). In 1955-56 I was secretary to a ministerial committee which included Tunku Abdul Rahman, Tun Abdul Razak, and also Abdul Aziz bin Ishak, and observed how prickly their relationship proved to be.

14 Musolf and Springer (1979), Chapter 5, 'Career Paths of Malaysian MP's', has some interesting material on the limited progress so far towards a *carrière ouverte aux talents*.

15 'A large segment of the Malayan public will pursue communal objectives only until the point is reached where communalism threatens domestic

tranquility or stability'; Means (1970), 403. As District Officer Seremban (in Negri Sembilan) in the autumn of 1945, I had to try to counteract the alarm and ill-feeling resulting from the Batu Kikir massacre (see Chapter 5, note 7). On both sides, Malay and Chinese, there was a geniune disposition to bury the past and search for a peaceful accommodation.

16   *FEER* (20 October 1978) on the debate about the Merdeka University project described in Chapter 12.

17   Musolf and Springer (1979), Chapter 3.

18   Ratnam and Milne (1967), Chapter IX. The whole book is a storehouse of fascinating observation. One enjoys such touches as the PMIP endeavour to discredit Tunku Abdul Rahman by spreading the story that he had danced the twist with a female competitor after a Koran-reading competition held during the month of fasting (p.121). On Malay politics in Kelantan see also Kessler (1978), passim.

19   Kessler (1978), 281. See also Milne and Ratnam (1974), Chapter 4 on the elections in Borneo over the period 1968-70. The besetting sin of Borneo political parties is the use of bogus 'independents' as candidates. The ruling or opposition coalition agrees (with difficulty) on the 'allocation' of constituencies between its component parties. No party can then put up an official candidate to oppose its partners in the constituencies allocated to them. But this constraint is evaded by putting up an 'independent' in the knowledge that if he wins, he will join the party which encouraged his candidature. See *FEER* (5 October 1979) for an account of such manoeuvres in the 1979 elections in Sarawak. The balance is often tilted by the marked preference shown by UMNO leaders in Kuala Lumpur for Muslim parties (which may be Melanau rather than Malay) as leaders of Borneo coalitions. But such is the distrust felt in Borneo that it would be counterproductive for any local Muslim party to declare its allegiance by becoming the local State outpost of UMNO itself: Milne and Ratnam (1974), 87-9.

20   The phrase is usually attributed to Tun Abdul Razak: *Straits Times* (19 September 1967).

21   Gerakan (also GRM for *Gerakan Rakyat Malaysia* — the Malaysian People's Movement) is not explicitly a Chinese communal party, but is predominantly Chinese in its leadership and its electoral support. It reflects the breakaway of part of the MCA leadership in 1959 (see above) and has its main base in Penang.

22   On the death of Tun Abdul Razak in January 1976 he was succeeded as Prime Minister by Datuk Hussein bin Onn (son of Datuk Onn who had founded UMNO in 1946). Although he commands the confidence of his supporters as a good Malay nationalist, he is a moderate. It is said that he postponed the publication of the Third Malaysia Plan, when he became Prime Minister, so that it could be revised to express his government's intention of relieving poverty in all communities and not just among the Malays: *FEER* (16 July 1976), 11. A quiet man, he has effective control of his party — so far at least.

23   The Datuk Harun affair was extensively reported in *FEER*. There have been other reported scandals. See *FEER* (3 November 1978), 29-30, (16 January 1976), 90, (6 October 1978), 72, and (24 August 1979), 14 on such varied matters as urban land development, purchase of armaments, opportunities

of investment reserved to Malays, and the administration of the smallholder rubber-replanting scheme. The causes and effects of corruption have been studied by a Malay sociologist (Alatas (1968)). The damage done by corruption is not confined to injustice or misallocation of resources. It becomes accepted in the national ideology as an ineradicable factor—'an unavoidable practice too deep-rooted to combat' (Alatas (1972), 104). There is then less resistance to it on a future occasion and a loss of confidence in the integrity of those who hold the reins of power.

24 Tilman (1964), Esman (1964), Ness (1967) are American academics who studied and/or worked in the bureaucracy. Esman (especially Chapters 6 and 7) gives a vivid account (despite the opacity of the language of a political scientist) of his endeavours to introduce various reforms and improvements.

25 The 'binding constraint' on growth is 'specific shortages of middle and high-level manpower': TMP, para 129. See Chapter 12.

26 *FEER* (3 November 1978).

9 The Management of the Economy

By the standards of developing countries the economy of Malaysia is strong and prosperous. Every year sees a growth of gross domestic product of the order of 6 to 8 per cent. But it is also subject to imbalances. It depends heavily on the fluctuating export earnings of a few key products such as rubber, palm-oil, tin, and more recently timber and petroleum; in 1978 these commodities yielded almost three-quarters of export income. There is a wide disparity of income between classes and communities. Three-quarters of a million households are reckoned to be below the poverty-line and the majority of them are rural Malays. Most of the 'modern sector' is still concentrated along the west coast of Malaya. These are political as well as economic problems. Since Malaya became independent, and especially since the New Economic Policy (NEP) was launched in 1970, there has been an active development programme which aims at growth, stability, and diversification and the gradual eradication of poverty. But some of these measures had their origins in the last years of the colonial regime. It may be useful to begin at that point.

Development down to 1957

By good fortune Malaya possessed rich and accessible alluvial deposits of tin of which the industrialized countries had need in the nineteenth century. Tin-mining imparted a momentum of growth from which Malaya acquired an infrastructure of ports, roads, and railways. Since the tin was found along the western side of the central Malayan range of hills, the network of communications — and also the influx of immigrant labour — was limited to the west-coast zone. The semi-subsistence economy of the Malays of eastern Malaya, and of the indigenous peoples of modern Sabah and Sarawak, was little altered. At the turn of the century the boom in rubber-planting began a second wave of development. This too was concentrated in the west-coast zone of Malaya since that area offered abundant land with the advantage of good communications. There was also some planting of rubber in Sabah and Sarawak which gave a modest impetus to development there. To this day, however, more than half the population of Malaysia and all its large towns are found in an area which is only about one-sixth of Malaysia as a whole.

Down to 1941 the government was content to encourage development by providing good communications, by making available agricultural land on attractive terms and essential economic and some social services of a satisfactory standard. The resulting economic development was described in 1954 by a visiting World Bank Mission as making of Malaya 'a geographical region where capital and labour belonging to other economies found it convenient to carry on certain specialized operations within the British monetary as well as political framework'.[1] Yet even at this period the government could not remain entirely passive. It was obliged to make choices and to determine priorities in order to promote or to stabilize the economic development which it had so successfully encouraged. In its land policy, for example, it gave preference to large-scale enterprises, generally financed and managed by European companies.[2] It was settled policy that the Malay peasant should be protected from what was perceived as the damaging effects of a modern economy and so encouraged to grow rice rather than rubber.[3] When the plantation industry needed to regulate the inflow of Indian labour, a legal basis was provided through the Indian Immigration Committee (Chapter 4). The wide fluctuations in world prices of rubber and tin in the period between the two World Wars led to arrangements for restriction by Malayan law of the output of these industries (Chapter 11). Occasionally the government made a positive intervention in the field of development such as the Krian irrigation scheme completed in 1906 (Chapter 4), and the establishment in the same area of government rice mills to break the monopoly of the Chinese rice-millers.[4] In 1922 a Co-operative Department was established to provide advice and encouragement (but not money) for co-operative credit and some agricultural marketing societies. In general, however, it was official policy to avoid the management of economic enterprises and major development schemes. As Krian had shown, these projects often cost much more than had been estimated, and some, such as the wharves at Prai opposite Penang, were a failure. Fluctuations in government revenue also induced a mood of caution. Expansion of public services in times of boom was followed by painful retrenchment during the ensuing slump. The benefit of essential public services was concentrated in urban centres where there was a considerable population, and among the mines and plantations where an economic return could be expected.

The restored colonial government of 1946 had a different and more interventionist philosophy. In 1950 it recruited for the first time a professional economist as a policy adviser — but then assigned to him a large burden of administration. The first national development plan covered the years 1950-55, though it was only a summary of departmental plans for capital expenditure.[5] 1950 also saw the establishment of a Rural and Industrial Development Authority (RIDA) under the chairmanship of Datuk Onn bin Jaafar, then UMNO president.[6] RIDA was the first — but not very successful — attempt at concerted government action to improve the social and economic condition of the Malay peasant.[7] The World Bank Mission referred to above produced the first comprehensive and expert survey of the facts, problems, and possibilities of the Malayan economy as a national and autonomous entity. In the same year, 1954, another group of experts, the Mudie Committee, proposed a government-directed programme of replanting estates and smallholdings with high-yielding rubber and gave the warning that 'this is probably the last chance that a large part of the natural [rubber] industry will have of getting its house in order before the storm breaks'.[8] The essence of the Mudie scheme was that money for replanting should be collected as a cess on exports of rubber and only returned to producers, as an acreage subsidy, if they replanted.

Malaya had had since the turn of the century an excellent system of registered title to land, based on the Torrens system of South Australia. But the sheer elaboration of registered title was a brake on progress. As part of the schemes for restricting the output of rubber there had been a ban since the early 1920s on the grant of land for rubber-planting. The effect of this policy was felt mainly by the smallholders who had no undeveloped land in their holdings; by contrast a typical estate company — when first established a generation or more before — obtained a large block of land which was still only partially developed. If the land hunger of the peasant population, growing by natural increase, was to be satisfied, the established procedure of individual applications for land and its subsequent clearing and planting by individual effort would have to be swept aside. The best way to develop new smallholdings was to clear large contiguous blocks of land and plant them as the estates did — and then divide them up. In 1956 the government established for this purpose a Federal Land Development Authority (FELDA). FELDA and the rubber-replanting scheme proved to be the mainstay of Malayan agricultural development over the ensuing twenty-five years.

A New Economic Strategy

For some years after the achievement of independence in 1957 the Alliance government was preoccupied with political and security problems; the civil service was in a state of upheaval through the replacement of British by local personnel in the higher grades. But the results of the 1959 federal elections (Chapter 8), in which the Alliance government lost ground in Malay rural areas, were a jolt to the regime. It would have to do more — and be seen to do more — for the welfare of the Malay peasant. The response was the establishment of a new Ministry of Rural Development under the personal control of Tun Abdul Razak, then deputy prime minister and recognized as the most effective organizer in the cabinet. Razak set about energizing the rather lethargic federal and State civil services by adopting the personal style and operational methods used by General Templer in his drive to win the Emergency campaign (Chapter 5). In every district office an 'operations room' was established with maps and wallcharts; there was also a 'red book' to record the local development programmes and the progress made in them.[9] Razak also set about modernizing the techniques of the civil service in the federal capital, using American experts as advisers.[10] As politics these initiatives were effective; as a development programme they made some headway. This was also the period of the mid-1960s when the pressure of Indonesian Confrontation and the euphoria over the creation of Malaysia strengthened the position of the Alliance government. But the upheaval of 1969 (Chapter 8) showed that there was still serious Malay discontent at the continuing economic backwardness of their community. In the reconstruction which followed in 1970-71 the NEP was an essential element. If there was to be political stability and constitutional government, there must also be major changes in the economy.

In its diagnosis of the Malaysian economy the NEP discerned two evils to be eradicated. First there was—and still is—widespread poverty: in 1970 just under half the total number of households in Malaya (there is no data for the Borneo territories) had incomes which were less than the minimum required 'to sustain a decent standard of living'. In rural areas the proportion in poverty was three-fifths and Malay family incomes were 10 per cent below the rural average.[11] The second major problem was a destructive 'identification of race with economic function'[12], friction between the communities was aggravated by the fact that Malays predominated in some activities such as rice-growing, in which poverty was exceptionally acute, but Chinese and other non-indigenous communities were equally predominant in more prosperous activities such as shopkeeping. There was also a wide disparity in the ownership of productive assets in the modern sector of the economy. In 1970 the Malays as individuals owned less than one-fortieth of the share capital of companies in Malaya, but foreign shareholders had almost two-thirds—and the non-indigenous communities the rest.[13]

The objectives of the NEP are to eradicate poverty, to restructure patterns of occupation and property ownership on a more equitable basis, and in particular to achieve 'the ownership and management by Malays and other indigenous peoples of at least 30% of commercial and industrial activities in the economy, and an employment structure at all levels of operation and employment that reflects the racial composition of the nation by 1990'.[14] It is not, however, intended that the Malay community should be transmuted entirely into a class of business magnates and rentiers. On the contrary, for the foreseeable future the majority of Malays must continue to be smallholders earning their livelihood in agriculture. But agriculture must be turned 'from a subsistence occupation to a business-oriented enterprise'. This result is to be achieved by increasing the productive assets at the disposal of the peasant farmer and by making available to him better technical services, credit, and marketing arrangements. To take advantage of these opportunities and to be able to enter new occupations he must be better educated. For poverty is associated with poor education. More than half of the poorly educated but only a fifth of the better-educated are below the poverty income line.[15]

The detailed programmes for achieving NEP objectives by stages are set out in five-year development plans covering each decade in two parts: the Second Malaysia Plan (SMP) 1971-75 inaugurated the new approach and the current Third Malaysia Plan (TMP) covers the period 1976-80; a Fourth Malaysia Plan (FMP) for 1981-85 is in preparation. The SMP appeared during the reconstruction of 1970-71 and put heavy emphasis on the urgent needs of the Malay community. The TMP, perhaps as a result of the personal influence of the present Prime Minister, recognizes that if the political objectives are to be attained, measures to relieve poverty must extend to all the poor of every community. 'Open intemperate debate and party politics based on sectional interests could divert the energies of the Malaysians from the tasks of nation-building'.[16] For example, the programme of rural improvement in the TMP extends to New Villages where the population is mainly Chinese; the land-settlement schemes are in principle open to Chinese settlers — partly to relieve poverty and partly to break down the identification of race with economic function. But the planners cannot go so far in this direction as might be desirable in case in doing so they should arouse Malay protests. The Chinese regard these plans as discrimination in favour of the Malays in their positive aspects, and as discrimination against themselves in the restrictions which they impose in order to facilitate the entry of Malays into the field of commerce and industry. Apart from the question of balance between the communities in Malaya there must also be an evening-up of economic development between the west-coast zone of Malaya and the more backward east-coast zone and also the Borneo territories.

Problems of the NEP

If the programme is to succeed, there must be a continuing steady expansion of the national economy as a whole. No one supposes that the condition of the poor, more especially the Malay poor, can be ameliorated by mere redistribution of resources at the expense of the better-off, many of them Chinese. This would be a recipe for a communal explosion as well as a political upheaval. The only practicable method is to enlarge the cake and allocate the increment so as to create fairer shares of the whole. It is a politically expedient philosophy for an essentially conservative regime which has made no serious attempt at redistribution within the communities. Among the Malays themselves the gap which separates the middle class of urban bourgeoisie and rural landlords from tenant or landless peasant in the villages is probably widening.

To achieve growth there must be a high level of investment in new resources. This is all the more necessary because the population continues to increase at a rate of about 3 per cent *per annum* — though there is a family-planning campaign which aims to reduce the rate to 2 per cent by the mid-1980s. Development expenditure by the government and government agencies makes a massive and increasing contribution to investment; it was expected to double over the period 1976-80 as compared with the rate in the previous quinquennium.[17] In raising money for its programmes the government can augment its revenue surplus by borrowing from the national Employees' Provident Fund (EPF), to which employers and workers must contribute to provide support for workers when they reach the age of retirement.[18] But after taking account of public-sector investment in 1976-80 there remained a huge 'resource gap' of about $10 billion which it was intended should be filled in roughly equal shares by private investment and by foreign loans.[19] As will be explained later, the flow of private investment has fallen short of the planned level. Sustained growth also requires reasonable stability of export earnings (Chapter 11).

The volume of investment is not the only problem. If the redistribution target is to be achieved so that by 1990 Malays and other indigenous peoples own at least 30 per cent of the commercial and industrial sector of the economy, there must be a massive investment by or on behalf of those communities. How is it to be done? Whenever a new company is floated, 30 per cent at least of its shares must be allocated on favourable terms to these *bumiputra* investors.[20] But it is beyond the financial capacity of Malays as individuals to take up securities on this scale. They are not men of wealth; investment of this kind is alien to them. The middle class may be able to invest. But the allocation of favourable investment oportunities can easily become a near scandalous system of 'spoils' for the middle ranks of UMNO and members of the Malay upper class.[21] But if the special block of securities reserved for *bumiputra* investors is not taken up, the opportunity will be lost and may never — as regards that company — recur. Accordingly the government has established and financed a number of '*bumiputra* institutions', such as the National Equity Corporation, to subscribe for securities to be held 'in trust' for the *bumiputra* communities until such time as they can be distributed to individuals.

This policy has been pursued with ingenuity and determination. The commercial empire of PERNAS will be described later. There are also government-sponsored unit trusts to assist the would-be small investor. Traditional attitudes and religious beliefs impede the spread of *bumiputra* investment in securities. As Muslims, many Malay peasants accumulate the savings of a lifetime to pay for a pilgrimage to Mecca by which they gain much esteem and pious grace. According to the leading Malay academic economist the cash was 'stored in tree hollows, under floorboards, stuffed in a mattress', until the day it was needed. At best it was invested in realizable village assets such as buffaloes or land.[22] The Islamic prohibition of usury prevented the investment of cash in loans bearing interest — but not participation in the profits of a business. In 1962 with the blessing of the Grand Imam of the al-Azhar University in Cairo, the great centre of Muslim learning, a scheme was launched for a Malaysian Pilgrim Management and Fund Board *(Lembaga Urusan Tabung Haji),* to which the intending pilgrim could pay his periodic contributions. The fund had been able from its investments to pay an annual bonus of about 6–8 per cent. When the contributor wishes to make the pilgrimage, the board arranges his passage and accommodation *en route*. It is a most enlightened and successful combination of tradition and of new methods; in 1978 there were more than 300,000 depositors and the accumulated assets were worth more than $250 million.

The general result of these various methods of mobilizing and investing capital for the *bumiputra* communities is to concentrate in the hands of a small group of Malay politicians and technocrats control of much of the private sector of the economy. It shifts the balance of power in favour of the public sector — without adequate methods of ensuring public accountability and disclosure. Insofar as the bureaucrats are Malay and some of the entrepreneurs are Chinese, it has its communal undertones.

The 30 per cent *bumiputra* participation requirement extends to management and employment. Here the constraint is the shortage of well-qualified and capable men for the senior posts. By the mid-1970s the number of Malays employed in manufacturing industry, mining, construction, and the service industries amounted to one-third or more of the total. But these overall figures masked the much smaller proportion of Malays in managerial posts. The majority were subordinate staff or manual workers. There is now a much-expanded programme of education and training at professional and sub-professional levels to increase the pool of available recruits for senior posts (Chapter 12).

The development of an indigenous entrepreneurial class of small businessmen raises problems of a different kind. Most of the existing firms are small family concerns or partnerships owned and managed by Chinese or Indian proprietors whose working language is a non-Malay vernacular. Cultural differences of that kind make it almost impossible for Malays to penetrate this sector of the economy as employees or partners in existing concerns. If you cannot join them, beat them, is the response. Government agencies such as MARA (the former RIDA in reorganized form) provide business training for Malays and also loans to establish or expand their ventures. Preference is given to Malay enterprises in the award of licences to run taxis or country bus services, or in making contracts for supplies required by government services. During the colonial period the Malays were almost shut out of commerce by the rapid expansion of alien firms. Further back in their history they were successful traders, albeit usually on a small scale.[23] To revive this tradition in a very different commercial world is not to be achieved overnight. However, some progress has been made. The policy of positive discrimination in favour of Malays is much resented by the small Chinese businessman who suffers its immediate effects. It also leads to the notorious 'Ali Baba' deception by which a Malay (Ali is a Muslim name) obtains a contract, licence, or franchise on behalf of a Chinese (Baba is the traditional term for a Straits-born Chinese). It is difficult to suppress. At a rather higher level of business organization the foreign manufacturer or importer finds that his path through official controls is rather easier if the distribution of his products is entrusted to a local firm which has a visible Malay element.

NEP requirements also affect policy on location of industry. The migration of Malays into the towns is causing some concern because their living conditions are sometimes unsatisfactory. Yet it is desirable that there should be more Malay workers in industry. Hence it is the policy that new factories, more especially those which are labour-intensive or which use local products, should be located outside the larger towns. Industrial employment is to be carried to the villages rather than have the villagers seek it in the towns.

The consequences of the NEP can also be seen in the organizational structure of the economy. To mobilize local capital there must be a securities market—the Malaysian Stock Exchange in Kuala Lumpur. But this is too small to provide a satisfactory market and is overshadowed by the larger and more active Singapore Stock Exchange. The companies listed on the Stock Exchange fall into two groups. The old-established rubber and tin companies were originally floated in London (plus a few 'dollar' companies also formed by overseas promoters in Singapore or Hong Kong). Their capital was subscribed by British and other foreign investors. A Malaysian investor could acquire their shares by purchase on the London market, but this was a remote and unfamiliar place. In the post-war period these British companies were pressed to obtain a local quotation for their shares in order to facilitate Malaysian investment and dealings. For a time the proportion of local investors, mainly Chinese, was small and they remained passive recipients of their dividends. By the late 1950s, however, local participation had increased; the market price of the shares fell below the price at which the underlying assets in Malaya could be sold to local purchasers unconcerned by the risks of foreign investment. From this situation began a series of local 'takeover' bids and the like, followed by asset-stripping. As a result many of the old British companies have either ceased to exist or have moved their seat of control to Malaysia with directors appointed by local interests (including in some prominent cases the Malaysian government acting through its parastatal agencies). There remain a few major plantation companies under British management and based in London. But their number is dwindling. Their middle management is Malaysian and they are required by 1990 to achieve a pattern of ownership compatible with NEP objectives. The government respects their technical expertise but is determined to have domestic ownership and control.

The other main group of companies quoted on the Malaysian Stock Exchange results from the development of new industries and commercial activities. For this purpose companies are registered in Malaysia though they may have a substantial minority shareholding held by a foreign manufacturerer. Apart from reserving a proportion of the shares for *bumiputra* investors, the foreign promoter may offer shares to the Malaysian investor generally, i.e., to the Chinese, or associate local interest with him in his new venture. There are also entirely local companies promoted mainly by Chinese businessmen. These flotations are supervised by an official Capital Issues Committee (CIC), and when appropriate by the Foreign Investment Committee (FIC), whose function is to ensure that NEP requirements are suitably observed in each case. The current Malaysian company statute is based mainly on the Australian model ordinance and is rather elaborate for its purpose in Malaysia. The establishment of a new industrial enterprise is also subject to the Industrial Co-ordination Act (Chapter 10).

The local investor is only gradually adapting his habit of mind to the pattern of these alien institutions. In contrast to the Malay villager, whose case has been considered above, the Chinese or Indian businessman has the habit of investing his profits or savings. But it has not been his tradition to put his money into large enterprises under remote, impersonal, and professional management. The position of a minority shareholder who has invested for the long-term gain is unfamiliar. He has in the past been more disposed by habit to invest in the purchase of land, for example a small rubber estate or a stake in one owned by a partnership of close associates or relatives, or he lends money to a kinsman for use in a business of which the lender has some direct knowledge. Until industrialization gained momentum in the late 1960s four-fifths of all Malaysian industrial concerns employed less than ten workers each. The small-scale family business was the typical unit.[24] When the investor tries his hand at buying shares, his object is to make a quick profit by speculation rather than a long-term gain.[25] This attitude renders him vulnerable to the activities of consortia who contrive to rig the market by buying in shares to raise the price (and the expectations of the general investor), and then unloading them. These malpractices do not escape the vigilant eye of the Malaysian central bank (Bank Negara Malaysia) which is the most important institutional regulator of the entire financial system. On occasion the Bank has felt compelled to read the riot act.[26]

The several objectives of the NEP applied to a fairly complex economy have caused a proliferation of special authorities and agencies. There is the Federal Industrial Development Authority (FIDA), Malaysian Industrial Development Finance Berhad (MIDF), Malaysian Industrial Estates Limited, the Federal Agricultural Marketing Authority (FAMA), the Farmers' Organization Authority (FOA), the Urban Development Authority (UDA), the Malaysian Rubber Development Corporation (MARDEC), the National *Padi* and Rice Authority (LPN), the Rubber Industry Smallholders' Development Authority (RISDA), the National Land Rehabilitation and Consolidation Authority (FELCRA), the Fisheries Development Authority (MAJUIKAN), the Livestock Development Authority (MAJUTERNAK). In addition to the federal agencies, the State governments have their State Development Corporations (SEDC). There is a serious and inefficient overlap of function between groups of agencies. Thus FELDA, established in 1956, undertakes major schemes of land development covering several thousand acres in each case. It clears the land and plants it with rubber or oil-palm or other crops preparatory to settling smallholders on 10-acre blocks. FELCRA's function is to open smaller areas for settlement so as to extend existing smallholders' acreage ('fringe alienation schemes'); it also consolidates holdings of uneconomic size into larger units. RISDA makes grants and loans to smallholders to assist them in the replanting of their existing holdings. The SEDCs also promote land-settlement schemes. For technical advice the smallholder can look to the Department of Agriculture, to the advisory service of the Rubber Research Institute of Malaysia (RRI), to RISDA which has established numerous Smallholder Development Centres (SDC), and to the local Farmers' Organization promoted by FOA. It is hardly surprising that employment has grown rapidly in the 'service sector' of the economy.

The planners themselves recognize that the growth of the agricultural bureaucracy has got out of hand — 'the shortage of trained and qualified personnel has been exacerbated by the establishment of numerous organizations with almost similar functions'.[27] It is, however, easier to expand than to streamline a bureaucrats' paradise.

In the new industrial sector of the economy also, there are important State agencies. When the NEP was launched in 1970, the main instrument used to establish a better balance of communal participation in industry and commerce was the *Perbadanan Nasional* (PERNAS) which operates as a state-owned holding company. It has principal wholly-owned subsidiaries engaged in construction, engineering, mining, property development, securities, trading, insurance, and contracts for the supply of goods to government departments. These major subsidiaries in turn operate through wholly-owned or joint-venture companies to carry on specific types of business. As examples one finds among the 60 to 70 active companies of the PERNAS group the manufacture of telecommunications equipment and of container transport, tin-mining (which is a major interest of PERNAS), the export of timber, and the processing of edible oils. Some are large enterprises and some are small. Some are tolerably well-managed and some are not. The PERNAS group is a huge state-owned conglomerate with assets in excess of $1 billion and 8,000 employees, of whom more than half at all levels are *bumiputra*, i.e., Malay. This commercial empire has been built up within a decade by active intervention and the abundant supply of government money. The trading subsidiary, for example, has been granted a monopoly of the trade with China. It also has major investments in large mining and plantation groups which were originally based in, and managed from, London. It is the declared objective of PERNAS to wrest control from foreign shareholders of these old-established concerns engaged in the exploitation of Malaysian natural resources. This strategy is a major qualification of the Malaysian government's disclaimer of any intention to nationalize foreign companies.[28]

When it became clear that there would be a rapid expansion of Malaysian petroleum production, the government established the *Petroliam Nasional Berhad* (PETRONAS) in 1974 'with over-all regulatory and developmental functions in all stages of development of the oil and natural gas industry'.[29] The exercise of these powers has led to predictable conflicts between PETRONAS and the international oil companies operating in Malaysia (Chapter 10). We shall come later to the Malaysian International Shipping Corporation (MISC), and the Malaysian Airways System (MAS), which are other major commercial enterprises under government ownership and control.

The growth of these large parastatal enterprises is a consequence of the NEP strategy of intervention to achieve the desired changes of ownership and control in the economic system. Such large concentrations of economic power and decision-making, without the discipline of competition or adequate parliamentary challenge, can be dangerous. There is a risk that resources will be wasted by inefficient management; private enterprise may be discouraged from expanding in fields dominated by these leviathans. Although they aim to effect a more equitable distribution of communal interest in industry and commerce, their immediate impact is one of communal discrimination — they are '*bumiputra* institutions'. The sheer size of their resources makes them a centre of political influence if not power. The argument that they are a necessary means to the acquisition of major assets of the economy to be held 'in trust' for the general body of the *bumiputra* communities is hardly valid. Trustees should be accountable to their beneficiaries — and this is not so here. Moreover, it is debatable whether national assets should be held with the declared purpose of ultimately transferring them to one sector of the nation. But they have achieved a result which is acceptable to the Malay electorate — for the time being at least — constituting centres of economic power which is visibly in Malay hands.[30]

Progress under the NEP

The objectives of growth, stability, and distribution make different calls on the economic system which is itself subject to fluctuations in world demand for Malaysian export commodities. But half-way through the twenty years of the NEP period (1970-90) some assessment can be made of results so far achieved.

The main cause of instability is the ebb and flow of world commodity prices. There are two possible counter-measures — price stabilization and diversification. The international schemes for the stabilization of the prices of rubber and tin are considered later in the context of Malaysian external relations (Chapter 11).

Since 1960 Malaysia has escaped by diversification from being a two-commodity economy. In 1957 rubber and tin produced one-third of Malayan gross domestic product and three-quarters of total export earnings. In a much larger economy rubber and tin now account for one-eighth of GDP and one-third of export income.[31] Palm-oil has become a major element in the economy; in 1960 palm-oil and kernels accounted for 2 per cent of exports — in 1980 they are estimated to yield 12 per cent. The most dramatic change has been the growth of petroleum production, which was negligible in 1970 (Appendix 2, Table 2) and now amounts to about 13 per cent of exports. The export of timber was the major industry of Sabah before Malaysia was formed and a useful but minor Malayan industry; it has expanded considerably during the 1970s. This is of course diversification into a wider spread of raw materials which still account for four-fifths of Malaysian exports. In a world threatened with scarcities Malaysia is strong as a producer of essential materials. But in the short term a serious world recession could hit the Malaysian economy hard since the prices of its main exports, other than petroleum, could fall disastrously, threatening the political as well as the economic stability of the country. Hence Malaysia is a determined proponent of price stabilization.

The considerable growth of the 1970s has been due as much to higher prices (despite a temporary setback in 1974-76) as to increased output. Rubber and tin, the traditional mainstays of the economy, have been rather disappointing. For reasons which are explained in the next chapter, output of both rubber and tin has been static—and tin shows signs of decline. Both are subject to substantial export duties which are levied at progressively higher rates as the price rises. This is the only practicable method of taxing the half-million rubber smallholders. It is the means of raising the money required to finance the replanting scheme. It also serves to stabilize the economy by siphoning off money at times of high prices. Otherwise, as happened during the Korean War boom of 1951-52, high commodity prices have an inflationary effect. The same system of export duty at progressive rates has been extended to palm-oil also. Since the oil-palm gives a much higher profit per acre than rubber, it was inevitable that land which was replanted or newly cleared for planting would come under oil-palm rather than rubber. But it is argued that rubber is now unduly heavily taxed; the government seems disposed to relieve the burden, but only marginally. Tin production is threatened by the exhaustion of workable deposits and sharply rising costs (including the price of oil). In deciding whether to risk his capital in a new mine, the Chinese entrepreneur counts on periods of high prices to give him the occasional bonanza. Progressive taxation related to high prices is therefore something of a disincentive.

The very rapid growth of the petroleum industry has exceeded the expectations of the Third Malaysia Plan, for 1976-80. It has served to offset the shortfall in other private-sector investment, and it has given to the government additional funds to finance the expansion of public-sector investment to fill the gap. It is not easy to discern exactly what has happened in the private sector. Funds which might have been invested have been applied to consumption or put under the floorboards (or salted away in overseas bank accounts). The measures taken to promote *bumiputra* participation in the economy have undoubtedly had a discouraging effect on the confidence of the Chinese businessman. It has also proved difficult to develop new industries, whether foreign or local enterprises. Government measures to fill the gap by investment in infrastructure, housing, and state enterprises are not an entirely adequate substitute.

An economy which continues so far to grow at the rate of 7 or 8 per cent *per annum* is very prosperous by any standard. The cause for concern lies in its dependence on world prices of its export commodities, on the exploitation of its limited resources in petroleum, and in the disproportionate share of public-sector investment in the total.

The same prosperity sustains a strong balance of payments with an annual surplus of $2 to $3 billion in recent years, and accumulated reserves sufficient to pay for more than eight months' retained imports. In increasing employment and diversifying the economy, government expenditure has grown in line with the rising revenue. It is a balanced budget, but like the balance of payments it is vulnerable to a world recession and a fall in commodity prices.

The objective of 'fair shares' requires the gradual elimination of poverty and a wider spread of ownership, employment, and opportunities in the modern sector of the economy. The measures taken to improve the position of the smallholder and their effect are considered in the following chapter. The main beneficiaries have been the smallholders who grow rubber, oil-palm, or coconuts. Greater productivity, larger holdings, better credit and marketing arrangements have raised their incomes. But there remains a hard core of unrelieved poverty among the tenant rice farmers, the fisherman, and the landless village labourers for whom new holdings have not so far been provided. These groups are mainly Malay, but in the remoter New Villages there is also unemployment and poverty among Chinese. The general improvement of social and economic conditions among a settled peasantry is a much more complex and intractable problem than moving them to take up new holdings developed on a large scale and at heavy expense. Yet both are necessary. The next chapter examines the different elements of the economy in order to review their progress and current situation.

Notes

1 'The Economic Development of Malaya': Report of a Mission organized by the International Bank for Reconstruction and Development (1955) ('the World Bank Report'), 645.

2 Lim Teck Ghee (1977), 90 and 117 on rubber land; Yip (1969), 152 on tin land.

3 Lim Teck Ghee (1977), 116 ff.

4 Short and Jackson (1971) on the Krian scheme: Lim Teck Ghee (1977), 156 on rice-mills.

5 'Critically deficient as an economic and political instrument for development': Rudner (1972). But it paved the way for better plans in later years.

6 RIDA resulted from a recommendation of the Communities Liaison

Committee established in 1949 on the initiative of Malcolm Macdonald, the Commissioner-General, to provide a forum in which the leaders of the communities could discuss their differences quietly and constructively (see Means (1970), 122).

7 The idea was the Datuk Onn, as the Malay national leader (and by 1950 Member for Home Affairs — see above, Chapter 6), should have abundant money and a free hand to promote schemes to improve the economic and social condition of the Malays. RIDA, however, foundered on the opposition of the State governments, most of which were by then at loggerheads with Datuk Onn, and the resentment of established departments (Agriculture, Co-operatives, etc.) at the arrival of this cuckoo in the nest. I was the first secretary of RIDA over the years 1950-52. RIDA struggled on, finding its function in schemes for training Malays for business activities and giving loans and grants for both commercial and village-improvement schemes. RIDA was overhauled and much enlarged in 1965 as *Majlis Amanah Rakyat* (MARA); see Tham Seong Chee (1979), 338-9 and below, Chapter 12.

8 Mudie, Raeburn and Marsh (1954) ('the Mudie Report').

9 Ness (1967), passim.

10 Esman (1964), Tilman (1964); see also Chapter 8, note 24.

11 TMP, para 490 and Table 9-5. Average annual income of a rural family in Malaya was estimated at $2,400, but the Malay level was only 86 per cent of this figure.

12 TMP, para 559.

13 TMP, para 119.

14 TMP, para 107. This leads to a 1990 target of Malay ownership of 30 per cent; other Malaysian 40 per cent; foreign 30 per cent. The reduction in the proportion in foreign ownership from 63 per cent in 1970 is compatible (on the planners' assumptions) with an absolute increase in foreign participation due to the rapid growth of the economy as a whole. TMP, paras 258-63.

15 Quoted from TMP, paras 294 and 490.

16 TMP, para 303.

17 The original TMP figure for public development expenditure over the period 1976-80 was $18,554 million (as compared with $9,820 for the SMP 1971-75 period). Agriculture was allocated 25.5 per cent, transport and communications 21.6 per cent, utilities 11.9 per cent, commerce and industry 9.5 per cent, defence and internal security 11.9 per cent, health and social security 7.6 per cent. See *FEER* (30 July 1976) for a long and interesting review of the TMP strategy.

18 In 1978 the EPF had contributors' balances totalling $6,514 million held for 3.3 million contributors. 95 per cent of the fund was invested in federal government securities. In 1978 alone the EPF provided $928 million for government loans, almost two-thirds of the total government borrowings. There are separate and smaller funds for the armed forces and the teaching profession and a Social Security Organization which insures employees against injury and disability. Malaysian external government debt was in 1975 a mere 11 per cent of GNP and Malaysia's standing as an international borrower was good.

19 According to the TMP mid-term review, private investment was increasing at an annual rate of only 7 per cent, which was well below the planned level.

In the latter part of the period it increased substantially — mainly as a result of abnormal and non-recurrent foreign investment in the expansion of Malaysian petroleum production.

20 The proportion reserved for *bumiputra* and other Malaysian investors varies with the type of enterprise. Those which use mainly local materials, or which sell most of their output in the Malaysian market, are required to allocate a higher proportion to local investors than those which import technology and offer access to foreign markets for their products. A general guide for the foreign investor is given in each year's Economic Report of the Ministry of Finance. See also the Annual Reports of the Bank Negara.

21 See *FEER* (6 October 1978). In a later interview (*FEER*, 13 April 1979) the deputy prime minister, Dr Mahathir, conceded that it was a case of 'Malay economic privilege being translated into political advantage. . . but another way of interpreting it is that even UMNO members are also *bumiputras*. And if they get their share, they are *bumiputras* getting their share'. He added that many of the Malay investors who had benefited were opponents of UMNO. It is reported, however, that quotas allocated to UMNO as an organization had come into the hands of individual officers of UMNO: *FEER* (31 August 1979), 63. From 1980 only parastatal institutions may subscribe for new shares allocated to *bumiputras*. On unit trusts see below note 30.

22 *FEER* (17 November 1978) reports an informative interview with Ungku Aziz, the Vice-Chancellor of the University of Malaya and doyen of Malay economic experts. He was the architect of the scheme.

23 Alatas (1977) has a chapter on this subject.

24 See Freedman (1957), especially pp. 87-8, on the Chinese preference for a family business structure of a personal character.

25 On the Chinese attitude to investment see World Bank Report (above note 1), 647. Yip (1969), 346-76 has some interesting material on the gradual transfer of shares of tin-mining companies to Malaysian ownership. See also K. R. Chou (1966).

26 *FEER* (26 December 1975) gives a circumstantial account of some malpractices leading to intervention by the Bank Negara.

27 TMP, para 957.

28 TMP, para 1042. See also *FEER* (7 September 1979), 59.

29 TMP, para 851.

30 In 1979 *bumiputra* shareholdings, mostly in the hands of *bumiputra* institutions, were worth about $2.2 billion. But despite a 'rapid burgeoning of the Malay middle class', who owned part of it, the general body of the Malay community obtained no benefit from it. The mere gift of securities to numerous Malays living in poverty would not solve the problem since they would be likely to sell these unfamiliar assets to obtain cash. The government apparently hopes to spread the benefits of ownership more widely through the wider use of unit trusts in which only *bumiputra* unit-holders would participate: *FEER* (2 November 1979), 53-4.

31 *FEER* (31 August 1979), 63. I have drawn on the articles published in *FEER* issues of 13 April and 31 August in offering this assessment of the latest position of the Malaysian economy.

1. Sir Hugh Low, British Resident, Perak 1877-89

2. Tengku Abdul Rahman, Prime Minister 1957-70, in May 1977

3. Tun Abdul Razak, Prime Minister 1970-76, in May 1974

4. Datu Hussein Onn, Prime Minister since 1976, in March 1979

5. General Sir Gerald Templer, High Commissioner of the Federation of Malaya, witnessed by six representatives from Tanjong Malim, opens replies to his confidential questionnaire to each household of the town asking for information on local Communists, March 1952

6. The Emergency Special constables guard factory installations against bandits who have already attacked the area, but who have been driven off

7. Malaya's first King, the Yang di-Pertuan Agong, inspects a guard of honour at the state opening of parliament in Kuala Lumpur in 1959

8. Federal elections, August 1974. Last-minute guidance for voters at a Setapak polling booth

9. Tapping a rubber tree: a thin sliver of bark is cut away to renew the flow of latex down the sloping cut for collection in the cup

10. Cocoa seedlings in a Sabah nursery. Cocoa is Sabah's third most important agricultural crop after rubber and oil palm

11. Harvesting an oil palm by cutting through the stalk with a chisel

12. Rubber smallholders weighing their latex at a collecting station

13. Harvesting padi

14. Settlers' houses on a FELDA development scheme near Segamat, Johore

15. Fishermen on the East Coast using the traditional lifting net

16. A gravel pump mine. A powerful jet of water breaks down the working surface. The slurry is pumped up to a sloping separation channel (palong) where the heavier ore is separated by gravity from the mud

17. Oil palm mill at Tanah Merah, Negri Sembilan

18. Electronics factory

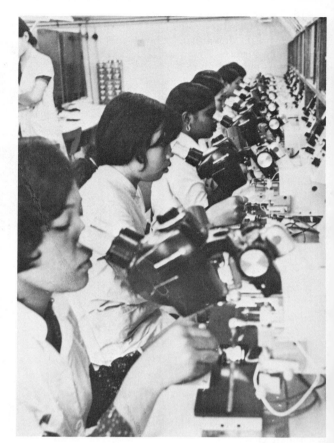

19. The timber company's logging station at Seputin, near Kapit

20. An oil-rig off the coast of Sabah, East Malaysia

21. Bird's-eye view of the Temenggor Dam

22.   A Malaysian patrol unit at the Malay-Thai frontier, July 1977

23.   Vietnamese refugees in Malaysia, 1979

24.   Malaysian troops in their dug-outs on Sebatik Island during Confrontation with Indonesia, 1964

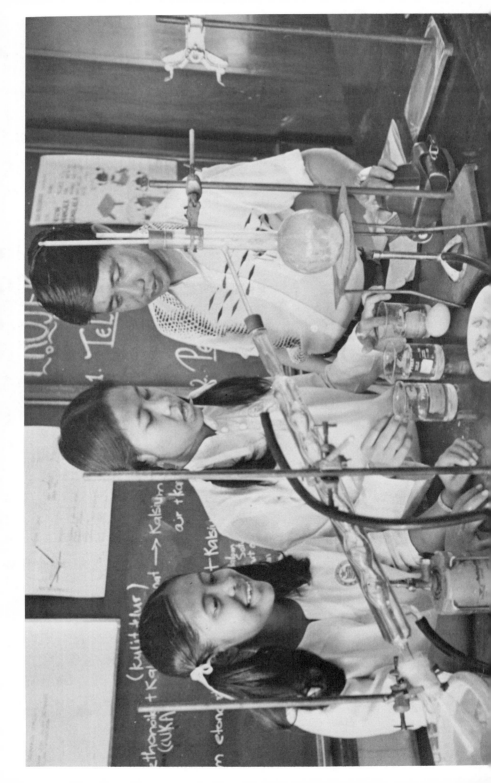

25. Science class in progress in Selangor

26. A Malay wedding. Surrounded by the women of her village, the bride waits in the bridal chamber for the coming of the groom

27. Kek Lok Si Buddhist monastery and temple at Ayer Itam in Penang, founded in 1891

28. Shophouses in Kuala Lumpur's Chinatown area

29. Kuala Lumpur market scene: the traders are mainly Chinese

30. The Ubadiah
Mosque, Kuala
Kangsar, Perak

10 Agriculture, Mining, Industry, and Trade

Agriculture

Malaysia has an abundance of land, sunshine, and water. The soil is not especially fertile and deteriorates rapidly if it is over-exposed to sun and rain. Some of the land is steep or inaccessible, but it is reckoned that out of 32½ million acres in Malaya less than one-third has so far been developed and there is ample land available for development at the present rate until the end of the century and beyond. Sabah and Sarawak are one and a half times as large in area as Malaya and have a huge reserve of undeveloped land suitable for agriculture.[1] To the indigenous cultivation of an essential foodstuff, rice, Malaysia has added two very successful tree crops, which give protection to the soil: rubber and oil-palm. It has hopes of adding another major commercial crop—cocoa—to its resources and of improving half a million acres under coconuts. It is a country whose prosperous economy is based mainly on its agriculture and its farmers.

In 1975 agriculture accounted for 30 per cent of gross domestic product and 45 per cent of export earnings. It employed 1.9 million people, just under half the total working population. Yet almost seven-tenths of the agricultural population had living standards below the poverty-line. In agriculture the main objectives must be to improve techniques, and to augment resources available to the working population on the land so as to lift them above the poverty-line. For reasons already described the future stability of the country depends on progress in this field.

Rubber

In 1978 Malaysia produced slightly less than half the world's entire output of natural rubber. It is the largest industry, in which about one-quarter of the working population is employed. The rubber-tree (*hevea brasiliensis*) is a native of the Amazon valley, but was imported to Singapore and Malaya for experimental work in 1876. Commercial rubber-planting began in the 1890s. From a mere

6,000 acres under rubber in 1910 the industry has expanded to over 4 million in the 1970s; it has not, however, grown significantly over the past decade, though productivity has increased. In brief there was first a period (1900-20) of headlong expansion under the stimulus of world demand for rubber to be used in making tyres for vehicles. The inter-war period (1920-39) was a time of boom and slump as productive capacity fell behind or outstripped world demand, which also fluctuated considerably. A key feature of natural rubber production is the traditional seven-year period between planting a tree and beginning to obtain rubber from it; the period of immaturity has been shortened by modern techniques to four to five years, and yield can be stimulated by the use of chemicals. But in the past and at the present time there is a time-lag of years between a major increase of demand and the consequent increase of supply. A mature rubber-tree has an economic life of about thirty years; once the capacity to produce has been created, it lasts for a generation at least. The two attempts at stabilization of world rubber prices (1924–28 and 1934–41) were a response to excess capacity, generated by the stimulus of scarcity some years earlier. The periods of adversity also saw a necessary reduction in costs of production in an effort to survive; economies were made and productivity was improved. The Japanese occupation (1942–45) did surprisingly little permanent damage, but it had two adverse long-term effects; it interrupted the progress of replanting with improved strains of rubber and it stimulated the growth of a synthetic rubber industry in America. As soon as the post-war rehabilitation work had been completed, there began a more comprehensive programme of replacement of old trees with high-yielding rubber-trees which greatly increased output per acre. Finally in 1956 FELDA was established to promote a massive expansion of planted acreage by opening new land for rubber smallholdings. But the growth of smallholdings was offset in some measure by the conversion of much estate acreage from rubber to the more profitable oil-palm in the course of replanting.

There are four distinct elements in the Malaysian rubber industry; each has its characteristics and its problems. These are the large estates of at least 500 acres (usually much more), the medium estates (100 to 500 acres), the smallholdings developed and owned by individuals, and the government-administered new land schemes under rubber. All holdings of 100 acres or more are classified as estates, but there are considerable differences of type among estates. A smallholding is for statistical purposes a holding of less than 100 acres; but the majority of smallholdings are family farms of no more than 10 acres — usually less than 5.

The large estates are the oldest element of the industry.[2] In the decade 1900-10 the price of natural rubber was high enough to induce a gold-rush by overseas investors, mainly British. In a typical case a public company was floated in London to acquire and develop 1000–2000 acres of land in the FMS, Malacca, or Johor. It might be undeveloped land, but more often it had previously carried a different crop such as coffee or tapioca. In some cases the British company purchased land from local proprietors who had planted rubber which was still immature. The intention of the promoters was to plant and maintain in the first stages as much of their land as the financial resources of the company could support; the expected profits would later be used to expand the planted area to the limits of the estate. Right down to the 1950s plantation companies continued intermittently to plant their 'reserve land', and so the average size of estates increased. There were also amalgamations and acquisitions. Expansion was necessary because the optimum size which would show economies of scale also grew. It is doubtful whether an increase in size beyond, say, 5000 acres reduces management costs on the estate. But for purposes of processing the crop, and general commercial management, larger units had greater strength. So companies found it profitable to acquire more than one estate by purchase, merger, etc. The London directors of these companies often had business connections with 'agency-houses', which will be described in a later passage on the trade system of Malaysia. The agency-houses were the merchants and distributors who dominated Malayan external trade during the colonial period.[3] Groups of plantation companies shared the services of agency-houses, which acted as company secretaries in London and as managing and selling agents in Malaya. The managing agents took control of the financial arrangements, the supply of materials and equipment to the estates, and the export, shipment, and sale of their rubber. The estate manager resident on the estate remained responsible for production, agricultural work, the control of labour, and other matters of management on the spot. Both the managing agents and the estate managers were answerable to the directors and there was a certain 'creative tension' between them. The London directors usually included managerial staff drawn from the agency houses who by their greater expertise dominated the boards to which in theory they were answerable as managers. By the 1970s the steady concentration of the rubber-plantation industry had gone so far that five major groups owned and managed more than half the 425,000 acres of large rubber estates; the same groups also had large interests in the production of palm-oil. The characteristics of these plantation groups are central control of policy on production and marketing; standard agricultural techniques used on all estates of the group; and on each estate an elaborate management structure—at the apex the manager (now usually Malaysian), his assistants in charge of divisions of the estate, junior field-factory and office staff, gang foremen (*kanganies*), and a labour force of several hundred workers, women as well as men, engaged in tapping, weeding (i.e., field maintenance), and processing. In some cases the latex is not processed on the estate but is transferred each day by tanker-lorry to a central plant shared by several estates. The large estates use the most advanced techniques of agricultural production and processing, and are the technological leaders of the industry.[4] Their critics argue that the essential techniques of rubber-growing and production are well within the capacity of smallholders aided by a good advisory service and the use of local processing centres for their latex. The smallholder is a more flexible producer since he has no overhead expenditure, and usually has other activities to which he can transfer his efforts to augment his income. There is a place in the industry for both types. But smallholder acreage is likely to continue its steady increase; estate acreage tends to contract as rubber estates are either subdivided to create smallholdings or converted to other crops such as oil-palm in the course of periodic replanting. An account has been given in the previous chapter of the gradual transfer of control and ownership of the plantation groups into Malaysian hands.

The rubber industry, and especially the large estates, have since the war been spurred to greater efficiency by the competition of synthetic rubber. Until the mid-1970s synthetic rubber made from petro-chemicals was comparatively cheap. It was sold at prices which were fixed for a considerable period ahead. In physical properties it was originally inferior to natural rubber, but over the years improvement of synthetic rubber has closed the gap. Both synthetic and natural rubber each have some uses for which they are preferred, but the main determinant of the industrial consumer's choice is price. In the past he has also tended to give synthetic rubber preference for its consistent and specific physical qualities. Natural rubber is more variable — it is an organic product and its primary processing on the estate or smallholding is not uniform; standards of cleanliness, for example, may vary. To compete in price the natural-rubber industry has raised its productivity so as to reduce its costs. The main means has been the replacement — over a long cycle of years — of low-yielding by high-yielding rubber. In the early days a rubber-tree was just a rubber-tree — one of the descendants of the strains imported in 1876. But in the 1920s there was experimental work in reproduction, mainly by budgrafting, of strains selected for their high yield. The replacement of the old rubber by the new strains began on the estates in the 1930s and was continued after the interruption of the war. Fertilizers, leguminous cover-crops, and chemical stimulants can also be used to increase output. As a result some 95 per cent of the planted area of estates is now under high-yielding rubber; the average yield is about 1,200 lb per acre *per annum,* as compared with about 400 lb before the war. Estate yields are also about a third higher than those on smallholdings planted with high-yielding rubber.[5] To compete in quality with synthetic rubber, natural rubber has been improved both in processing and in technical grading. Some estates produce concentrated latex instead of dry rubber for making special kinds of rubber products. Dry rubber is also produced as 'block rubber' of much higher consistency than the traditional 'ribbed smoked sheet' (RSS). A considerable proportion of Malaysian rubber exports are graded under the Standard Malaysian Rubber (SMR) scheme which gives the consumer a predicted range of physical properties according to the grade which he may choose to buy. With the passing of the era of cheap petro-chemicals the competition of synthetic rubber is no longer a threat to the existence of the natural rubber industry. The outlook for the technically progressive sector of the industry is more favourable than at any time since 1945. The Malaysian government is now concerned that output should continue to grow in line with world demand in the 1980s.[6]

The small estates in the 100–500 acre range make up about 250,000 acres of land under rubber. These are generally properties owned by absentee Malaysian Chinese or Indian owners, sometimes family groups or partnerships. As was explained in the previous chapter, land is still the traditional and esteemed investment medium for the savings or other surplus capital of the middle-class town-dweller. Too often the owners leave the property in the charge of a resident foreman, and are content to receive the share of the profits which he remits to them without being concerned (neither is he) with long-term measures of improvement such as replanting, which in the short term reduce income. However, about two-thirds of the acreage of this group is now under high-yielding rubber, though agricultural standards generally are not high. A few of the more farsighted proprietors arrange with the manager of a nearby large estate that he will act as visiting manager to inspect and advise. This relatively unimportant sector of the rubber industry is likely to continue on its undynamic way unless the government enforces more rapid improvement.

Any holding of less than 100 acres is classified as a smallholding, but the large majority are small family holdings owned and worked as an adjunct to the cultivation of rice, coconut, etc., as a mixed farm. Most of these holdings were planted with rubber in the first quarter of this century. When rubber-planting began, the pioneers were the estate proprietors, and the government was disposed to restrict rubber-planting to them. In 1906, for example, the British Resident of Selangor, whose knowledge of the subject was better than most officials, instructed that land which was accessible because it fronted on to public roads should be reserved for 'scientific planting', i.e., estate development.[7] In fact smallholders' methods were more efficient than those of estates until the latter began to replant with high-yielding rubber during the 1930s.[8] This was because the smallholders, unlike the estates, did not 'clean weed' their land; it was found by experience that this practice caused erosion. The main reasons for the official discouragement of rubber-planting by smallholders were the apparent inefficiency of their cultivation methods, the fluctuating returns, the temptation to the smallholder to take a quick profit by sale of newly-planted rubber land, and the view that the smallholder was better employed in his traditional function of rice cultivation. The sale of smallholdings under rubber led to the passing of the Malay Reservations Enactment of 1913 with very far-reaching effects (Chapter 4). But there was no stemming the tide; rubber was a more profitable crop than rice.[9] The land offices were inundated by applications from Malays for land on which to plant rubber; they also converted existing holdings from other crops to rubber despite official efforts to restrain them. When the second period of rubber restriction began in 1934, smallholders in Malaya were producing as much rubber as the estates and from a rather smaller acreage.[10] But in developing rubber land the Malay villager did not aim to concentrate exclusively on this one crop; or if he did, he was unable to obtain the 8–10 acres of land which he needed if his family holding was under rubber alone. The majority of holdings under rubber were of no more than 3 to 5 acres. Such land was subject to Islamic law of inheritance and so it was often subdivided at least once in a generation. The inadequate size of the Malay smallholding is a major problem.

For quite different reasons it was also official policy to refuse, save in exceptional circumstances, applications for land for smallholdings from Chinese or Indians. They were transient workers who might be expected to return to China or India rather than settle in Malaya. From about 1922 there was a general restriction on the alienation of land for rubber-planting to anyone; this policy was introduced in support of the schemes for restricting output of rubber from existing planted land. The ban, which continued with only slight remission until after the war, was more of an impediment to smallholders who had no unplanted land than to plantation companies which, as explained above, often had substantial areas of 'reserve land' within their boundaries.

Replanting with high-yielding rubber offered the same advantage to smallholdings–much-increased income in the long run, as to estates. But for two reasons the replanting of smallholdings has always lagged behind. For technical reasons it is not practicable to replant successfully on a smaller area than, say, an acre. This is no problem to an estate which, if it replants 3 per cent of its area each year working to a 30-year cycle, is likely to replant each year much more than one acre; 3 per cent of, say, 2,000 acres is 60 acres a year. But the smallholder who has about 4 acres in all must then replant a quarter of his entire holding in one year instead of 3 per cent. The second factor is the interval of 6 or 7 years between felling the old trees and obtaining a crop from the new ones. An estate working to a 3 per cent annual replanting programme may have a fifth of its area out of production at all times. But it can sustain itself with the income from the other four-fifths. The smallholder who replants the minimum of an acre a year will have a decreasing income for a few years and then none at all until his earliest replanted acre comes back into production. The loss of income on this scale is a severe disincentive to replanting.

This problem is resolved if the smallholder can be given new land to increase the size of his total holding. When the new land, planted with rubber, has come into bearing, its high yield will probably compensate him in full for the loss of income during immaturity if he then replants his old land. But in the more densely populated areas there may be no suitable undeveloped land within a reasonable distance of his existing holding. Where there is such land, however, at the edge of an existing block of smallholdings, it is developed in this fashion under a 'fringe alienation' scheme. Replanting costs money — as well as reducing income temporarily. Cash grants (related to acreage) are made by instalments over the period in which the rubber is immature. The smallholder also gets technical advice and encouragement. In particular, replanting requires for its success special measures to restore the fertility (partially depleted by growing the old stand of trees), and to maintain optimum conditions for the growth of the new trees.

A Rubber Industry Smallholders' Development Authority (RISDA) dispenses financial and technical aid to smallholders who replant their land. Of the total of about 2,320,000 acres of smallholdings (other than those on land-settlement schemes), approximately two-thirds has so far been replanted with high-yielding rubber, much of which is still immature. The Third Malaysia Plan called for replanting of the remainder at a rate which would complete the task in about ten years.[11] But actual progress in the first half of the period was less than half of this requirement. The trees standing on these unreplanted holdings are long past the end of their normal economic life and can hardly be worth tapping. In the end some holdings may have to be abandoned to revert to jungle or, if they form part of a block of adjacent holdings, surrendered when their owners move to new land-development schemes. They could then be replanted as a block and the total area divided into new holdings of economic size. But such a procedure represents a major upheaval in village life with all the social problems which arise from that.

Rubber smallholders also need efficient processing facilities and a good marketing system so that they can produce rubber of satisfactory quality and obtain a larger proportion of its value. Ambitious schemes for processing at large central factories have proved cumbersome and expensive.[12] The present strategy is to promote the establishment of over two thousand 'smallholder development centres', so that each smallholder can bring his latex to a small but adequately equipped centre near his holding and carry out the simple processing by his own labour. The same centres serve as stores and distribution points for fertilizers, weedicides, and other materials. The government agency in charge of processing and marketing schemes is the Malaysian Rubber Development Corporation (MARDEC), which in 1978 handled directly some 80,000 tonnes of rubber at large plants with about double that capacity.

The fourth element of the rubber industry is the smallholdings developed on the new land-settlement schemes by FELDA. Blocks of land of 4,000 acres or more are cleared of jungle by the use of machines and paid labour, which may include the prospective settlers. The land is planted with rubber (or oil-palm), using the same methods and technique as estates. When the rubber-trees are mature, the land is divided into holdings of about 10 acres, of which about eight are under rubber, and the rest are a house site and land available for other crops. Eight acres is about the optimum size for a family holding; a tapper can tap about 4 acres a day, but works his holding on an 'alternate daily' system like the estates. The latex is processed at a central factory. In these circumstances the income of a smallholder is very much larger than he could get from his old and much smaller holding with its poor rubber. He is required over a period of years to repay part of the cost of development of his land. The FELDA programme has been carried forward boldly and effectively since its inception in 1956. FELDA has some 300,000 acres in various stages of development as rubber land, and the pace is accelerating to a rate of about 50,000 acres *per annum*. This method is undoubtedly expensive and it remains to be seen how much of the contribution due from the smallholders can be recovered. Costs could be reduced—but with some loss of efficiency—by greater use of the labour of the new settlers on a co-operative basis. Settlement in large areas under central direction is also a change in the village way of life (Chapter 13).

Yet another government agency, the Federal Land Consolidation and Rehabilitation Authority (FELCRA), attends to the rehabilitation of neglected land, the supervision of 'fringe alienation' schemes, and the like. Whereas FELDA puts the bulldozers in, FELCRA has to work by different and less wholesale methods. New smallholdings may be created in two other ways. Occasionally an estate is sold for fragmentation. The buyer divides up the land and sells it off as smallholdings. This transfer of land from the estate to the smallholder sector reached a high level in the late 1950s and early 1960s, but has since declined. About 400,000 acres have been so transferred since the war.[13] It is a process which has caused hardship to the labourers, mainly Indian, who were employed on the estates before sale (Chapter 13). It has, however, been a valuable source of rubber land available for acquisition by Chinese smallholders who cannot readily participate in the government schemes. Of the smallholders registered with RISDA about one-third are Chinese, but the average size of their holdings is larger than for the Malays: about 8 acres. Finally the State governments also promote small-scale land settlement schemes.

In Sabah and Sarawak the rubber industry has about 750,000 acres, of which the major part is smallholdings.[14] Replanting with high-yielding rubber has made very slow progress and the average yield per acre is way below the Malayan level. If the 100,000 acres of planned replanting over the period 1976-80 is in fact achieved, it will have to be continued for decades to complete the task.

As the Malaysian rubber industry moves into the second half of the NEP period (1970-90), it faces neither new threats to its existence nor new roads to salvation. The problems have been identified and effective remedies have been found. It is a matter of slogging away, particularly in those areas, such as replanting of smallholdings, where progress to date has been slow. The question of price stabilization will be considered later (Chapter 11).

Palm-Oil

Ever since rubber began to dominate the Malayan economy three-quarters of a century ago, there has been a search for at least one other—preferably more than one—crop to supplement it. To protect the topsoil from erosion on sloping ground, any major crop must be a tree which provides some permanent cover. Coffee, which preceded rubber at the end of the nineteenth century, was itself the successor to other unsuccessful crops.[15] Coconuts, the 'consols of the East', have failed to deserve their reputation. In the period between the wars tea was planted at both high and low altitudes, but it has not been a success. Cocoa, after much trial and experiment since 1947, now seems to be an established crop—we will come to that later. The one great achievement in agricultural diversification has been the development of an oil-palm industry, which has grown so much that Malaysia is now the largest single producer of palm-oil in the world.

It is said that all the oil-palms of Southeast Asia are the progeny of four palms grown at the Bogor experimental garden in Java, from seed imported from West Africa in 1848. The oil-palm was grown in Malaya as an experimental and ornamental tree from the late nineteenth century. In the first commercial plantings of 1917 the seed used was of the Deli (Sumatra) type, but its exact provenance is not recorded. The rubber plantation companies at first viewed the new crop with misgiving; the edible oil market was dominated by other oils and by very large industrial consumers. In the 1930s, however, three plantation groups developed large oil-palm estates in Johor and in north-west Malaya. By 1947 the aggregate planted acreage of the three pioneers — British, Danish, and French — had reached 78,000 acres. When the outlook for natural rubber looked black in the mid-1950s and a major programme of replanting old rubber land was beginning, the general body of plantation companies began to plant oil-palms — much of this was on land which had previously been under rubber or coconut. By 1962 the planted acreage in Malaya had doubled to 153,000 acres. There was also some planting of oil-palm in Sabah. Apart from spreading the risks of price fluctuation by diversification, the main attraction to the plantation companies was that oil-palms generally gave a much higher profit per acre than rubber at that time (and down to the present time). Accordingly in the early 1960s FELDA began to include oil-palms as well as rubber in its development schemes. Thereafter planted acreage and output expanded at a fantastic rate. By 1978 planted acreage was about 2 million acres and output had reached 1.7 million tonnes, which was 46 per cent of world production and a much larger proportion of world exports (as the West African territories retain part of their output for local consumption).

The increase in output reflected improved technique as well as expanded acreage. The oil is extracted from the soft pericarp which surrounds the kernel. New strains of palm were developed with fruit in which the pulp is a larger proportion of the fruit (the *tenera* strain). The oil-palm is, however, a more demanding crop than the rubber-tree. It generally grows better in coastal areas than in the drier inland areas. To obtain optimum results it requires the carefully controlled application of fertilizers, and the harvesting of the fruit bunches on an 8 to 10-day cycle so that they are brought in when they are neither under- nor over-ripe. For the same reason they must be processed at the mill without delay — otherwise the quality of the oil deteriorates. Unlike rubber-processing, powerful, complicated, and expensive machinery is required to extract the oil from the fruit and to purify it. Hence the economies of scale call for large oil-mills with the capacity to process the fruit harvested from several thousand acres under palms. The minimum is about 4,000 acres per mill, but some serve as much as 25,000 acres — as the size of the area increases so does the cost of transport to the mill by lorry or light railway. The economic life of an oil-palm is limited by its height which increases with each year of its life. There comes a point when the fruit bunches, which may weigh 50 lb each, are 30–40 feet above the ground and cannot be cut down by waving a harvesting knife on the end of a long pole. It may be possible to breed a satisfactory 'dumpy' palm or to invent a workable mechanism for harvesting at a height, but these possibilities are still at the experimental stage. The development of high-yielding strains will be made more rapid and reliable if new techniques of vegetative propagation replace conventional plant-breeding by seed.

If the palm-oil price remains at a profitable level, further expansion of oil-palm acreage may be expected both by FELDA and (if new land is made available) by estates. In 1978 FELDA had 633,000 acres under oil-palms and produced from the mature acreage 340,000 tonnes of oil. Smallholder production requires a different organization from the outright allocation of, say, 18 acres to an individual producer. FELDA has been experimenting with various forms of group-working. The block system, under which groups of settlers work about 300 acres on a co-operative basis, comes nearest to combining the autonomy of village life with the technical requirements of oil-palm cultivation and harvesting. Wherever it has a substantial output FELDA establishes its own central mills; elsewhere the fruit is sold to nearby estate mills.

Palm-oil production is more profitable than rubber, but it is less labour-intensive. It affords employment on the scale of about 18 acres per family as compared with 8 acres for rubber. The world price of palm-oil fluctuates considerably in line with the general movement of edible oil prices. Vegetable oils are mutually interchangeable (within limits) in the manufacture of margarine and for other purposes. The key indicator is usually the price of soya-bean oil, which is produced in much larger quantities than palm-oil. At one time almost the entire Malaysian output of palm-oil was exported as a purified but essentially crude product. However, the bulk of it is now sold to local refiners and exported as refined oil. In addition to the oil obtained from the fleshy fruit, another valuable oil is extracted from the crushed kernels. Palm-oil is a Malaysian success story. The outlook is good.[16]

Coconuts

The coconut-palm grows best on low-lying coastal land. Most smallholders have a few palms as a source of food, but some 100,000 families in Malaysia (one-third of them in Sabah and Sarawak) depend on the sale of copra as the main source of their income. It is not a profitable crop. Most of the former coconut estates of the west coast of Malaya have converted to oil-palm. A moderate increase in smallholdings has raised total Malaysian acreage from just under to just over 800,000 acres in the 1970s. But more than half the growers are below the poverty-line due to the uneconomic size of holdings, the low productivity of over-age palms, and the poor standard of upkeep. Many of them are aged fifty or more since the younger generation has tended to move away to the towns or the new land-settlement schemes.[17] In spite of this gloomy situation it is possible to rehabilitate and improve coconut land by replanting with improved strains of palm and by better processing and marketing. But the most effective means of raising profitability of coconut smallholdings is interplanting with cocoa.[18]

Cocoa

In the period since the war hopes of establishing cocoa as a third major commercial crop in Malaysia have risen and fallen as each problem of agricultural technique has been solved and then succeeded by another. In terms of soil conditions, partial shade, etc., cocoa is a demanding crop. But the recent success of a number of estates in growing cocoa on a commercial scale suggests that the point of 'take-off' may have been reached. In 1979 acreage had reached 150,000 acres and output—three-quarters from Malaya and the rest from Sabah—30,000 tonnes.[19]

Other commercial crops

In the century and a half of Malaysian commercial agriculture, pepper, gambier, tapioca, sugar-cane, coffee, tea, tobacco, and pineapple have come on stage with a flourish only to make an exit as a failure or retreat to the back of the stage. Coffee, which led the field in the 1890s, has almost disappeared. Tea estates in lowland Malaya have not been a success, but those in the Cameron Highlands are more flourishing. Gambier and tapioca are grown on a small scale, but they exhaust the soil. The cultivation of pepper is now mainly in Johor and Sarawak, where it covers upwards of 20,000 acres. Tobacco is one of the old crops which is making a modest comeback.[20] Sugar was a major crop in north-west Malaya in the first half of the nineteenth century. It survived various vicissitudes until displaced at the end of the century by rubber, to which the estate-owners converted their land. There has been a revival in recent years and some 25,000 acres is now under sugar.[21] But these new estates have yet to demonstrate their long-term viability. Malayan exports of tinned pineapple have to compete in a world market which is very discriminating over quality (Malayan pineapples are not the best).

In addition to the crops which are grown on a commercial scale, there is a substantial production on smallholdings of fruit and vegetables for sale in the local market. Fruit-growing is a valuable sideline for the Malay smallholder. The production of vegetables is often combined with pig-rearing by Chinese farmers, since the pigs provide the necessary manure for intensive cultivation of vegetables. Although these are small farms, they produce in the aggregate a large quantity of foodstuffs and account for a considerable acreage.

Rice

There are two different methods of rice-growing in Malaysia.[22] 'Wet rice' (*padi sawah*) is grown on flat land which should be flooded to a controlled depth of a few inches throughout the several months of the growing season. 'Dry rice' or 'hill rice' (*padi bukit*) is grown in new clearings on hillsides in a manner which exploits the fertility of the land. Dry-rice cultivation has been discouraged in Malaya and is of little importance. In Sabah and Sarawak this shifting cultivation continues in remote areas, but the aim is to replace it by wet rice which gives a much higher yield per acre.

Within Malaya the cultivation of wet rice displays considerable differences of technique between different regions of the country. On the plains of the north-west and north-east, and also in the Krian, Sungei Manik, and Tanjong Karang districts of the west central coast, there are very large areas of 50,000 to 200,000 acres of land, almost all of which is under *padi* grown with water supplied from very large irrigation schemes. These are the granaries of Malaya, where the cultivator grows more rice than he himself consumes and has a surplus for sale as the main source of his cash income. Elsewhere in Malaya there are much smaller strips of land under rice. In a typical case there is a strip of varyng width which runs down the valley bottom alongside a stream. It is bounded on either side by rising ground on which stand the houses of the cultivators with their orchard and rubber land behind. In this milieu rice is grown for home consumption as a traditional crop; the farmers obtain their incomes from the sale of rubber or fruit or as wage-labourers. In the main areas of rice cultivation the land is usually tilled by a plough drawn by buffaloes. But in some places the buffaloes are driven round and round the flooded fields so that their hooves churn up the soil. Elsewhere the land is prepared for planting with the hoe. The rice seed is sown in nurseries and the seedlings are planted in the fields by hand – a laborious task which custom assigns to the women. There are local variations in nursery and planting-out techniques. Although wet-rice cultivation is widespread and is associated with many cherished village rituals of pagan origin, it is not as ancient and dominant an element of Malay culture as tradition asserts.

In any kind of wet-rice cultivation, success depends on a controlled water-supply and work in the fields completed by all holders of adjacent land to a common timetable. It has been explained that after an early and expensive experiment in building an irrigation scheme at Krian in Perak, there was a pause until about 1930 (Chapter 4). It is only in modern times that water has been supplied to most rice lands in Malaya from concrete dams, through irrigation channels running over a large area and cut to exactly defined levels. Until this vital change was made, the cultivator relied on damming a stream with a flimsy brushwood dam or on rainwater running off the high land. In some seasons at least he had the discouragement of losing his crop by drought or flood. Rats and other pests and straying buffaloes could also do irreparable damage. Since the 1930s, however, it has been the objective to assure a controlled water-supply everywhere except in the smallest rice lands. In the post-war period the momentum increased with the construction of very large irrigation works in Kedah in the northwest and in Kelantan in the north-east. These schemes, completed in the 1970s, cover about 300,000 acres of rice land altogether. The main benefit of such a scheme is to raise productivity. It may incidentally expand the area of rice land by bringing water to more land at the margin.

There has been some major development of new virgin lands for rice cultivation, notably the Trans-Perak, or Sungei Manik, scheme along the lower reaches of the Perak river, and the Tanjong Karang scheme on the north-west coast of Selangor. It was estimated in 1956 that there were then about 750,000 acres of undeveloped swampland. But it was overlaid by sterile peat and would require prolonged treatment to render it fertile.[23] The cost of opening new land, with all the ancillary development required, is prohibitive. There are similar possibilities—and similar constraints—of new land development in Borneo, more especially in Sarawak. For the time being at least it is more economic to secure higher output by raising yield per acre, rather than by opening new land for rice.

In the drive for higher output—and also the relief of poverty among rice-farmers—the key element is double-cropping. A normal main rice crop matures in about seven months from planting. In the five-month off-season it is possible to take either a second quick-growing rice crop or some alternative crop. During their occupation of Malaya, the Japanese introduced Taiwanese strains of rice for planting as the second off-season crop. This experiment was not successful, but over the ensuing years plant geneticists have developed suitable strains of Malayan rice. A second crop in the same year requires irrigation to assure a water-supply in the off-season; chemical fertilizers must be used to maintain fertility; the timetable imposes on the rice-farmer a more demanding cycle, since he must work instead of resting or celebrating after his main harvest. The cycle might be speeded up to save time by the use of tractors to draw the ploughs. But difficulties of technique have not yet been resolved, and mechanization is uneconomic in an agricultural community which suffers from under-employment and low incomes. There has been a sustained effort to extend double-cropping; by 1980 about two-thirds of Malayan rice land will be irrigated in such a way that double-cropping is possible.[24] At best double-cropping is a precarious means of increasing output; in the 1977-78 season, for example, total crop fell by a quarter because a severe drought caused a failure of the double-cropping programme.[25]

Sabah and Sarawak have about 450,000 acres of rice land—about half the Malayan acreage. But much of it is under hill rice and so the yield is lower and double-cropping is not possible. But the proportion of wet-rice cultivation is increasing, and with improved irrigation comes the possibility of double-cropping. The more primitive agricultural systems of Borneo will not reach Malayan standards for decades to come.[26]

In spite of its declared objective of breaking down communal specialization of economic function, the government shows no sign of opening rice cultivation to the non-Malay communities—nor is there much demand from them since rice is not as profitable as other crops. Where the Chinese have become rice growers, they have been efficient and successful.[27] Hence the continuing poverty of the rice-farmer is almost entirely a Malay problem. The man who both owns his land and takes a double crop is relatively prosperous. At the other extreme, poverty dogs the tenant farmer who grows a single annual crop. But even this contrast is only relative; it is reckoned that about 70 per cent of the former are below the poverty-line as compared with 90 per cent of the latter.[28] It is a very large problem since about 140,000 families depend on rice-growing as the main source of their livelihood. It is also a localized problem; nine-tenths of this group are settled in the north-west and north-east.

The poverty of the rice-farmer reflects pressure on the land. More than half of them have farms of less than 3 acres, and four-fifths have less than 5 acres. As already explained, there is no prospect of opening large areas of new land for rice-growing. The aim is to move the surplus population from the rice-growing areas to the new land-settlement schemes where they could grow rubber or oil-palm—thus there will be a double upheaval: a change of residence and of technique. The rice-farmers who remain must also cope with major changes. Their holdings must be consolidated into units of a more economic size; their annual working cycle must be adapted to the more intensive rhythm of double-cropping. The rice-farmer, if he is to escape from poverty, must also retain a higher proportion of the value of his output. Here there are two factors—one the subject of loud complaint and the other veiled in discreet silence. Unlike the rubber smallholder whose income flows throughout the year, the rice-farmer needs seasonal credit, in cash or kind, to meet his living expenses during the growing season and to pay any cultivation costs such as fertilizers. Under the traditional *padi ratus* or *padi kuncha* system, he obtains goods or money by pledging part of his future crop to the local middlemen who resell it to the rice-millers (or buy as the millers' agents). In this way the rice-farmer may lose up to half the value of his saleable surplus. The high cost of this credit reflects the unreliability of the rice-farmer as a debtor as much as the avarice of the middleman, who is usually a Chinese shopkeeper. In the later years of the colonial period attempts were made to break this system by the encouragement of co-operative credit and marketing societies among the growers, by the establishment in the main rice-growing areas of government-owned rice-mills to break the commercial monopoly, and by offering to buy rice at a price fixed each season at about the expected market level. In recent times government funds have been injected into the co-operative system through special lending agencies, and a Federal Agricultural Marketing Authority (FAMA) operates on a wider scale to buy and mill rice. Fertilizers are distributed to encourage double-cropping; this and other technical assistance is given through a network of 'farmers' organizations' (FO), with its inevitable Authority (FOA) to provide the higher co-ordination.

Less is said of the burden of rent paid by the tenant farmer to his landlord. Rice lands are generally within the limits of Malay Reservations, where the ownership of land is confined to Malays, sometimes well-to-do neighbours, but often absentee landlords of the Malay middle and upper class. Agricultural tenancy among rice-farmers is a modern phenomenon resulting from pressure of population on the land, fragmentation due to division on inheritance, and the heavier cost of developing wet-rice land.[29] There is some legislation to protect the tenant farmer, but the absence of published information suggests that it is a neglected as much as an intractable problem. It needs radical treatment to enlarge the size of holdings and make the occupier the owner of the land which he works.

The rice industry has also to be considered as part of the national economy. The territories of Malaysia have never been self-sufficient in rice. In the pre-war period more than half the total domestic consumption was imported mainly from Thailand and Burma. Since the 1930s the aim has been to make the country as self-sufficient as possible. This factor, as much as the social needs of the Malay rice-farmer, has been the justification for heavy investment in the construction of irrigation works. With the steady increase of population in the traditional exporting countries of Southeast Asia, the supplies available for purchase are likely to decrease. There is a government agency for the purchase of imported rice (LPN), and the maintenance of stocks for resale through the local commercial network of distribution. In a year in which the local crop is good, Malaysia produces about three-quarters of the rice which it consumes.[30] The proportion is unlikely to increase.

Fisheries

The east and west coasts of Malaya are in effect the bases of two distinct fishing industries. On the west coast two-thirds of the fishermen are Chinese, who fish in offshore as well as inshore fishing-grounds using power-driven trawlers. The west coast fronts on to the sheltered, though occasionally stormy, waters of the Straits of Malacca. In these waters it is also possible to maintain elaborate fixed fishing-traps in the shallows along the coast. The urban centres along the west coast provide a readily accessible market to which the catch can be swiftly transported by lorry. But up in the north-west on the coast of Kedah, there is a less developed fishing industry in which the fishermen are mainly Malay.

On the east coast, which is exposed to heavy seas during the north-east monsoon season at the turn of each year, it is impossible to maintain fixed fishing-traps. At the height of the stormy weather fishing by boat also is suspended for a few weeks.[31] The fishing communities of Kelantan and Trengganu are entirely Malay, and their organization, although it has adapted itself to such innovations as power-driven boats, reflects a traditional and highly complex economic system.[32]

This is one of the problem areas of Malay rural poverty. Government assistance programmes include subsidies for the purchase of equipment and improved arrangements for credit and marketing. On the coast fishing harbours and jetties have been built together with packing sheds and cold stores. Total fish landings have increased, but not the average catch per unit of fishing-gear, which is the measure of productivity. The decline is due to the depletion of fish stocks within the existing range of the fishing-fleet. It may be possible to extend the fishing to distant waters by the use of larger craft. But such a change will impose on the fishermen major changes in their traditional way of life. A better solution may be to move some of the fishermen to settle on the new land-development schemes. This change would probably be acceptable since many fishermen, despite their seagoing tradition, come from communities or even from families, which also grow crops. It is a very mixed economy along the north-east coast of Malaya.

Animal Husbandry

The rearing of animals for meat or milk, and poultry for eggs or meat, is a small part of the agricultural economy. Malay villagers keep buffaloes partly for drawing the plough on their rice land, and partly for occasional slaughter to provide meat in quantity on a special occasion such as a wedding feast. The grazing of dairy cattle and goats is more often in the hands of north Indians. Indian Hindus keep cows, but their religious practices prohibit their slaughter for meat. A small but expert Veterinary Department has been as much concerned with economic development as with animal health. The former is now in the hands of a special agency (MAJUTERNAK). In Malaysia the limiting factors on animal husbandry are insect-borne diseases and the general lack of good grazing. If land is cleared of jungle and put to no other use, it soon becomes covered by coarse grasses which have little or no nutritional value.

Timber

The Malaysian rain-forest contains considerable quantities of valuable hardwood timber, for which there are export markets in countries such as Japan and Australia. When land is cleared for agriculture, it is the practice to extract the saleable timber before the rest is burnt. It is necessary to preserve forest-cover on steep land as a soil-conservation measure. But this is compatible with the controlled and selective extraction of valuable timber. Logging and sawmilling has always been a substantial but secondary activity in Malaya. In Sabah, however, the exploitation of vast reserves of timber provided the main impetus of economic expansion in the years after the war. Until 1952 the right of export was the monopoly of one British company. When timber concession rights became more freely available, this precipitated something of a gold-rush which yielded substantial fortunes to some Sabahan Chinese businessmen, and which added to the rather unsavoury atmosphere of Sabahan politics in the 1960s.

The bonanza is now ended. The supplies of growing timber which are both readily accessible to loggers, and can be felled without damage to the essential forest-cover, are dwindling. Malaysia is now committed to a policy of managing its forest reserves as a permanent and continuing source of timber-supply. As a part of this policy it has become necessary to switch the areas of exploitation from the lowland swamps to the drier hill-slopes. This change in turn requires more stringent measures of soil conservation. Timber and sawn logs accounted for about 17 per cent in value of Malaysian exports in 1970; by 1978 the value of these exports had almost trebled, but as a proportion of the total it had fallen to 15 per cent. Sawmills are a useful local industry; the production of wood products such as veneers, chipwood, plywood, etc., has grown both to meet local demand as for export.

Mining

Tin

The Malayan tin industry (there is no tin in Sabah or Sarawak) has outlived several expert forecasts of impending exhaustion of its ore reserves.[33] The size of available reserves which it is economic to work is not static, but varies with the efficiency and cost of working methods and the world price of tin. In the first quarter of the century there was a major improvement in methods of mining. In recent years the price of tin has risen sharply.

When Chinese immigrants first arrived to work as tin-miners in the mid-nineteenth century, they began to develop the richest alluvial deposits at shallow depths.[34] A rectangular pit was dug by hand to a depth not usually exceeding 30 feet to remove the nonproductive overburden and reach the ore-bearing strata. Baskets of ore were carried up out of the mine slung at the ends of a pole across the shoulders of a labourer who walked up an inclined treetrunk. In this country of heavy rainfall an open pit soon fills with surface water. The Chinese adapted from its use in the rice-fields of south China a form of chain-pump (*chin chia*), driven by a waterwheel from a nearby stream. This was their only mechanical device. The first attempts at mechanized mining, using steam-pumps, were made by British companies in the 1880s. These were badly managed and failed. But the sale of their surplus equipment to Chinese miners aided the first beginnings of mechanization. The two most widely used modern methods of tin-mining, the gravel-pump and the dredge, were introduced early in the twentieth century, but their full impact was not felt until the 1920s. A gravel-pump mine is essentially still an open-cast mine—a hole in the ground. The vertical working face of the ore-bearing stratum is broken down by directing on to it a powerful jet of water. The slurry from the bottom of the mine is then raised to the surface by pumping it through a pipe. It is there run over an elevated, sloping wooden runnel (the *palong*—which is the characteristic visible sign at ground level of a mine). Low barriers across the runnel check the flowing mixture, and the heavier tin ore is thus retained and recovered. A dredge works in a large mining pool, on the surface of which it floats. Its revolving chain of buckets lift ore and earth from depths of up to a hundred feet or more below the surface. The dredge excavates the pool at the front and fills it in behind by discharging its tailings (i.e., waste) at the back; the pool thus moves forward over the area to be mined carrying the dredge with it. On the dredge the mixture of ore and earth is separated by more sophisticated devices (jigs), which also function by differences of specific gravity. A modern dredge costs millions of pounds to install; the heavy initial cost cannot be recovered unless the dredge works over several hundred acres of land during a period of 15 or 20 years. A gravel-pump mine costing about $100,000-200,000 is a much more modest investment with usually a shorter life. It is better adapted to small and difficult sites for which a dredge is unsuitable. But the running costs of a gravel-pump mine, including oil used as a fuel for its pumps, are heavy, and rising almost as rapidly as the price of tin itself. Offshore dredges sometimes lift the ore from considerable depths by the use of a suction-pipe instead of buckets. There is one lode mine in Malaya.[35]

By improved technique it has been possible to work profitably land containing very low proportions of ore. When the Kinta valley, the richest tin-field in Malaya, was opened in the 1880s, the Chinese miners reckoned to recover up to 6 *katis* (8 lb) of tin ore from each cubic yard of soil which they lifted. Some modern dredges are working profitably at a recovery rate of a quarter pound of ore per cubic yard.[36] The same land has in some cases been reworked a second or even a third time to recover the tin left behind by earlier miners. But as the dredges come to the end of their existing working sites, they are dismantled for the last time. To dismantle a dredge and rebuild it elsewhere (with considerable replacement of worn-out or obsolete parts) is very costly, and there are few suitable areas left for dredging. The number of dredges has fallen by about a third over the past twenty years. The future lies with the more flexible gravel-pump technique, unless new and extensive mining areas are discovered and made available. The creation of Malay Reservations reserved to agriculture in 1913 effectually closed considerable areas of Malaya to prospecting. In the post-war period the difficulties of the Emergency period also discouraged prospecting. But some new areas of dredgeable size have been found, and there is also prospecting for tin in the offshore areas at the mouth of Malayan rivers. Apart from following the ore out to sea it may be possible to trace it back into the lodes from which it originated. In any new mining ventures *bumiputra* participation will be the price of obtaining the necessary mining rights. There is already one such joint venture.

The recent sharp rise in metal prices has in a few years almost quadrupled the price of tin. This must have its effect in making it economic to mine marginal ground. But the rise in the price of oil, which accounts for about one-third of gravel-pump mining costs, has a contrary effect. Malayan output of tin, which reached a peak of 72,600 tons in 1970, has fallen back to about 60,000 tons. The slow decline seems likely to continue. But in terms of value, falling output may be offset by rising price. Tin-mining is no longer a major source of employment.

Other Minerals

Before and after the war Malayan iron ore was produced for export to Japan. The two main deposits have now been exhausted and the mines were closed in the 1970s. The former small-scale production of bauxite is also virtually at an end. Japanese interests are working a copper mine in Sabah;[37] prospecting for copper deposits is in progress both in Sabah and in Malaya. At one time coal of a fairly low grade was produced for use by the Malayan Railways. But when the railway changed over to diesel locomotives, the colliery closed.

Petroleum

The first working oil-field in the Malaysian region was and still is in Brunei, which is surrounded by Sarawak territory but is not a part of Malaysia. The production of oil in Sarawak has expanded rapidly in the 1970s with the development of offshore wells. Prospecting for offshore oil is also in progress along the coasts of Malaya. Increasing volume combined with rising world prices will make petroleum a major element of the Malaysian economy—as long as the deposits last. In 1979 production was expected to exceed 300,000 barrels per day (as compared with less than 20,000 in 1970). Output on this scale was estimated to be worth $3½ billion annually, but with prices still rising this may be too low. In 1978 government revenue from the petroleum industry already exceeded the combined yield of export duties on rubber and palm-oil.[38] Petroleum accounts for 13–15 per cent of export earnings.

As explained in Chapter 9, this sudden windfall has been a most welcome aid to economic expansion; it has filled a gap caused by shortfall in other production and investment. Although Malaysia may again be a net importer of oil in the mid-1980s, it is hoped that by then there will be substantial exports of natural gas from the field at Bintulu in Sarawak now in course of development. The state-owned corporation PETRONAS, established in 1975, has a legal monopoly of the exploitation of Malaysian oil and natural gas. Its aim is to replace the original system of exclusive concessions granted to international oil companies in return for royalty payments with a system of joint-production arrangements and participation by PETRONAS in 'downstream' processing and distribution. All this is in accord with the general practice of the larger oil-producing countries. But the international companies have an unhappy memory of the Indonesian fiasco in which the state-owned oil corporation (PERTAMINA) became over-extended and collapsed.[39] Until 1976 PETRONAS (with PERNAS described in Chapter 9) was part of the power-base of the ambitious Tunku Razaleigh (now Minister of Finance). But some rather inept dealings with the producing companies threatened the continued expansion of production. Responsibility for this key subject was transferred to the office of the Prime Minister and some of the regulatory powers conferred by the Petroleum Development Act remain in abeyance. But in this as in other fields of the economy the government is very much master in its own house.

Despite its importance to the national economy, the petroleum industry stands apart from it. The oil-wells are far away from the main centres of political power and population. They generate vast wealth but do not create local employment on a significant scale. A developing country has always a difficult choice to make in determining the rate at which to permit the exploitation of finite and limited natural resources such as oil or minerals. The doubt has been expressed whether 'the new oil policy is mortgaging the future for present expediencies'.[40] It remains to be seen.

Manufacturing Industry

Factory industries share with petroleum output the distinction of being the most rapidly expanding sectors of the economy. The long-term NEP projection (1970-90) estimates that manufacturing output will rise from 12 per cent of gross domestic product in 1970 to 26 per cent of a much larger total in 1990, when it will have outstripped the old agricultural industries to become the largest single sector in the economy and provide 38 per cent of export revenues.[41] As a sector of rapid growth it offers favourable opportunities of finding employment in the modern side of the economy for Malays. By 1975 Malay employees were one-third of the total workforce at all levels in industry.[42]

The expression 'manufacturing industry' comprehends a wide variety of enterprises. Some are 'resource-based': they exist to process local materials such as rubber, timber, or pineapples. Others make use of imported components or materials — for example the manufacture of textiles, or the assembly of components to make television receivers. These latter industries have been established in Malaysia either to make use of abundant local labour or to gain access on favourable terms to the local market protected by tariffs. Some firms are owned entirely by local proprietors, mainly Chinese; others have been established by foreign enterprises which provide part of the capital and often valuable know-how and established links with overseas markets. The range of manufacturing technique is wide — a sawmill is a very simple process, but the manufacture of electronic equipment, even if it is little more than assembly work, is more complex. There are also considerable differences of size between the different sectors of manufacturing industry. In terms of value of output, the most important manufacturing industries are the processing of food and edible materials such as making canned pineapples and beverages and the refining of palm-oil; the manufacture of textiles which uses imported materials; the sawmills for local timber and the factories which make wood products and furniture; the manufacture of fertilizers and industrial chemicals from imported raw materials; the processing of rubber for export and the manufacture on a limited scale of rubber products such as tyres for the local market. There are several small petroleum refineries using mainly imported crude oil, a steel-mill and a heterogeneous group of light engineering and assembly plants which produce metal products of various kinds. In 1954 the experts of the World Bank Mission rightly predicted that Malayan industrialization would develop on 'a pattern of individually small advances over a wide range of industries'.[43] Apart from its heterogeneity, Malaysian manufacturing industry is essentially on a small scale. In this field Malaysia is not a major world producer as it is in respect of rubber, palm-oil, and tin.

The industries which process some local materials and a few

which exist to supply local needs had their beginnings back in the period of colonial rule.[44] In the early years of independence industrialization was particularly directed at import substitution. A Federal Industrial Development Authority (FIDA) was established to undertake technical and economic research and advisory work. Industrial estates were established and finance for new industries on satisfactory terms assured through MIEL and MIDFL. Under a system of tax remissions for pioneer industries the profits of a new venture could be exempt from Malaysian tax for up to eight years. The offer of tariff protection against the competition of other foreign suppliers may induce a foreign manufacturer to establish a Malaysian factory or assembly plant. The first response to these measures was very small. It was reckoned that over the decade 1957-67 industrialization in Malaya created only 20,000 jobs.[45] In the early stages of such a programme, progress is inhibited by shortages. Because there has hitherto been little demand, there is a lack of trained specialist staff—cost accountants, works supervisors, personnel officers, marketing managers, etc. Every new industry needs the complementary goods and services of others—components or semi-finished products to be bought in, and specialist services to be hired as required. But every advance in a particular area is a general accretion to the pool available for subsequent ventures.

In the early 1970s the tempo of industrialization quickened. The creation of new jobs in manufacturing industry rose to ten times the rate of the 1960s.[46] Moreover, the new factories were sometimes merely the first phase of enterprises planned to double or treble their original size as they became established.[47] These newer and often larger ventures had a different purpose from the earlier efforts at import substitution. They planned to export at least part of their output to overseas markets. Exports of manufactured goods more than trebled.[48] Success, however, had its attendant problems. The upsurge in industrialization was the result of a move into the relatively lush pastures of Malaysia by Japanese and Hong Kong companies. The inducements offered were perhaps over-generous. The expansion of textile manufacture, for example, was almost chaotic. There was little prospect that the output of these new plants could be exported. On the contrary, the recession of 1974-75 caused a contraction of world demand and the raising of barriers against cheap imports of textiles from Southeast Asia.[49]

There were other problems arising from the success of the industrialization programme. The erection of tariff barriers to protect pioneer industries makes the Malaysian consumer a captive to domestic high-cost producers and denies him supplies from a cheaper foreign source. The need to contain inflation and to buy in the cheapest market has always been a different but conflicting objective of Malaysian policy. Administrative control of the new industries was more easily effected in dealings with large foreign concerns which needed government assistance, or at least approval for their projects, than with local, mainly Chinese, concerns which by tradition go their own way and seek to avoid involvement with government agencies. These factors and the NEP philosophy of intervention to 'restructure' the economy led to the enactment in 1975 of an Industrial Co-ordination Act (ICA) as 'a comprehensive law to control manufacturing industries in the country so that industrial progress can be carried out in an orderly manner'. The general effect is that an official licence is required for the establishment of any industry except on a very small scale. The declared purpose is 'to ensure that there are not too many firms in the same line of industry'.[50] It is not the intention to impose a central direction of industry on socialist lines, but to stimulate growth along the lines which the national interest requires.[51] However that may be, the ICA also provides the means to enforce NEP requirements of increasing *bumiputra* ownership, management, and control of the economy. Foreign companies generally manage to accommodate themselves to the ICA without too much difficulty; it is part of their common experience of investment in developing countries. Their main problem is not the manufacturing plant itself, but the establishment of a distributor network which is satisfactory to them and which contains the necessary *bumiputra* participation. To Chinese business interests the ICA has become a bugbear. They protest vigorously at the restrictions and obstacles which they say it imposes on them. In circumstances such as these, the rigour of the law comes to be tempered 'with a reasonable degree of pragmatism'.[52] The similar difficulties over the powers of regulation of the petroleum industry given to PETRONAS have already been mentioned.

Whatever the causes — probably multiple rather than simple — there has been an unwelcome shortfall in industrial expansion during the later 1970s.[53] The main problem is the inadequacy of the domestic Malaysian market and the difficulties of penetrating overseas markets. The 13 million people of Malaysia include many whose poverty and simple living standards prevent them from being regular buyers of manufactured goods. When Malaysia was first established in 1963, Singapore was eager to promote a Malaysian free market for local manufactures. The project was examined by an expert committee under the French economist Jacques Rueff which concluded that Malaya and Singapore at that time were consumer markets of about equal size, since the smaller Singapore population had a higher standard of living. It was estimated that the combined market of the two territories would be 'only just adequate to support efficient production', and that as a separate entity Malaya could not support a programme of industrialization.[54] In the aftermath of Singapore's expulsion from Malaysia the plan was dropped, and Malaysia has since sought a solution in the wider context of Southeast Asian co-operation through ASEAN (Chapter 11).

Industries require power to operate their machines. The limited indigenous reserves of hydrocarbon materials, coal and oil, have been considered above. There is no plan as yet for the generation of electricity from atomic power. But a country which has a rainfall of between 100 and 200 inches *per annum* should be able to produce hydro-electric power. The constraint here is the immensely heavy cost of installing major dams and other plants. But as the price of alternative types of energy rises, hydro-electric schemes begin to look more attractive. A feasibility study has been made of a possible hydro-electric scheme on the Rejang river in Sarawak, which would produce an initial 1,400 megawatts (increasing later to 2,200 megawatts). This would be sufficient to supply all the present requirements of Malaysia and Singapore at half the cost of the present supplies. But it would entail an investment of $1.1 billion.[55]

For the moment, however, the planners direct their attention to more modest and humdrum possibilities. In a country which produces mainly agricultural raw materials and which as a growing problem of rural unemployment, it should be possible to expand labour-intensive, 'agro-based', small-scale industries. The rubber-processing centres, the sawmills, the rice-mills, and the like are individually a drop in the ocean, but collectively they are as useful as the more ambitious, high-technology, capital-intensive factories on the industrial estates.[56]

Trade

The Trade System
The traditional entrepôt trade with other countries of the region

has lost much of its former importance. Singapore, which is the main entrepôt port, is no longer a part of Malaysia, though they remain major trade partners. The trade of Penang with northern Sumatra, south Thailand, and Burma is of purely local significance to Penang. Malaysian exports go mainly to Japan, the European Community, and the United States, which between them absorb almost three-fifths of the total; the same regions supply more than half the goods imported into Malaysia.[57] These trading relationships are further considered in the context of Malaysian foreign policy (Chapter 11). The rice which is needed to make up local production to the level of consumption comes, as it always did, from Thailand and to a lesser extent from Burma. The growing sophistication of the economy has led to a steady increase in the proportion of imports represented by plant and machinery; it has risen from one-eighth in 1955 to one-third of a much-increased volume of imports in 1978. The export trade is still dominated by raw materials which account for about three-quarters of the total. But it is a more diversified trade, including palm-oil, timber, and petroleum, as well as rubber and tin. Within the category of manufactured goods exported there is a growing proportion of electronic and metal products.[58]

The structure of commercial organization in foreign and domestic trade has adapted itself only gradually to the changes in the pattern of trade. In the nineteenth century much of the foreign trade was handled by the 'agency-houses',[59] which first established themselves as distributors of British manufactured goods from Singapore and other major ports in the first half of the century, when Britain was the workshop of the world. The proceeds of sale were received in the local currency, the Spanish or Mexican dollar. This money was invested in the purchase of 'Straits produce' collected in from the region, which was then shipped back to Europe to pay for the manufactures. In the course of this trade the agency-houses became local agents for the shipping lines, insurance companies, etc., with which they did business. In the latter part of the nineteenth century they were increasingly involved in organizing and financing tin-mining and plantation production. They made advances to a planter to be repaid by the coffee, rubber, etc., which he undertook to consign to them. When the rubber boom began early in this century, the new plantation companies floated in London relied on the agency-houses, with their know-how and local connections, and used them as managing agents to oversee the estate management and to handle the commercial side of the new enterprise. Some of the new companies were promoted by the London associates of the Eastern agency-houses. Out of this system came the plantation groups; a number of plantation companies shared the management services of the same firm, acting as secretaries to the companies in London and as agents in Malaya. In particular the agency-houses shipped and sold the estate produce which was the most remunerative part of the connection. They continued their purely commercial trade, known to the management as 'pots and pans', but the developing Malayan economy now required more sophisticated products. The agency-houses therefore developed technical and after-sales services to secure the distributorship of more complex manufactures.

The larger agency-houses had branches 'up country' in the more important towns. But most of the goods which they imported were sold, sometimes from the quayside at the port of entry, to Chinese merchants who in turn resold them to smaller Chinese traders and retailers in the local towns. The nexus which held the system together was the supply of credit: the trader lower down the distribution system obtained goods on deferred payment terms. In the towns the Chinese and Indian merchants were associated in 'chambers of commerce', or specific trade associations such as rice- or textile-importers. In the pre-political era down to 1941 these commercial associations, like the management committees of Chinese schools, often served a more general function as community associations. Through the same commercial links flowed a return trade in rubber and other produce purchased from smallholders and small estates. There was a similar two-way trade in imported manufactures and local produce between the ports of the Straits Settlements and the adjoining territories of the region. Again the local distribution network was mainly Chinese and the agency-houses were usually the importers into the region and the exporters from it. The regional rice trade, however, was in the hands of Chinese merchants since the rice-millers in the exporting countries were also Chinese.

As the Malayan market for manufactured products has grown, and the share of it taken by producers in countries other than the United Kingdom has become larger, the agency-houses have lost their dominant position.[60] Foreign manufacturers sometimes preferred to establish their own distribution networks in association with Chinese firms. The old system has given ground under the weight and diversity of an expanding trade in special products of many kinds. But it is by no means defunct. The agency-houses retain their distributorships over a wide field, and they have branched out into new activities such as joint ventures with local interests, and the installation as well as the supply of specialized equipment.[61]

To the Malay élite who now control the bureaucratic machine of import and trade licensing, the former Anglo-Chinese monopoly is an affront. Measures have been taken both to penetrate and to bypass it (Chapter 9).

Banks and Currency[62]

Until 1941 the main elements of the banking system were the British 'exchange banks', which had grown with Malayan international trade and which existed to provide the services that it needed (and also banking services to the plantation, mining, and commercial enterprises within the country), the local Chinese banks whose customers were mainly the local Chinese merchant community, and some Indian banks of the same type including, however, the specialized Chettiar banking firms (Chapter 5) which provided loans to smallholders among others. It was a heterogeneous and rather alien system, but it served its purposes. In the conscious development of Malayan financial institutions and markets in the 1950s there was considerable debate over the potential role and powers of a central bank.[63] To impose a new regulatory mechanism on the existing system would be a major innovation. The central bank (now Bank Negara Malaysia) was established in 1959 with the temporary aid of some senior staff seconded from the Australian central bank. The Bank Negara has flourished and developed into a major force in the economy. Its success owes much to the personal contribution of the first Malay Governor of the Bank, who has held his office for many years past.[64]

Until 1966 there was no change in the colonial currency system by which the governments of the territories which joined Malaysia (and also Brunei) appointed commissioners who issued a common currency backed by 100 per cent sterling cover. But from 1966, in the aftermath of Singapore's expulsion from Malaysia, the governments of Malaysia, Singapore, and Brunei began to issue their own currencies which for a time circulated side by side with the old currency. When sterling was devalued in 1967, the link with Malaysian currency was broken. The Malaysian *ringgit* (dollar) is a fiduciary issue exchangeable into foreign currencies at floating rates. The currencies of Malaysia and Singapore have no fixed rate of exchange, but are readily interchangeable on an informal basis. Monetary policy is conservative and there are fully adequate foreign-exchange reserves.

The main function of the Bank Negara is to regulate the local banking system. The long-established British exchange banks have been joined by a number of other foreign banks which have branches in Malaysia. The first local Chinese bank was established (in Singapore) in 1903.[65] About a dozen other Chinese banks made their appearance up to 1941; the British banks also extended their services to the Chinese business community. Originally the Chinese banks were small institutions. But expansion and amalgamation in recent years have produced some large and financially powerful Chinese banks which can hold their own with the international banks. Although the importance of the Chettiar banks has diminished, there are a number of Indian banks of a more general character.

Over the last two decades banking has expanded and become a normal service even in the smaller urban centres. There are about forty separate banks, of which about half are 'domestic', i.e., Malaysian-based, with about 500 branches throughout Malaysia. As part of its programme of drawing the rural community into the 'modern' economic system, it is official policy to encourage the spread of branch banking into the smaller towns.

The regulation of the major banks, foreign or Malaysian, is a technical exercise of the normal central bank function on which the periodic reports of the Bank Negara provide much detailed information. There is now a well-developed Malaysian money market and a number of specialized financial institutions such as merchant banks,[66] whose function is both to make loans and to provide advice and other technical services. Some of the small local banks with gross assets of less than $100 million conduct their business with less professional expertise than their larger brethren, and they are subject to the watchful supervision of the Bank Negara. Their boards of directors tend to consist of a single senior executive who in fact runs the bank, and a group of local businessmen whose main interest lies in extracting bank loans on favourable terms. Loans are sometimes made without adequate scrutiny of the borrower's prospects of repayment.[67] It is the object of official policy to create larger and better-managed banks by a process of merger.

Transport and Communications

The road and railway links developed in the colonial period were designed to serve the needs of the tin and rubber industries which were centred on the west coast of Malaya. Trade flowed by road, rail, and coastal shipping between the centres of production and the major ports of Singapore and Penang. In the 1930s an east-coast railway line was built to open up the backward part of Malaya and provide links with Singapore and (through the Thai railway system) with Bangkok. There was a minor and unsuccessful scheme of railway construction in Sabah.[68]

The major deficiencies of the system as a national communications network were the lack of east–west links across the Malay Peninsula (which contributed to the military débâcle of 1941-42), of all-weather roads along the east coast of Malaya, and of any road links at all between the east and west coasts of Sabah and the settlements along the coast of Sarawak. These deficiencies have been gradually remedied since the end of the Second World War.

Passenger travel in Malaysia has been revolutionized in the post-war period by the development of internal air services, which connect the main towns of Malaya and also fly between Malaya and the Malaysian territories in Borneo. At one time Malaysia and Singapore had a joint national air service, but this co-operation, like much else, was a casualty of the break-up of 1965. The state-owned Malaysia Airways System (MAS) provides services over international routes as well as for internal needs. For short journeys in Malaya there are adequate bus services running over a rural secondary-road system which has much improved.

In plans for the improvement of Malaysian communications there is always a determination to outdo or to shake off 'big brother'—Singapore, with its historic role as the commercial capital of the region, and its current aspirations to retain that position. It is not easy to escape domination by the third largest port in the world, but Malaysia will not fail in that objective for lack of determination. The long-term plan for port development provides for four major ports in Malaya. There is no hope of reviving the ancient glories of Malacca, but there are already two major ports on the west coast, Penang and Port Klang (previously Port Swettenham). Port Klang has been doubled in size by developing a second port at a new and better-placed site to supplement the original port, which itself has been much improved. The port of Penang also has been enlarged and its mainland wharves at Prai, long derelict because of silting, have been restored to use. A third major port is being developed at Pasir Gudang near Johor Bahru at the southern end of the Peninsula. It is a port designed to handle the export of the produce of southern Malaya, rubber, palm-oil, etc., which previously was exported through Singapore. On the east coast there was in the past no major port, partly because there was less need of it and partly because this coast is exposed to the north-east monsoon. The development of a new port at Kuantan has been retarded by technical difficulties. It is intended that Kuantan should develop into a major urban centre with a population of 200,000.[69] There is also to be a major port in Borneo, at Bintulu in Sarawak, through which liquefied natural gas will be exported when the Sarawak off-shore fields come into production about 1982.[70] These port-expansion projects include modern equipment for container handling, 'roll on-roll off' cargoes, the handling of timber, etc. At Penang and also at the new port in Johor there are shipbuilding and ship-repair resources. Much of the massive investment in these projects has been provided by Japan either directly or through the Asia Development Bank.

When expansion is planned on such a large scale as this, there are inevitably mistakes and delays which prove costly. The progress of the port-expansion programme has encountered such difficulties. So has the ambitious plan to establish a state-owned international and local shipping-line, Malaysian International Shipping Corporation (MISC), which is scheduled to grow to a million tons of shipping by 1980. A country which is divided by a wide stretch of sea and which has a large foreign trade in bulk cargoes would naturally — and very reasonably — wish to ship a substantial portion of its trade in its own ships. Moreover, the Malays have a seafaring tradition (Chapter 2), and an aptitude as seamen. But the world is over-supplied with shipping, including the national 'flag-carriers' of many developing nations. To launch a large business successfully in such a market requires good timing, good judgement — and sometimes good luck. It is unlikely that MISC will prove to be one of the more profitable state enterprises — at all events not before the new trade in liquefied natural gas begins in the 1980s. In 1975 MISC had a fleet of 500,000 tons deadweight, including eight general cargo vessels and a number of specialized carriers. Over the period 1976-80 the planned expansion included nine more bulk-carriers and five LNG carriers. But it appears that the LNG carriers will be delivered by the builders some years before the LNG cargoes are available.[71] There is also some doubt about the successful operation of the other bulk-carriers in the volatile international shipping world.[72]

In shipping, as in many other sectors of its economic expansion, Malaysia is not an island unto itself, but a part of a regional and world economy whose circumstances and fluctuations may affect its domestic position. The next Chapter deals with the commercial aspects of Malaysian external relations, among other topics.

Notes

1 In Malaya the developed area in 1973 was 9.2 million acres plus 11.8 million acres of forest land which was 'logged and disturbed'. In Sabah and Sarawak less than a fifth of the 48.5 million acres had been developed. In 1975 Malaysia as a whole had 34 million acres of land suitable for agriculture, of which half was still undeveloped: TMP, Table 11-1 and para 191. The figures of smallholder acreages given in this Chapter should be regarded as approximate: they are the aggregates of a large number of estimated planted areas of small size. 'EconRep' is used in these notes to indicate the annual Economic Report issued by the Malaysian Ministry of Finance with the Budget; 'ARBNM' indicates the Annual Reports of the Bank Negara Malaysia (the central bank).

2 Drabble (1973) is the definitive study of the growth of the rubber plantation industry down to 1922.

3 Puthucheary (1960) reveals the interlocking connections of the agency-house system. See also Allen and Donnithorne (1957).

4 Since 1926 there has been a central Rubber Research Institute (RRI) which undertakes basic research and provides advisory services to the rubber industry as a whole.

5 See Appendix 2 Table 3.

6 *FEER* (16 February 1979).

7 Annual Report of the British Resident Selangor (H. C. Belfield) for 1906. Barlow (1978), 38: Drabble (1973), 72: Lim Teck Ghee (1977), 72-9 and 116-20. As Commissioner of Lands FMS Belfield had previously written a handbook (Drabble, 25) describing the potentialities of rubber as an estate crop.

8 Bauer (1948a), 58: Barlow (1978), 149.

9 Bauer (1948a), 60-5 demonstrates that a peasant cultivator could obtain more rice by growing rubber and buying rice with the proceeds than by direct rice cultivation. See also Lim Teck Ghee (1977), 186-7.

10 Bauer (1948a), 98. Elsewhere Bauer (1946) demonstrated how the economics of smallholder production differed from those of estates. The largest element in the estate cost of production is the wage paid to rubber-tappers. As the number of trees which a tapper can tap in covering his daily 'task' is

limited, it pays an estate to maintain a relatively low planting density of about 100 mature rubber-trees per acre. In that way well-grown trees give the maximum output per tree, and also per tapper, in return for the wage paid. But a smallholder who works his own holding (or shares the output with a sharecropper) has no cash wage costs. As the smallholder has less land than he can work in a full day's task, it pays him to increase the number of trees per acre (up to as much as 200 mature trees per acre) in order to obtain the maximum income from his given acreage. The trees are not so large and it takes more labour, which costs nothing, to tap the holding. To the expert trained in estate methods it looks like bad husbandry, but it gives a higher yield per acre. This fact was not realized when yields per acre were assessed for the purposes of the rubber restriction schemes (see Chapter 11) by regulation officers who had been trained as planters on estates.

11 Over the TMP period (1976-80) it was planned that 200,000 hectares of rubber smallholdings should be replanted. But over the first four years (1976-79) only 80,000 hectares were replanted under RISDA supervision. The FELDA target for the TMP period was 50,000 hectares, or 10,000 *per annum*. After achieving this rate in the first two years, FELDA increased its programme to about 20,000 hectares *per annum* for the remainder of the TMP period: EconRep 1978-79.

12 The annual capacity of MARDEC plants in 1978 was 156,000 tonnes. On these plants' efficiency see Barlow (1978), 323-31.

13 Barlow (1978), 230.

14 In 1978 Sarawak smallholdings produced 97 per cent of total output and Sabah smallholdings 65 per cent, a total for both territories of 51,700 tonnes: ARBNM (1978), 106.

15 J. C. Jackson (1968) is the definitive study of nineteenth-century plantation agriculture. See also R. N. Jackson (1961).

16 Much less has been written about the Malaysian oil-palm industry than its older rubber industry. H. S. Khera (1976) is a well-researched modern study. See also Lim Chong-Yah (1967), Chapter 5 and also Allen and Donnithorne (1957).

17 EconRep (1979-80), 163-7 is an informative general survey of the state of the Malaysian coconut industry. The outlook is rather better in Sabah and Sarawak than in Malaysia.

18 Between 1963 and 1978 about 130,000 acres of coconut smallholdings in Malaya were rehabilitated in various ways, but the current rate of progress is no more than 10,000 acres *per annum*: EconRep (1979-80), 167. Over the period 1971-75 some 52,000 acres, mainly on the west coast of Malaya, were interplanted with cocoa: TMP, para 942.

19 EconRep (1979-80), 113.

20 EconRep (1979-80), 116-17. Tobacco is grown as an additional crop by rubber and rice-farmers mainly in the north-east of Malaya. It is reckoned that a typical 2½-acre plot (1 hectare) gives a cash income of between $1,700 and $3,400. But it is a difficult crop both to grow and to cure properly. Local output is sold to cigarette manufacturers in Malaya.

21 In 1978, 63,000 acres were harvested, but a substantial part of this total was in Negri Sembilan where the one large sugar project collapsed in 1979. 1978

output at 70,000 tonnes was 20 per cent up on the previous year. But even this peak quantity was only one-tenth of the volume required to keep the refineries, installed to process the local crop, fully employed. 394,000 tonnes of raw sugar were imported in 1978 to augment the throughput of the refineries: ARBNM (1978), 112. There are all the signs of an unbalanced and unstable industry.

22   J. C. Jackson (1972), Short and Jackson (1971), Cheng Siok Hwa (1969), Lim Teck Ghee (1977), Sharom Ahmat (1977), Zaharah bt Haji Mahmud (1970), and Kessler (1978) describe either the origins of the modern rice industry in Malaya or the historical context in which it developed. See also Lim Chong-Yah (1967) and the World Bank Report on more strictly economic aspects. The main body of technical and some economic data is found in articles in the Malayan Agricultural Journal.

23   Final Report of the Rice Committee 1956, para 105. The World Bank Report, 297-300 offers a cost-benefit analysis of schemes for opening new rice-land which is unpromising. In the long term the best prospects of major expansion of rice acreage may lie in the river valleys of Sarawak.

24   It is difficult to interpret the numerous statements about double-cropping. It appears that in 1979 only one-third of the total irrigated rice-lands were in fact double-cropped: EconRep (1979-80). There are optimistic predictions in TMP, paras 936 and 964.

25   In the 1977-78 season, when drought precluded double-cropping in the important Muda area of north-west Malaya, the total Malaysian rice crop was 897,000 tonnes only, as compared with 1.2 million tonnes in the previous season, and 1.46 million predicted for 1978-79: EconRep (1978-79) and (1979-80), 109.

26   In 1979 Sabah had 100,000 acres and Sarawak 150,000 acres of land suitable for wet-rice cultivation, but only 15,000 acres could be double-cropped: EconRep (1979-80), 109. Sarawak, the main centre of dry-rice cultivation, had a crop of 61,200 tonnes from this culture in 1978: ARBNM, 109.

27   The outstanding case is the Chinese settlement at Sekinchang in the Tanjong Karang area.

28   TMP, para 499. The figures relate to cultivators who grow rice as their main crop. There are in addition about 160,000 households which grow rice for domestic consumption only.

29   Kessler (1978), 64-71 describes how tenant farming developed as a consequence of the introduction of wet-rice cultivation in Kelantan.

30   1978-79 was a good year (after the disastrous drought year 1977-78) and current production was estimated to suffice for 85 per cent of current needs: EconRep (1979-80), 109.

31   Firth (1946; 2nd ed 1966) is one of the recognized classics of social anthropology—a masterpiece of observation and analysis of complex economic and technical aspects of Malay fishing on the east coast. The 1966 edition has an additional chapter recording the author's further observations when he revisited the same fishing village in 1947 and again in 1963.

32   TMP, paras 501, 538, 898-9, 946, 959, 973-5. Firth (1966) describes the introduction of power-driven fishing boats and the economic and social consequences. Parry (1954) describes the basic fishing methods in use.

33   Fermor (1939), 159 in 1939 estimated known tin deposits at about 1 million

tons (metal). Since that time 1½ million tons have been extracted and the end is not yet in sight.

34   The discovery of rich tin deposits at Larut in Perak in 1848 marked the beginning of a large-scale tin-mining industry. Between 1850 and 1875 exports quadrupled – about 2,400 tons *per annum* over the years 1844-48 and about 10,000 tons *per annum* over the period 1869-73: Wong Lin Ken (1965) in Tregonning (ed.) (1962) at p.31. See also Yip Yat Hoong (1969), 392.

35   Yip Yat Hoong (1969), Wong Lin Ken (1962, 1964 and 1965), and also Ooi Jin Bee in Silcock (ed.) (1961) give detailed accounts of the technical and economic history of Malayan tin-mining.

36   Straits Budget (25 April 1962) quoting the government Mines Department.

37   The Japanese copper-mine at Mamut in Sabah has not been a great success so far. At the end of five years of its estimated 15-year life it had an accumulated loss of $66 million. It exports about 90,000 tonnes of copper concentrates annually: *FEER* (26 October 1979), 92.

38   *FEER* (3 November 1978), 53, (31 August 1979), 61, and (5 October 1979), 103. About a third of current production now comes from wells off the coast of Trengganu on the east side of Malaya.

39   D. W. Fryer and J. C. Jackson (1977) (the companion volume on Indonesia in this series) describe the affair in detail.

40   *FEER* (13 April 1979), 37.

41   TMP, paras 200 and 211.

42   TMP, para 1040.

43   World Bank Report, 121.

44   World Bank Report, 417-38 and Puthucheary (1960), Chapter VII.

45   Straits Budget (21 June 1967), 4.

46   108,300 new jobs in 1971-75: TMP, para 1015: i.e., 20,000 *per annum* as compared with 2,000 *per annum* before (see note 45).

47   TMP, para 1015.

48    $591 million in 1970 and $2.1 billion in 1975. TMP, para 52.

49   *FEER* (3 January 1975), 35.

50   Official statement quoted in *FEER* (3 August 1979), 36.

51   *FEER* (30 July 1976).

52   *FEER* (3 August 1979), 37.

53   *FEER* (28 July 1978), (13 April 1979), and (31 August 1979).

54   Report on the Economic Aspects of Malaysia by a Mission of the Bank for International Reconstruction and Development 1965.

55   *FEER* (19 May 1978), 45.

56   Employment in manufacturing industry was planned to increase from 398,200 in 1975 to 568,100 in 1980. Most of the increase was expected in agro-based industries: TMP, para 1055.

57   EconRep (1978-79).

58   Machinery and transport equipment accounted for 38 per cent of 1978 exports of manufactures: EconRep (1978-79).

59   Allen and Donnithorne (1957), Hyde (1973), Puthucheary (1960), Cunyngham-Brown (1971), Mills (1942).

60   In 1971 the United Kingdom was still Malaysia's third largest supplier (after Japan and Singapore); in 1978 the United Kingdom ranked fourth after

Japan, Singapore, and the United States, and its share of Malaysian import trade had declined from 14 to 7 per cent. Japan, the United States, and West Germany had over this period increased their shares: information sheet published by U.K. Dept. of Trade.

61 Puthucheary (1960), although now out of date in detail, is still the best account.

62 Allen and Donnithorne (1957), Chapter xi; J. L. Boyce in Cowan (ed.) (1964); Compton Mackenzie (1954); Hyde (1973); Lim Chong-Yah (1967), Chapter 8; World Bank Report; Kanapathy (1970), Chapter 5; Caine, Silcock (1961b), Tan Ee Leong, Siew Nim Chee (the last four all in Silcock (ed.) (1961)). See also the annual and quarterly reports of the Bank Negara Malaysia.

63 World Bank Report, 228-31 and 645-8, Watson and Caine (1956) followed by various articles in the *Malayan Economic Journal* (1957-59).

64 Tan Sri Ismail bin Mohamed Ali is a Cambridge graduate in economics who was one of the first two Malays recruited direct to the Malayan Civil Service. Before joining the Bank Negara initially as deputy governor he had served as an executive director of the World Bank.

65 Tan Ee Leong in Silcock (ed.) (1961).

66 *FEER* (21 September 1979), 55 for an informative article on the merchant banks.

67 ARBNM (1975) gives a fairly scathing account of this sector of Malaysian banking.

68 Tregonning (1965), 56. The railway was intended to link the west and east coasts of North Borneo. Owing to changes of plan only a small stretch was built along the west coast. But it served to make land accessible for rubber-planting.

69 TMP, para 642.

70 *FEER* (9 February 1979).

71 TMP, para 1230 on the expansion programme; *FEER* (14 April 1978) on the LNG carriers.

72 *FEER* (15 June 1979), 44.

11 Defence and Foreign Policy

In twenty years of independence Malaysia has gradually evolved a realistic and limited policy of strengthening its external relations and internal security, by disengaging from ties with Britain and developing a closer association with its neighbours in the Southeast Asian region through ASEAN (the Association of South-East Asian Nations). This is a country which could never afford to fight in a major war. Tunku Abdul Rahman said in 1968 when he was Prime Minister that 'he would rather surrender than involve his country in widespread destruction'.[1] The Malaysian defence forces are therefore organized, trained, and equipped for the maintenance of internal security if it should be threatened either by an internal upheaval or by foreign intervention.

Defence and Internal Security

When Malaya became independent in 1957, there was still a continuing internal security problem, the Emergency campaign against the MCP guerrilla forces. Although the real threat had been broken by 1957, the Emergency was not officially terminated until 1960. Meanwhile, the security forces engaged in mopping-up operations included a substantial British and Commonwealth element which Malaya could neither replace nor immediately dispense with. At that time Britain was still much involved in Southeast Asia, where she still had colonial territories and also obligations as a member of the South-East Asia Treaty Organization (SEATO). SEATO had been formed in 1955 on American initiative to screen Southeast Asia from the risk, as it then appeared, of Chinese aggression. Malaya was unwilling to join SEATO since, apart from other factors, an open alignment with an anti-China alliance might aggravate tensions within the multi-communal Malayan society. Britain and Malaya therefore made a limited Anglo-Malayan Defence Treaty[2] which provided for mutual aid. The treaty also stipulated that British forces stationed in Malaya should not be employed in operations outside Malayan or British territory—should not be committed to any SEATO military operations, without the prior agreement of the Malayan government.

An Indonesian–Malayan Treaty of Friendship was signed in 1959, a rather perfunctory gesture of recognition of common culture and common interest in stability. There had been a military revolt in northern Sumatra in 1957-58, which had shown how easily an internal disturbance could escalate into a diplomatic problem. The revolt was soon suppressed, but the rebels had used the established trade-links between Sumatra and Malaya (and also Singapore) to export produce and earn money with which to purchase arms. In 1961 Malaya made her first essay in regional cooperation by promoting the Association of South Asian States (ASA) comprising Malaya, Thailand, and the Philippines. But President Sukarno of Indonesia declined to join a group of which he would not be the acknowledged leader. ASA in fact had a very short life since the dispute between Malaya and the Philippines over Sabah in 1962 effectively wrecked it.

When the Malaysia project was launched in 1961, it raised a new problem in Anglo-Malayan defence relations. Malaysia would include Singapore, but Britain wished to retain the use of her Singapore base for possible SEATO operations. It was agreed in negotiations over the formation of Malaysia that the base might still be used 'for the preservation of peace in Southeast Asia'.[3] For reasons which have been explained (Chapter 7), this phrase sounded sinister in Indonesian ears; was it a covert threat of subversion in her territory? The Philippines for quite different reasons did not wish to see northern Borneo as *terra irredenta* absorbed into an enlarged Malaya. When Malaysia was formed in September 1963, both Indonesia and the Philippines refused to accord it diplomatic recognition. Thereafter Indonesia waged undeclared war, 'Confrontation' (*Konfrontasi*), on Malaysia. A trade embargo was imposed which did severe though temporary damage to the entrepôt trade between Singapore and Penang and nearby parts of Indonesia. Attempts were made at sabotage and subversion in Malaysia; there were armed raids on Malaysian territory and on vessels at sea. These forays in and around Malaysia were a fiasco. The large number of Indonesians settled in Malaya remained loyal or at least acquiescent. The small number who attempted subversion were soon rounded up; a few Malayan political leaders were interned on charges of intrigue with the Indonesians.

Popular reaction in Malaya to Indonesian aggression among both Malays and Chinese helped the Alliance government to trounce the opposition in the federal elections held in April 1964 (Chapter 8).

In Borneo there was a common land frontier between Indonesia and Malaysia. 'Volunteers' from the Indonesian armed forces made raids across the boundary, but were chased out by British, Gurkha, and Malay troops who used to the full the advantages of air-cover and mobility obtained by the use of helicopters. In August 1964 Indonesian raiders reached Malaya itself by air and by sea, but in very small numbers. When one of these groups had been rounded up, Indonesia asserted that they were merely a party of traditional dancers returning from abroad whose aircraft had come down in Malaya owing to engine trouble. The Philippine government had drawn back from active measures against Malaysia. The Thai, Japanese, and even the American, governments tried at various times in 1964 to act as conciliators. But a meeting of heads of government of Malaysia, Indonesia, and the Philippines, held in Tokyo in June 1964, broke up before its work had begun, since it became clear that Sukarno was contemptuous of all forms of compromise. Malaysia was nonetheless conscious of its vulnerability to misrepresentation as a 'neo-colonial' state in the eyes of the Afro-Asian bloc, among which Indonesia still had some influence. After the raids on Malayan territory, Malaysia took its case to the United Nations Security Council. The exhibition of the weapons (of Russian make) taken from the dancing party was too much for the Russian delegate who presided over the Council on this occasion; he ordered their instant removal in case they were loaded. As is usual, an innocuous resolution merely calling on both parties to abstain from the use of force, was drafted behind the scenes as a compromise. It was nonetheless vetoed by the Russian delegate. The general sympathy for Malaysia was shown by its election to a place on the Security Council in 1965. Indonesia then withdrew in a huff from the United Nations.

The limited reconciliation between Indonesia and Malaysia which was achieved in 1966 was an indirect consequence of the collapse of the Sukarno regime in the previous year. By 1965 Indonesia was spiralling into economic collapse. Sukarno held on to power by the support of the army commanders and the Indonesian communist party (PKI). In this unstable situation the PKI made a bid to seize power for itself alone by the destruction of the generals. Sukarno himself was probably aware of the PKI plans for a *coup* and willing to see it succeed if it kept him in the seat of power as president. In the course of the *Gestapu* affair (*Gestapu* is the acronym for '30 September movement') a number of Indonesian senior commanders were brutally murdered. But a previously unknown general, Suharto, who commanded the strategic reserve, was judged too unimportant to merit assassination. Suharto rallied the army forces in counter-measures which led to mass killings of the PKI leaders and many of their followers throughout Java. For the time being at least the PKI had been destroyed as a political force. Sukarno was allowed to survive as the puppet of Suharto and his colleagues until Suharto became president in 1967-68. Thus the way was cleared for a new deal with Malaysia.

The Indonesian generals had lost all enthusiasm for the undeclared war of Confrontation with Malaysia. It had yielded no praetorian triumphs. On the other side, the Malaysian government was concerned lest Singapore, expelled from Malaysia in 1965, should come to terms with Indonesia, in order to revive its entrepôt trade, before Malaysia itself had restored normal relations with Indonesia. These considerations led to the Indonesia–Malaysia Agreement of 1966 which contained only three operative clauses; public opinion in Sabah and Sarawak was to be tested by holding elections; diplomatic relations were to be restored; hostile acts should cease. This settlement left unresolved the underlying causes of tension between the two countries. The leaders of Indonesia, Suharto as much as Sukarno, look forward to the day when Indonesia, the largest and most populous state in Southeast Asia, will dominate the region. But Sukarno's successors have a more realistic understanding than he ever had of the constraints imposed by economic weakness and administrative disorganization. It suits them therefore to play for time; the Indonesian 'go slow' over plans for regional industrialization are discussed below. The permanent pattern must not be set in the mould of the present balance of power. Malaysia on its side has reason to fear domination by the sheer size of its huge neighbour in any bilateral relationship such as the short-lived project for merger of Indonesia and Malaya (*Indonesia Raya*) planned by Sukarno and the Malay nationalists in the last days of the Japanese occupation in 1945 (Chapter 6) and Sukarno's Maphilindo scheme of 1963 (Chapter 7), in which Malaya was first to sever all connections with other allies outside the region. The Confrontation episode was an object lesson in the risks of allowing any dispute within Southeast Asia to escalate. A broad-based regional accommodation was essential.

As will be explained, ASEAN is not primarily a defence organization, though it does diminish the risk of attack. Malaysian defence
is a matter now for Malaysia itself. The Anglo-Malayan Defence
Treaty of 1957 served its purpose up to the mid-1960s. It then
withered on the vine as Britain decided to withdraw her forces and
(in 1971) to close her base in Singapore. Malaysian defence forces
have expanded considerably since Malaya achieved independence
in 1957, but they are still of moderate size and only lightly
equipped. These forces, land, sea, and air, are mainly Malay in personnel from privates to generals. Attempts to develop mixed units,
other than technical services, have met with little support either
from the Malay or from the non-Malay side. Hence the armed
forces, like the police and the civil service, are mainly a Malay
preserve. Their operational function is to maintain internal security
by the use of troops in small detachments – to patrol in search of
elusive opponents rather than to fight set battles. From the
Emergency campaign of the 1950s they have inherited much practical expertise in these tactics. The main scene of activity is the inaccessible country towards the Thai frontier in the north. After years
of frustration, a more effective co-operation with Thai forces during the late 1970s has given to the security forces the upper hand in
the long-drawn chase after the MCP guerrilla bands. But specialization has its price. When the crisis takes a different form, such as the
disturbances of May 1969, or the control of the Vietnamese refugee
influx of 1979, the response of the Malaysian armed forces has
sometimes appeared clumsy and uncontrolled.

Foreign Policy

The Role of ASEAN

In detaching itself from foreign entanglements Malaysia was moving in line with its neighbours. Sukarno had argued that any foreign
bases in the Southeast Asia region were a threat to the stability of
every state in it. The disastrous American involvement in Vietnam
was a lesson for all to see. But if the Southeast Asian states were to
detach themselves from foreign defence arrangements, they must
also reach an understanding among themselves that none would attack or interfere in the affairs of another. They also had common
interests to pursue. These rather vague aspirations led Indonesia,

Malaysia, the Philippines, Thailand, and Singapore to join in forming ASEAN in August 1967. ASEAN was founded without clear-cut objectives and lacks any commitment to specific measures of unification which, with a strong central organization, gave momentum to the European Economic Community in the previous decade. Eight years after its formation ASEAN was still 'little more than a weak association of anti-communist regimes whose mutual differences and conflicts outweigh any impetus towards real cooperation and unity'.[4]

ASEAN is not a defence organization. It would have little value if it were, since the combined military resources of its member states would hardly suffice to repel a major external attack on their scattered territories. It would be difficult to establish an acceptable and workable command structure. In 1967 there were still large American military bases in the Philippines and a substantial military 'presence' in Thailand, including bases for American bombers used in the Vietnam war. The member states differed in their attitudes to the great powers. Indonesia and Singapore for different reasons were much more suspicious of China than the others. But the lack of a comprehensive military organization does not impede bilateral arrangements. Malaysia and Thailand co-operate in containing the communist guerrilla forces lodged in their inaccessible frontier region south of the Kra Isthmus. Malaysian and Indonesian forces co-operate in drives against the remaining communist forces in their frontier region along the southern border of Sarawak. At the height of the crisis over Vietnamese refugees in 1979, there was talk at least of combined measures to prevent them coming into the region by sea from the north. The existence of ASEAN serves to lower the temperature of old grievances about *terra irredenta,* such as the Malay area in southern Thailand and the Philippine claim to Sabah. ASEAN meetings of ministers or civil servants provide a forum for exchange of views on problems, regional or external, of common concern. The existence of ASEAN promotes a habit of thinking in regional terms. The Malaysian view is that it must develop at its own slow pace.

On this languid and inconclusive basis ASEAN continued until the communist takeover of South Vietnam in 1975 jolted the member states into agitated reaction to a new threat. For some time before there had been talk of enlarging ASEAN to bring in South Vietnam, Cambodia (as it then was), Laos, and even perhaps Sri Lanka and Burma. Some inconclusive overtures had been made. The first effect of the new situation in Indo-China was to divide the ASEAN states. No one could forget that the Japanese had used the same territory as their jumping-off point for the invasion of 1941. Thailand thought that its best safeguard was to become conspicuously neutral by disembarrassing itself—with minimum ceremony—of the remaining American forces in its territory. But the Philippines did not follow this example. At this stage it was still possible to envisage the recruitment of the communist regime in Vietnam to a would-be neutral ASEAN bloc since Vietnam was not then firmly in the Russian camp. The ASEAN members were in some disarray over their attitude towards China. Malaysia had re-established diplomatic relations with China following a visit to Peking by the Prime Minister, Tun Abdul Razak, in 1974. Thailand and the Philippines eventually did the same, but Indonesia, with memories of Sukarno's Jakarta–Peking axis, and Singapore with her very large Chinese population, preferred not to do so.

In the search for neutrality, Vietnam has proved a severe test of ASEAN policy. Neutrality requires a willingness of the great powers to abstain from involvement in Southeast Asia. The old colonial powers, Britain (Malaysia), France (Indo-China), the United States (the Philippines), and the Netherlands (Indonesia), recognize that their own important interests in trade and investment are best safeguarded by non-involvement, provided always that other great powers do the same. SEATO is dead.[5] Japan, which has perhaps the largest economic interest to protect, has learnt from the disastrous wartime 'Co-Prosperity Sphere' that common economic interests are best pursued by inconspicuous and essentially commercial ties.

The position of China is more complicated. There is an important flow of trade between China and Southeast Asia. There are several million ethnic Chinese settled in the region as minorities. In the period between the wars the KMT government of China took the line that these overseas communities were still Chinese nationals and sought to extend its political influence among them (Chapter 5). In 1949 the bogy of Chinese intervention took on a new life since Chinese nationalism among the overseas Chinese was now combined with communism; for countries like Malaya this was a potent mixture. But despite some ritual encouragement of Chinese communists in Southeast Asia over the radio, the government of China has on the whole followed a policy of non-intervention even when, as in Malaya and in Indonesia, the local Chinese have been in conflict with the government of the country. The regime which has succeeded Mao Tse Tung in China seems even more likely to continue this policy.[6] But China cannot be indifferent to manoeuvres on its southern flank by its arch-enemy Russia.

The conflict between China and the Soviet Union over Vietnam threatens to disrupt the peace of Southeast Asia. When it took control in the south, the communist government of Vietnam was still (in 1975) comparatively independent of both China and Russia. Over the years 1975-78, however, it became a Russian satellite. The Russian motive for effecting this change is easy to see. Since the 1920s it has been Russian policy to relieve pressures on other fronts by giving aid in Southeast Asia to the enemies of its enemies nearer home. For that reason Russia promoted the spread of communism in the Southeast Asian colonies of the European powers — though it could not have flourished if local conditions had not been so favourable to it. When Russia became an ally of the Western powers in 1941, the communists in Malaysia and elsewhere were instructed to co-operate with the colonial power. Since China became a major foe of the Soviet Union, Indo-China has been a useful means of threatening China from the south. The disruptive conflict has escalated into a 'second Indo-China war'[7] of great ferocity.

In 1979 the struggle spread into Kampuchea (formerly Cambodia) as the forces of the Vietnamese regime, led by Pham Van Dong and allied with Russia, drove out the Pol Pot government and installed a no less oppressive Kampuchea National Front in its place. In mid-1979 Chinese troops made a brief but menacing incursion into northern Vietnam. A flood of peasant refugees and many of the defeated Pol Pot forces crossed the border into northeastern Thailand. Kampuchea, devastated by war, faces the grim prospect of famine.

It is too early yet to assess the full consequences of the chaos in Indo-China on the ASEAN nations to the south. The most immediate and dramatic event was the sea-borne flight of the Vietnamese 'boat people' southwards towards Malaysia, Indonesia, and the Philippines which had begun late in 1978 and which swelled in 1979 to a movement from Indo-China to neighbouring territories of some 400,000 people (including the refugees who moved by land into Thailand). The exact number of those who fled by sea will never be known since a considerable proportion of them were lost by drowning in their perilous transit across the South China Sea. Malaysia alone played unwilling host to more than 70,000 (with perhaps another 50,000 in Indonesia). It seems that the movement of the boat people was quite deliberately enforced by the Vietnamese government which wished to be rid of its ethnic Chinese minority who, as in Malaysia itself, included many merchants, shopkeepers, and small traders. In the cause of 'socialist transformation' of Vietnamese society these citizens were first forced out of business and then intimidated into paying—in gold—for permits to leave the country. Others merely fled without the dubious advantage of official permits. They crowded on board aged small steamships or took to the sea in overloaded sailing vessels. In addition to the ethnic Chinese, who made up the majority, the Vietnamese government also disembarrassed itself of a considerable number of its political opponents in the same way. Apart from the domestic reasons for this enforced movement the Vietnamese regime was possibly seeking to disrupt the economy and society of the ASEAN countries as recipients of the influx of refugees. It was also an opportunity to infiltrate communist agents into those countries.

If disruption of the host countries was an objective of Vietnamese policy, it came close to success. The flood of men, women, and children who drifted to the shores of east-coast Malaya in their sinking vessels were in great physical distress. It became clear that the more Malaysia accepted, the more would come after them. When its refugee camps were full, the Malaysian government took measures to exclude later arrivals. The armed forces were deployed along the east coast, thus weakening the military hold on the troubled northern frontier zone. It is said that over 260 vessels with 40,000 people on board were towed back to sea from Malaysian coastal waters to prevent them landing. Some of these rejected entrants may have reached Indonesia, which protested at the transfer of the burden, and some died at sea. A statement by the Malaysian Deputy Prime Minister, Dr Mahathir bin Mohamed, that troops had been ordered to shoot refugees on sight was hastily amended; 'shoo on sight' was the unconvincing revised version of the remark attributed to a political leader known for his forthright words. But whether it was a calculated indiscretion or not, these words served to concentrate the minds of the Western powers on the size of the problem and the near desperation of the ASEAN governments. In their view the latest events in Indo-China were the indirect consequence of the disastrous American intervention in Vietnam in the 1960s. It was this original cause which had led to the catastrophic 'destabilization' of the region. If the rest of the world expected the ASEAN nations to receive the refugees in their hour of need, it was up to the other countries, with their greater resources, to take over responsibility for resettling the refugees throughout the world. The problem was considerably relieved at an international conference held in Geneva in July 1979. The developed countries increased the size of their commitments to accept refugees for settlement. Pressure was brought to bear on Vietnam to halt the problem at its source. There were indeed signs that the Vietnamese government had 'under-estimated the extent of the uproar triggered by the mass exodus and is now concerned at its isolation on the international scene'.[8] At all events, whether for reasons of self-interest or otherwise, the Vietnamese government took steps — as it always could — to reduce the flow of refugees to manageable proportions.

The direct cost to Malaysia of receiving, controlling, and feeding the refugees in 1979 was expected to be of the order of $100 million. In addition their presence caused an upsurge of racial feeling among the Malay communities of the east coast to whom this influx of Chinese and other foreigners seemed a deliberate threat to the Malays in their one remaining stronghold in Malaya. Before condemning the Malaysian government for its drastic measures, with their occasional inhumane consequences, one should take account of the near-hysteria whipped up against them by their Malay political opponents.

Although the refugee problem was a shared burden of the ASEAN powers, their reactions to it differed — as might be expected of this loose coalition. Thailand was very conscious that in allowing Kampuchean Pol Pot forces to cross its frontier it was exposing itself to an invasion by their pursuers. Malaysia too was very concerned lest the war should thus be extended to Thailand, its immediate neighbour to the north. Although somewhat discredited, the "domino theory", i.e. that Southeast Asia will be overrun by stages from the north — as happened in 1941-42, dies hard. The only great power which could give effective aid to the ASEAN nations against invasion by Vietnam is China. But — to varying degrees — the ASEAN nations fear Chinese intervention too. Assuredly no American president is ever likely to commit troops of his country to another war in this region. The decision of the British government to accord diplomatic recognition to the new government of Kampuchea was seen as a feeble gesture of appeasement and one which gave away a bargaining counter.

There are however some signs that the Vietnamese government may be seeking an accommodation with the ASEAN group. The

ASEAN response is to urge Vietnam to disengage itself from its links with Russia. It otherwise risks a second invasion by Chinese forces. The Vietnamese view is that the ASEAN nations are not true neutrals if they retain American bases (in the Philippines) and some links with China. The status of a "neutral" is very much in the eye of the beholder.

It seems likely that ASEAN will continue its slow progress towards a closer association of its members. The habit of concerted diplomatic action and the development of economic ties may draw the member states together. But it is not a strong or cohesive group.

Foreign Trade

The importance of foreign trade in the Malaysian economy can hardly be underestimated. It absorbs about half the national output and provides half the goods consumed in Malaysia. The particular objectives of trade policy are to widen the markets for the growing volume of manufactured goods, and to sustain the world prices at which Malaysian staple export commodities are sold. In both fields membership of ASEAN offers some advantages, though actual achievement has been less than expectation.

The population of the ASEAN states is about 230 million, as compared with 13 million in Malaysia alone. Poverty is even more widespread and acute than in Malaysia. The ASEAN market for consumer goods may be smaller than mere population size might suggest, but it is a consumer of fertilizers and other agricultural materials on a substantial scale. An expert study had demonstrated that the domestic markets of individual ASEAN states for these and some other products were insufficient to support industries of economic size, but that ASEAN as a whole could do so if it established a common market.[9] The obvious obstacle to all such schemes is that in creating an enlarged market one or more countries may gain more or lose more in the short-term balance than others. This difficulty can be tackled either by adopting a fixed timetable for progressive reduction of all tariffs by stages so that the long-term outweigh the short-term effects, or by instituting a series of bargaining 'rounds': negotiations at intervals, in each of which every participator can bargain for reductions item by item so as to secure gains to offset its concessions. A determined effort made in 1975 to launch an ASEAN scheme came to an abrupt halt mainly owing to the unwillingness of Indonesia to go along with the other states. Indonesia reckons that in the long term it must, as the largest state of the region, dominate the others. But in the short term it has one of the weakest economies. It did not wish the others to take advantage of its current weakness to gain a headstart by building up industries, with the aid of the detested 'multinational' corporations, to supply the Indonesian market.[10] A second attempt was made in 1976 under which each territory, including Indonesia, was to have a defined share of the supply of agricultural fertilizers, etc. The manufacture of superphosphate to supply the ASEAN market was allocated to the Philippines; soda ash to Thailand; urea to Indonesia and Malaysia; and the manufacture of small diesel engines to Singapore, already heavily industrialized and not an agricultural area. In each case the new plant was to be jointly owned and to have the right to supply the ASEAN area free of import duties. But several years later this ingenious scheme was still at the planning stage. ASEAN is full of good intentions, but lacks the will and the strong central directing organization which is needed to carry through co-ordination of this kind.

The other problem of industrialization which Malaysia shares with her ASEAN partners (and many other developing countries) is how best to secure fair terms of entry for her manufactured goods exported to foreign markets outside the region. The essential features of the problem are well understood and have been explained in the Malaysian context (Chapter 10). Industries migrate to countries where wage costs are relatively low. The host countries encourage this movement by establishing 'free trade zones' usually near to a port or airport. In addition to freedom from import and export duties, these industries are given 'tax holidays' on their profits for a period of years, and can minimize their profits by artificial transfer-pricing. This is a regional rather than a national system, since the manufacturing operations in different free-trade zones are often vertically integrated. Operations which require advanced technology are located in industrial centres such as Hong Kong or Singapore, where skilled workers are available. Assembly work is carried out using female labour mainly in other countries where labour costs are low. Between Japan and India there are about forty of these free trade zones and their number is increasing. The benefits to the economies of the host countries are less than might appear. The initial costs of setting up infrastructure in the form of industrial estates and transport facilities are often considerable. But the new industries are 'footloose' and prone to move on to another country if the terms offered there are more attractive.

These schemes create jobs, but they are isolated from the national economy of the host country and contribute little to it. The assembly of electronic equipment and the manufacture of textiles are two typical but contrasted examples of industries which find the system useful to them.[11]

Manufacturing industry, whether developed by the artificial stimulus of free-trade zones, or more firmly rooted in one country, must either sell its products within the domestic market or find export markets. In Malaysia the possibilities of import substitution within the home market have now been fully explored and, as explained above, regional import substitution programmes have faltered under the imperfections of ASEAN economic co-operation. Goods manufactured in Asian countries where labour costs are low become 'cheap imports' when they reach the markets of the industrialized countries of the West. To safeguard employment in their own declining industries where wage costs are higher, the industrialized countries impose tariffs or quotas against Asian imports. Endless international conferences have so far failed to produce a clear-cut solution to this fundamental conflict of interest between the industrialized 'North' and the developing 'South'.[12] This is not a specifically Malaysian nor even an ASEAN problem; it affects the 'Group of 77' (developing nations) in whose negotiations Malaysia plays its part.

There is competition between developing countries or groups of such countries to secure the most favourable terms for their exports, both manufactures and raw materials, in the markets of the industrialized countries. As a member of ASEAN, Malaysia can do better for itself than by negotiating on a simple bilateral basis. The negotiations in 1978 between the ASEAN states and the European Economic Community are a fair specimen of their kind.[13] The agenda included trade in both manufactured goods and primary commodities, investment in the ASEAN area by EEC concerns, technical and financial aid, cultural co-operation, and even a wider scheme of semi-political co-operation. The ASEAN negotiators tried, but without much success, to secure for the ASEAN group the same concessions as the EEC countries had granted under the Lomé Convention to the 'associated states' — former colonial dependencies in Africa and the Caribbean of continental members of the EEC. The EEC insisted that it must reserve the right to limit the inflow of manufactured goods from ASEAN countries. It also offered various forms of assistance in promoting development and the establishment of new industries in the ASEAN area. The end result was that ASEAN gained something — more perhaps than its individual members could have obtained in separate negotiations — but no more than the EEC is prepared to concede to groups of developing countries (other than the privileged 'associated states' with which France and certain other EEC countries wish to preserve their political and economic influence).

The former system of Commonwealth preference in import duties, in which the territories of Malaysia participated as former dependencies of Britain from 1932 onwards, has been phased out. In its place has come a generalized system of preferences (GSP), accorded by industrialized countries to the exports of developing countries — but subject to selective quota limits on the volume of trade, and to discrimination between the exports of advanced developing countries, of which Malaysia is one, and the more backward countries whose case for selective aid is more compelling. The GSP system applies to raw materials, if otherwise subject to import duties, as well as to manufactures. About one-eighth of Malaysian exports, mainly palm-oil, sawn timber, electronic products, textiles, and canned pineapples, have the limited benefits of the GSP system in their main markets. As explained above, Japan, the European Economic Community, and the United States are Malaysia's main trade partners. The flourishing oil-producing countries of the Middle East should be a valuable new market for Malaysian exports, but lack of expert knowledge of local conditions has so far restricted the growth of trade with that region.

About three-fifths of Malaysian exports of manufactured goods are machinery and transport equipment such as printing machinery, electrical appliances, diesel and motor-engine parts, etc. The prospects of expanding production and export of this type of relatively advanced product depend on importing technology and other resources from abroad. The rapid growth of Malaysian production of textiles and footwear in the mid-1970s has since been checked by the restrictions imposed on imports of these goods in other countries and the severe competition of other exporting countries. The export trade in products manufactured from local materials such as canned pineapples and other food products, wood products such as veneers, chipwood, plywood, etc., is more securely based but this trade is not expected to grow rapidly.[14]

Commodity Price Stabilization

The proportion of Malaysian export earnings gained from the

traditional pillars of the economy, rubber and tin, has fallen from the three-fifths in 1960 to about one-third in 1978. In the past both commodities have been subject to violent price fluctuation in world markets which has been a disrupting influence on the Malaysian economy. Rubber in particular is the main source of income of almost half a million smallholders whose economic welfare is a dominant concern of the Malaysian government. The lessons of past experience have been applied in current efforts to stabilize prices. The underlying problem is, as it always has been, inelasticity of demand and of supply. Demand for tin and rubber is determined by demand for tin cans and rubber tyres and some other products in which they are used as raw materials. But this induced demand is not affected by the prices of tin and rubber since those prices are only a small part of the cost of producing the end-product. If rising consumption leads to scarcity and high prices of the raw materials, the most likely effect is a substitution of other materials such as aluminium or synthetic rubber. But that is a medium-term rather than an immediate effect. On the supply side, output can be marginally increased by short-term measures. But any long-term adjustment requires that rubber-trees shall be planted and grown to maturity, or that new tin-mines shall be opened. Either takes years to achieve. In the period between the wars periods of scarcity and of high prices led to an expansion of productive capacity. But when that new capacity eventually became available, the trade cycle was at a low point so that the additional output merely added to the glut and depressed the price still more. Malaysia is an efficient producer of both tin and rubber compared with some at least of its competitors. In strict theory it might be profitable to endure a period of low prices in order that less competitive neighbours should be forced out of business. But even a high-cost producer will continue production so long as the current price exceeds his *direct* costs of production. There is always the hope that the volatile price will rise again until it covers total costs. This is particularly apposite to fixed assets such as rubber estates and tin-dredges which have a long life and cannot readily be sold or converted to other uses.

In these circumstances even a low-cost producer finds it attractive to join in regulating the flow of supplies onto the world market rather than have a long period of cut-throat competition which may ruin everyone. The first international rubber regulation scheme ran from 1924 to 1928 and the second from 1934 to 1941. The first international tin agreement came into operation in 1931, was extended by stages to 1941, and revived in 1956 to continue to the present time. Agreement was reached in 1979 on a new rubber stabilization scheme. In all these arrangements Malaya (and later Malaysia) has played a leading part. Experience suggests that a satisfactory stabilization scheme must have two elements. First, there should be a substantial buffer stock which absorbs excess supplies when the price falls below an agreed level and releases stocks when the price rises above an agreed level. On this basis it is a profitable enterprise which gives a return on the capital invested in it. The operating price levels have to be fixed by agreement between producing and consuming countries. Since no one can estimate precisely the equilibrium price at which supply will equal demand at all stages in the cycle, the price levels have to be renegotiated from time to time. But a buffer stock cannot relieve a major imbalance of supply and demand. It is a short-term stabilizer. If there is a serious and continuing glut, the buffer stock exhausts its cash and the producing countries must then resort to the second weapon in their armoury, restriction of output.[15] This is usually done by assessing the potential output of each producing territory; the government of that territory then allocates its national quota between individual producers. Each individual producer is allowed to produce a prescribed percentage of his rated capacity during a period typically of three months at a time. There are two main drawbacks to regulation schemes. At the level of international co-operation the countries which are high-cost producers demand that the world price shall be sustained at the level at which they can made a profit. Within each territory the assessment of productive capacity of individual producers, especially smallholders, is a rigid form of control based on inadequate data. It can—and in Malaya it has—led to unfairness.[16]

The history of the international tin scheme since its revival in the 1950s is a sequence of encounters between the producers who want to set the 'floor' and 'ceiling' prices at higher and higher levels and the United States as the largest consumer of tin. The United States has had a powerful bargaining weapon in its 'strategic stockpile' of tin. During and after the war a huge quantity of tin was accumulated to safeguard the American economy against an interruption of supplies such as occurred in the period 1942-45. More recently, however, the Americans have decided that they hold more tin than is necessary as an emergency stock, and they have been running it down. In its own interest as a seller and to avoid total disruption of production in the countries which provide the world with most of its tin (these include Bolivia, Indonesia, and Nigeria, as well as Malaysia), the United States seems to have accepted that stockpile disposals must not depress the world price of tin below the level at which established producers can achieve profits. Tin-mining consumes oil and other forms of energy and so the cost of producing tin is rising with the price of oil. But the habit of co-operation between producers and consumers is now well established. The tin regulation scheme is a well-tried mechanism which is accepted despite its occasional imperfections.

For twenty or thirty years after the war, natural-rubber producers had to survive in reluctant competition with a price stablizer imposed upon them—synthetic rubber production (Chapter 10). There was no question of supporting the level of prices by restricting the flow of supplies. The consumers were already using increasing proportions of synthetic rubber of steadily improving quality. But a new era began in 1973 with the sharp rise in the world price of petroleum, since synthetic rubber is made from petro-chemicals. Natural rubber became cheaper than synthetic and American manufacturers ceased the remorseless expansion of capacity to produce synthetic rubber. But this was also a period of world recession in which the price of natural rubber fell sharply owing to reduced total demand. It became politically imperative for Malaysia to stabilize the price of natural rubber at a level which would yield a satisfactory income to its smallholders. The first move towards reconstituting international regulation of natural rubber output came in 1970, when Malaysia and Indonesia took the lead in establishing an Association of Natural Rubber Producing Countries (ANRPC), which also included Thailand, Sri Lanka, and Singapore (as a major centre of the world rubber trade). The ANRPC group produce about nine-tenths of world output of natural rubber, but, as with ASEAN, conflicts of interest make it difficult to concert common action. During the 1974-75 slump, Malaysia imposed domestic restraints on output, but with only temporary and partial effect. From 1976 to 1979 there were protracted negotiations under UNCTAD auspices to establish a rubber stabilization scheme under joint control of producers and consumers. The main points at issue were the levels at which the buffer stock should intervene in the market and the size of the stock. The United States as a large consumer pressed for a very large buffer stock and no 'supply rationalization' (the jargon for restrictions on output). But no scheme can offer any prospect of success without some restriction in the last resort both on current output and on creation of new capacity by the planting of additional rubber-trees. The scheme agreed in 1979 has complex provisions for a large buffer stock whose operations are to be related to the movement of the market price above or below a reference price, which can be renegotiated at intervals. Producers and consumers are to consult when necessary over measures to be taken by producers which may affect output. In view of the present size of the rubber smallholding sector of the Malaysian industry, and the political influence of smallholders as electors, one may doubt whether outright restriction of output, such as was practised between the wars,[17] is any longer practicable. But the government of the Netherlands East Indies solved the problem of restraining output by imposing very heavy taxes on exports. The new scheme is not expected to come into operation until 1981. Voting-control and the financing of the large buffer stock (a maximum of 550,000 tonnes) is to be shared equally between the producers and the consumers as separate groups. The scheme must be regarded as the major achievement of Malaysian commercial diplomacy in the period of independence.[18]

Notes

1   *FEER* (15 February 1968), 266.
2   The Anglo-Malayan Defence and Mutual Assistance Treaty: Cmnd 263 (1967).
3   Joint Statement of the Governments of the United Kingdom and of the Federation of Malaya: Cmnd 1563 (1961). This and the document referred to in note 2 are reproduced in Gullick (1967) as documents 14 and 15.
4   *FEER* (20 February 1976).
5   The SEATO treaty has not been rescinded, but the military organization to operate it was disbanded in 1977: *FEER* (10 March 1976), 16.
6   Purcell, a former Adviser on Chinese Affairs to the Malayan governments and later an eminent academic authority on China and the Chinese, vigorously rebutted the argument that China had expansionist designs on Southeast Asia. See Purcell (1962) p.315. See also Wang Gungwu (1979). The most persuasive argument is China's abstention from any effective support of local Chinese communities or political movements in Southeast Asia. But she also declines formally to sever ties of fraternal solidarity with communist movements in the region.
7   *FEER* (4 August 1978). See *The Times* (25 September and 23 October 1978) on the cool ASEAN reaction to Vietnamese overtures at that time.
8   *FEER* (27 July 1979). The story of the Vietnamese refugees and the ensuing diplomatic moves is fully reported in a sequence of articles published in *FEER* during 1979.
9   *FEER* (21 November 1975) gives a very full account of the 'Robinson

Report' ('Economic Cooperation for ASEAN') published in 1973. As one example, manufacture of plate glass is not economic on a smaller scale than 100,000 tons *per annum*. No one ASEAN state offers a market for even half this quantity, but the ASEAN group could absorb one and a half times that tonnage.

10   *FEER* (23 January 1976), 47.

11   *FEER* (18 May 1979), 76: *FEER* (3 August 1979) on movement of labour-intensive industries from Singapore to Johor where labour costs are lower. On the Japanese attitude to these problems see Shinohara (1979).

12   *FEER* (2 February 1979), 76 on the general ASEAN disenchantment. It was also expressed by the Malaysian Minister of Finance in his address to the Wilton Park Conference on 6 November 1979 (together with some hints of an OPEC-style producers' cartel to raise prices and restrict supplies).

13   *FEER* (24 November 1978), 47. The agreement was ratified in December 1979.

14   United States, EEC, Japan, and Australia took 60 per cent of Malaysian exports and supplied 62 per cent of imports in 1979: EconRep (1979-80), 42. The exports included a substantial proportion of raw materials as well as manufactured goods.

15   On the origins and working of the successive tin and rubber regulation schemes see Yip Yat Hoong (1969), Eastham in Silcock (ed.) (1961), Bauer (1948a) and (1948b), Drabble (1973), McFadyean (1944), and Benham (1949). Drabble gives the best account of the origins of the 1924-28 rubber regulation scheme and Bauer (1948a) is the classic study of the scheme in the 1930s. McFadyean is the official history.

16   The potential yield of Malayan smallholdings was underrated in assessing the production quotas: see above note 10 to Chapter 10. The second disadvantage to smallholdings was that they could not develop areas of high-yielding rubber during the currency of the two schemes. Their holdings were too small to replant (for reasons explained in Chapter 10) and new planting, i.e., planting additional land with high-yielding rubber, was not possible either because the regulation scheme forbade it, or, in periods when it did not, because it was government policy not to alienate land for rubber-planting. The estates could, however, replant and, when new planting was permitted, had available 'reserve land' within their boundaries. Bauer himself accepts that 'the discrimination against the smallholders. . . should not be ascribed simply to "colonialism" in the sense of the exploitation of the dependence of a colony to promote metropolitan economic interests' (Bauer 1957). In the early stages – but not later on – the government failed to comprehend the effects of measures which it had initiated for the efficient working of rubber regulation as this was perceived at the time. The plantation section of the industry had more political influence at that time than the smallholders had. Thus far it has been tacitly assumed that Bauer's analysis is substantially correct – though he probably overstates his case. Not everyone, however, agrees – more especially on the subject of the yield of smallholdings at the time. See Benham (1949) (who had been Economic Adviser to the Commissioner-General for some years after the war). Bauer's second major study (Bauer 1948b) is a very controversial document and to my knowledge a number

of officials in both the Agricultural Department and the RRI disputed its factual accuracy.

17 When the Malaysian government took measures to restrict output (in order to raise prices) in 1975, it did not attempt to impose direct restrictions on smallholder production.

18 The protracted negotiations over the period 1975-79 were regularly and fully reported in *FEER*.

12 Education, Language, and Culture

Education

The changing pattern of the Malaysian education system is a legacy of the mistakes of the past, a mirror of the society which it serves, and a formulation of aspirations for the future. There is no difficulty in discerning the last of these — 'the overriding objective is national integration and unity'.[1] Such a statement implies, however, that education is a lever used to roll aside a rather large boulder blocking the path to the future. One has to begin with the past to see how the present was born and what constraints limit its future development.

Education down to 1945

In pre-colonial times Malay society attached little importance to general education. In the nineteenth century a Malay Sultan or chief might employ a wandering Malay schoolmaster from the Straits Settlements as tutor for his sons. But many aristocrats of the 1870s were illiterate.[2] The writing of state documents such as treaties or diplomatic letters was a specialized craft subject to many formal rules; it was a task delegated to 'secretaries', (professional scribes). But religious instruction played a much larger part. At puberty Malay boys attended a Koran class at the house of a local teacher to be taught to read the Koran (without learning the meaning of the Arabic in which it was written) and to be instructed in the basic beliefs and practices of Islam. A minority continued their religious studies as adults by attending as full-time students a *pondok* school,[3] under the supervision of a teacher of local or regional renown. The general body of the laity were also instructed by sermons and at prayer meetings at the mosque or local prayer-house (*surau*). The highest prestige was reserved for the devout who made the pilgrimage to Mecca, or studied at the al-Azhar University in Cairo or some other foreign centre of learning. From the more advanced students Malay society drew its Islamic clergy and teachers in the village communities, and Rulers and chiefs, if devout, obtained their advisers on Islamic law and belief. In modern times the system has become more bureaucratic; each State has its Department of Religious Affairs and students take degree courses in Islamic studies at universities in Malaysia. There is also a much more active and pervasive contact between Malaysian Islam and the learning and social movements of the Middle East.[4]

The British enclaves of the Straits Settlements were outposts of an Indian Empire in which education through the medium of English was already producing a small but growing number of educated men to fill subordinate posts in government and commercial offices. In the Straits the chaplains of the East Indian Company were forbidden to undertake missionary work, but interested themselves in founding schools for education both in English and in Malay. The first English-language school, the Penang Free School, dates from 1816 and it is believed that the first classes for teaching Malays in Malay were held at that school in 1821.[5] A considerable number of schools were established in the second quarter of the century, mainly under missionary influence. Stamford Raffles had a vision of founding a great regional centre of education at Singapore; the lesser men who followed him made it another secondary school. When British rule was extended into the Malay States, more English-language schools were established in the towns. As the urban population was mainly Chinese, Indian, and Eurasian, the schools drew most of their pupils from those communities. These ventures were on a limited scale since there was very little money available, and the intention was merely to produce a pool of educated staff for whom employment could be found.

The first generation of British administrators in the Malay States were Victorian Englishmen whose home country had recently developed a system of universal primary education.[6] Something on these lines, they felt, should be provided for the Malay population for whose welfare they had assumed responsibility. Lack of buildings, trained teachers, and textbooks, stood in the way and in the allocation of funds education had a low priority. The response of the Malay villager was unenthusiastic. 'The staple industries of the district, i.e. cutting *ataps,* clearing jungle, or working fishing-stakes, do not require that their sons should read or write'.[7] For social and religious reasons the Malay community was even more opposed to sending its daughters to school. This attitude changed with time as it became clear that an education opened the way to employment which, even if lowly, produced a better income than a peasant farmer could earn. By 1920 it was noted that 'the awakening of the Malay race to the advantages of education, vernacular or English, has been rapid and widespread. Education is the daily topic of the Malay press'.[8] It was not, however, a liberal education. The object was to 'make the son of the fisherman or peasant a more intelligent fisherman or peasant than his father had been'.[9] Swettenham, whose strong views left their mark on official policy for many years after his retirement, was determined to avoid the mistakes, as he saw it, of British educational policy in India. Malay education must not give 'a smattering of knowledge that only makes them discontented with their lot in life'.[10] In making the young Malay peasant literate his mind would be opened only to technical information on farming matters and to moral instruction designed to inculcate such missing virtues as punctuality and diligence in his work. The teaching of English in particular was to be shunned since it might let in all sorts of dangerous thoughts. There were a few British administrators who supported a more enlightened policy. One of them, R. J. Wilkinson, in a few brief years of work in the education department around 1900 left a legacy which is a shining exception to the rest. But after his departure from the education field in 1906, the narrow view prevailed.[11] Wilkinson saw that colonial rule and the stifling effect of Malay education policy had a demoralizing result. His object was to develop from the base of Malay language and culture towards the attainment of a more vigorous and wide-ranging Malay intellectual life. In this he was half a century ahead of his colleagues and — one must add — of many Malay aristocrats of his time. The specific weakness of Malay vernacular education as it expanded in the period between the wars was that it led nowhere. The Malay pupil who completed a six-year course — and many dropped out without doing so — was only qualified for employment as a police constable or a driver and the like. There was no secondary education in the medium of Malay. A small proportion, however, of the ablest pupils at Malay schools was selected for transfer to the English-medium secondary schools in the towns. On entering these schools they spent two years in a 'special Malay class' in which they learnt English in order to merge with the mainstream of the more advanced classes later on. It gave them an opportunity, but at the cost of detaching them from Malay village life to become part of the English-educated élite for whom there were opportunities of employment in clerical or technical posts in the towns.

Yet the genie escaped from the bottle. It had always been recognized that the achievement of satisfactory results, by any standard, in the Malay schools required a proper system of training Malay schoolmasters. The breakthrough came in 1922 with the establishment of the Sultan Idris Training College at Tanjong Malim to replace previous inadequate teacher-training facilities. To the SITC came students selected on ability from village schools throughout Malaya. Dussek, who was headmaster of the college from 1922 to 1936, described it as 'a Vernacular University in embryo'.[12] There may have been some pardonable exaggeration in this, but it indicates a totally different attitude. In particular the SITC picked up where Wilkinson had left off in the development of Malay literature and culture. It also became a centre of Malay nationalism and social reform. The graduate returned from the SITC to spend his life teaching in village schools, but with a different vision — and a very sound basis in teaching methods. When Malay nationalism found political expression with the foundation of UMNO in 1946, its strength at the grass-roots lay in the support of the general body of Malay teachers, better-educated than most other members of the village community.

Education for the sons of the Malay ruling class followed a different path for political reasons (Chapter 4). Here the decisive step was the foundation — on Wilkinson's initiative — of the Malay College at Kuala Kangsar. Wilkinson had planned it as a school both for the sons of the aristocracy and for selected pupils from the peasant class. But this aspect was deferred until, in the 1920s, it became the practice to reserve half the places for pupils selected on merit and half for candidates nominated by the State governments from their upper class. In its initial stages the MCKK was commended to the Malay aristocracy for its character-building virtues borrowed from the English public school. This was misunderstood. Wilkinson, by now a British Resident, found in 1910 that it was conceived as 'a sort of reformatory for idle and refractory boys of good family'.[13] Public school ethos was suitably adapted to Malay aristocratic values. The boarders, for example, were divided into three groups — royalty, sons of major chiefs, and others — and accommodated separately with maintenance allowances for their board on a descending scale.[14] But the school was a success, becoming both a valued Malay institution and the training-ground for the generation of Malay administrators who provided the chief ministers of the Malay States under the federal constitution of

1948.[15] Apart from the privileged few who went to Kuala Kangsar, a considerable number of other Malay boys of the upper class were educated in the ordinary English secondary schools. This system opened up a gap between the main body of the Malay community, confined within the limits of the Malay vernacular schools, and the English-educated élite. The increasing social mobility by which able boys of the peasant class could get scholarships and so enter the élite has not closed the gap.

The Chinese who immigrated to Malaya were, like the Malays, of peasant stock, but they came from a society which placed a high value on literary education of an archaic type as a qualification for public office and leadership in rural China. When the immigrant Chinese made their homes in Malaya as permanent residents, they established schools for their children in Malaya, and supported them from their own resources since the government at first accepted no financial responsibility. These Chinese schools, primary and secondary, became prominent institutions of the community.

In this case also the period around 1920 was something of a watershed. The republican revolution in China produced great changes in education which spread to Malaya.[16] The more obsolete elements of the old education were swept away and a single dialect of Chinese (*Kuo Yu*—the national language) replaced the numerous regional dialects as the medium of instruction. With these changes came a strong current of Chinese nationalism expressed in anti-Western form in such subjects as Chinese history. The Malayan governments instituted a system of inspection and control of Malayan Chinese schools to curb these tendencies. This supervision had its constructive as well as its restrictive aspects, and established the first tenuous links between the Chinese schools and the general stream of Malayan education.[17] From 1924 onwards the government made modest *per capita* grants towards the cost of running the Chinese schools.

The leading exponents of nationalism in the Chinese schools were the schoolmasters, many of them born and educated in China. They were poorly paid and had no guarantee of re-engagement by the same school management committee at the end of the school year. Lack of security led to 'the inevitable shifts and straits, and lack of professional dignity and social status, which attaches to poor itinerants, packing up bag and baggage for the annual mass migration to new jobs in other schools'.[18] Their textbooks imported from China were devoid of Malayan content of any kind. The

223

school buildings and equipment were often poor. It is not surprising that standards of teaching and of discipline were low. There was also discontent and frustration among their pupils, especially those who progressed to the Chinese secondary schools. They had no recognized qualification which would equip them in their search for employment or opportunities of higher education. They were confined within the world of Chinese business and alienated from Malayan society as a whole. Many Chinese middle-class parents, especially the Straits Chinese, preferred to send their children to be educated in the English secondary schools.

Proprietors of estates were required by law to provide primary education for the children of their labourers. As most of the labour-force were Tamil-speakers, the majority of the Indian Tamil schools were situated on rubber estates; the balance were in the towns and were government schools provided for the children of government labourers. Standards in estate schools were generally poor — 'clerks, *kanganies,* and even literate labourers would function as part-time teachers. . the school was often a dilapidated shed'.[19] A qualified teacher employed in an estate school was looking for the opportunity of better-paid employment in schools in urban areas. Like the Chinese and Malay schools, the Indian vernacular schools were isolated from the rest of the educational system.

The most flourishing part of the system was the English secondary schools in the towns, maintained both by the government direct and by missionary bodies in receipt of government grants. These schools provided courses on Western lines leading to external examinations of the 'School Certificate' type; a few offered sixth-form courses leading to university entrance qualifications. The curriculum was overweighted with academic rather than technical subjects, since the majority of the pupils aimed to enter the government clerical or other subordinate services, or to find a job in the offices of European firms whose main requirement was that the candidate should have a good knowledge of English. Apart from medicine there was no opportunity of pursuing a course of university or professional education in Malaya. Raffles College founded in 1928 offered courses in English, geography, history, and other subjects leading to a diploma. There were also limited opportunities of vocational and technical training for subordinate posts. A few Malayan students went on to universities in the United Kingdom and other foreign countries. The Queen's Scholarship founded in

1885 was the premier award for overseas study; it was greatly prized and included among its holders some of the most distinguished Malayans of their generation. But it was a mere drop in the bucket. The whole question of university education was under examination at the time of the Japanese invasion.

In Sabah and Sarawak financial constraints and difficult communications prevented the development of any widespread educational system at all. The few schools were mainly missionary foundations in the towns.

Secondary Education

In the period 1942-45 education suffered a severe setback everywhere. Apart from physical damage to buildings, etc., there was an upheaval as the Japanese made ineffectual efforts to spread the teaching of their language. When reconstruction began after the war, the political climate had altered completely. It was no longer acceptable to leave four different types of school to teach in four different languages. The citizens of Malaya of the future would be the children born in the country. They must share a common experience at the formative stage of growing up. But this objective was easier to recognize than to introduce into the system. A committee set up in 1949 to review the state of Malay education exceeded its terms of references by recommending that the separate vernacular school systems should be merged to form a 'national school' system based on the use of Malay and English.[20] There was a pause during which this novel idea was considered and one or two more committees wrestled with the intractable problems of establishing a unified school system and of finding the money with which to pay for it. The next landmark was the report of the committee appointed in 1956 when the Alliance ministers first took the reins of power into their hands. The chairman was the then Minister for Education, Tun Abdul Razak, who was later to be deputy prime minister and Prime Minister (1970-76). The committee's terms of reference required it to devise 'a national system of education acceptable to the people of the Federation as a whole. . making Malay the national language of the country, whilst preserving and sustaining the languages and culture of the other communities living in the country'.[21]

A national system of education clearly requires that there should be a common syllabus and common teaching-material in the form of textbooks. Moreover, this material should be Malaysian and not alien. History should be Malaysian history and not the Wars of the Roses or the imperial dynasties of China. Since Malay is the national language, it is considered that there should be secondary and university education available exclusively in the Malay language. In practice this accords special treatment to the Malays, but as a community they have 'special rights' in education and it is open to a non-Malay to be educated in this way if he chooses.[22] The controversial issue is the choice of language through which the non-Malay student should be educated. The colonial regime assumed — with some doubts — that English as an international language and a proven instrument of assimilation would prevail or at least be an available option.[23] But the strength of English as an established element in the system and its obvious economic advantages made the Malay nationalists fear that it would swamp the alternative of Malay if there were a choice. The recent experience of Singapore, where parental choice has favoured English-medium schools, indicates that this is a correct assessment. Confronted with this sensitive issue the Razak Committee, headed by a politician of a pragmatic disposition, contented itself with the declaration that Malay as the national language should be 'the main medium of instruction', but made no recommendations to that end other than a review of the position in ten years time.[24] It was, however, decided to withdraw official recognition from secondary education in Chinese and Tamil by terminating the conduct of school-leaving examinations (beyond the primary level) in both of those languages.[25] Given the choice of securing a recognized qualification for employment through the medium of either English or Malay secondary education, the majority of Chinese and Indian pupils opted for the former. In 1967, when the ten years had elapsed, the enrolment at English secondary schools was twice as large as at Malay schools and in the towns even Malay parents showed a disposition to prefer the English medium.[26]

The resentment of the Malays, more especially the teaching profession, at the continued dominance of English secondary education was one of the grievances which the government set out to relieve in planning its new policies during the interregnum of 1969-71. In 1970 it was decided that over the period down to 1982 there should be a progressive conversion to Malay as the sole medium of instruction in all government-aided schools in Malaya. In the first year the lowest class in primary schools was to change over to Malay only, and each year the next higher class in sequence of seniority would be converted. The change-over would be complete at the primary stage by 1975. A gradual change was necessary to permit the retraining of non-Malay teachers, to give them sufficient proficiency in Malay, and the production of Malay textbooks. There was, however, one exception to the 'all Malay' policy; any other language such as English or Chinese could be taught through the medium of that language. English was to be retained at all stages as 'a strong second language'. So a Chinese child would in infancy learn a south-China dialect at home; at school he would be taught through the medium of Malay from the outset, but would probably also learn the *Kuo Yu* dialect of Chinese and also English, being taught those two languages direct and not through Malay. But in learning history or physics, for example, Malay would be the medium of his instruction.

Apart from the linguistic upheaval, the schools have had to cope with a massive increase in numbers. There are four recognized stages of the school system: primary (6 to 11), lower secondary (12 to 14), upper secondary (15 to 16), and post-secondary (17 to 18). Until 1965 only primary education was freely available to all who sought it. Then came the Malayan Secondary Schools Entrance Examination (MSSEE), which weeded out all but the minority whose general ability and aptitude for academic study made them suitable for secondary education. Pupils who might have benefited from vocational education at the secondary stage were eliminated. During the early 1960s there was considerable disquiet at the very high rate of wastage at the MSSEE stage; in Malay-medium schools it was as much as 85 per cent.[27] In 1965 it was decided that promotion to the lower secondary stage should be automatic, with the object of providing 'comprehensive' education for three more years. In addition to the core subjects, there should be a choice of vocational and practical subjects. There was no transitional period and so the sudden influx of a greatly increased number of pupils of very mixed ability and attainment placed a great strain on the system. A crash-programme to train additional teachers led to a fall in standards. The admirable concept of comprehensive education proved difficult to realize, since it required all sorts of new courses and equipment which could not easily be provided. Expert opinion is that this sudden change was 'a bold experiment. . .dictated by political expediency. .prematurely launched'.[28]

To the problems of over-rapid expansion is added the tradition of rather arid academic teaching. 'Memorization and close reproduction of facts and details is exalted above the students' understanding, interpretation, and application of knowledge learnt'. Teachers struggle to teach mixed-ability classes of up to fifty through the medium of a language which is not spoken by teacher or pupil outside the classroom. Add to this 'the overloaded curriculum, the overloaded syllabus, the heavy examination orientation'.[29]

In Sabah and Sarawak the first priority was to expand the education system from its inadequate pre-war scale. The Chinese schools had, as in Malaya, been left very much to their own devices; it was now the aim to achieve a more unified system. It was also necessary to train local candidates to fill the more senior posts in the government, if the states were to progress towards self-government.[30] When the two states negotiated the terms of entry to Malaysia, they were conscious of the relative backwardness of their education systems and eager to retain English as the main medium of instruction, since Malay is not an indigenous language to the same extent as in Malaya. Some safeguards were obtained, but the federal government is determined that education in Borneo shall 'be progressively integrated with the national system'.[31] This has been one of the issues over which conflict has arisen on occasion.

In addition to the government-aided schools there are private schools which anyone may attend if he is prepared to pay relatively high fees. In particular some of the Chinese-medium schools opted out of the government-aided system in order to preserve their own style and method. But these are not flourishing; they have generally failed to liberate themselves from the constraints of communal solidarity and so to provide an education which will stand on its merits as a good education. Those who have the resources prefer to seek their education overseas. In the main this exodus is at the university rather than the secondary school stage, but there are some pupils at foreign schools.

Two particular problems of secondary education deserve final mention. The schools reflect the values of their society in undervaluing vocational and technical training. In the colonial period the main opportunity of employment for an educated man was as a clerk in the government or business world. White-collar jobs were better paid and carried higher status than manual labour or even blue-collar work. Yet it is now recognized in official planning that 'specific shortages of middle and high level manpower' are a 'binding constraint' on the growth of the economy.[32] Demand for professional and technical staff is growing at a faster rate than any other sector of the job-market. The need is for men trained in engineering, agriculture, and the manifold skills used in manufacturing industry. At the other extreme there is an impending surplus of non-science graduates which will have to be curtailed.[33] A proportion of the missing technical experts must be graduates, but the majority need less advanced training. Apart from providing the opportunities to acquire these skills it is necessary to 'reorientate people's attitudes towards a vocational and technical bias in education'.[34] For various reasons, however, the growing demand for technical staff has been met by developments outside the secondary school system to be described below.

The other fundamental need of the secondary school system is for more and better teachers. On leaving school a future teacher at a secondary school attends a two-year course at a residential training-college; Malaysia now has about twenty of these.[35] The main deficiency in numbers is at the graduate teacher level; in the mid-1970s it was estimated that there was a shortage of about 10,000 with an acute deficiency among graduate teachers of mathematics and sciences. But the problem is more one of quality than of quantity. The rapid expansion of lower secondary education in the mid-1960s 'turned out thousands of ill-equipped lower secondary teachers. . . the teaching profession does not attract the best-qualified people or those sincerely dedicated to teaching. . . the morale of teachers is low'.[36] These comments must be seen not as a criticism of the teaching profession, many of whom are shining exceptions, but as a reflection of official and popular priorities. A society gets the teaching profession which it deserves.

Technical Training

The rapid expansion of technical and vocational training at sub-professional level is due to two causes. The first has been sufficiently described — there is an acute shortage of trained personnel. The second is the obvious correlation between education, more especially of a practical kind, and a better standard of living. A survey of poverty in the early 1970s established that 50 per cent or more of the uneducated or poorly-educated sector of the population lived below the poverty-line, but only 20 per cent of the better-educated.[37] It is this which underlies much of the drive for better educational opportunities for Malays. The problem was recognized by RIDA, established in 1950 as the first attempt at rural improvement. RIDA did not flourish, but it remained in being when the 'Economic Congress of Indigenous Peoples' called for a better programme in 1965. RIDA was re-formed and strengthened as the *Majlis Amanah Raayat* (MARA), which established a MARA Institute of Technology (MIT) with its headquarters outside Kuala Lumpur but branches throughout Malaya. It offers courses in Accountancy, Administration and Law, Business Management, Art, Architecture, Applied Science, Engineering and Computer Science, and Mathematics, with such practical applications as food technology, land-surveying, and library science.[38] There may be some grandiloquence in using these titles for essentially practical instruction at technical college level, but they illustrate the wide range of skills which the developing Malaysian economy requires. In 1980 more than 9,000 students — almost all Malay — were taking MIT courses. To give them practical training, arrangements are made to attach students to industrial and commercial firms with the incidental advantage of working with employees of other communities. Many of the new Malay recruits to the modern sector of the economy have come by way of MIT. In addition there are other centres of technical training, including the Abdul Rahman College (primarily a business studies school established on Chinese initiative, but not exclusively Chinese in personnel) and a Polytechnic. Enrolment for training of this kind is expanding rapidly; it increased fourfold during the 1970s. Malays make up four-fifths of the total, though the range of their subjects is very wide — from engineering and applied science to courses in 'art and language' and 'humanities'.[39] At a lower level there are Industrial Training Institutes, trade-schools at which school-leavers, ex-servicemen, and apprentices can obtain practical workshop skills.

In Sabah and Sarawak there are some technical training facilities, but there is less demand here for workshop and commercial skills. Four-fifths of all employment is in agriculture, and this situation will not change significantly for some time.

Universities

At the present time university education is the most controversial element in the Malaysian education system. The other communities have acquiesced in the changes enforced by the Malays at the secondary and sub-professional training level, so long as there was reasonable equality of opportunity in the universities. But this is no longer the case. To understand the current situation it is necessary to look briefly at the recent past.

On the eve of the Japanese occupation of Malaya there was a plan for merging Raffles College with the King Edward VII College of Medicine to form a university college. When the project was revived after the war, it took the form of a full University of Malaya established in existing buildings in Singapore. It was split into a University of Singapore and a University of Malaya (on a campus at Petaling Jaya near Kuala Lumpur) in 1960. Singapore had meanwhile acquired a second university, the Nanyang University, established in 1956 on the lines of Western-style universities in China, for students who had been educated in Chinese schools. In its early years the Nanyang University had a troubled history marked by uncertain academic standards and lack of external recognition, mediocre staff, and an inward-looking concentration on all things Chinese. This had its bearing on the Malaysian attitude towards the scheme for a Merdeka University, described below. The University of Malaya as it developed in the 1950s and 1960s was essentially a Western-style centre of learning and research offering courses through the medium of English. High standards induced a fairly narrow and specialized range of studies.

To the Malay political leaders in the 1960s, many of whom had been educated at English universities in the immediate post-war period or in the English professions such as the Bar, university education was the gateway to the commanding heights of the economic, political, and social system.[40] These opportunities must be secured for the Malays if they were to retain control of an increasingly sophisticated national economy.[41] The champions of Malay as 'the main medium of instruction' were determined that Malay should become the language of all Malaysian universities. As a first step the Education Review Committee of 1960 recommended that the University of Malaya should become bilingual — use Malay as well as English — to accommodate the Malay students who were passing through the new Malay-medium secondary schools. It was also necessary to establish additional universities to meet the growing demand. As a result of a survey in the mid-1960s[42] a college, later the Science University, was established at Penang and a National University (*Universiti Kebangsaan*) in Selangor in 1969-70; in the early 1970s the long-established Technical College and also the College of Agriculture were upgraded to become universities offering degree courses in their subjects. The National University — as the Malay title suggests — was designed to show that a university teaching in Malay only could produce satisfactory results.[43] It declared its readiness to admit students of any community if they had the required qualifications. Both this university and the university at Penang offered rather broader courses than the University of Malaya.

As part of the review of education during the interregnum of 1969-71 there was a survey of universities.[44] This brought to notice a disturbing failure of Malay students to obtain their due share of university education in technical subjects.[45] It was decided that positive steps must be taken both to increase the total number of Malay students at universities and to ensure that—in keeping with the general NEP philosophy—the number of students enrolled in each subject should correspond with the communal composition of the population as a whole.[46] The words of the present Malay Minister of Education state very clearly the policy adopted and the justification, as the government sees it:

> We are trying to bring youngsters from the rural areas into the centres. . . bring them to the universities. . . send them overseas. But can we allow them to compete in normal circumstances? Certainly not. You find a Malay third-grade pass getting a scholarship to go overseas instead of a Chinese first-grade. Conclusion: racial discrimination. But we have no choice but to do what we are doing. The Malay student who gets a third-grade lives in the rural areas. If he was exposed to the same facilities he might well get a Grade I. That is what the National Economic Policy is all about. This is what discrimination is about.[47]

The results of a decade of this policy of 'positive discrimination' are striking. In 1970 Chinese students at Malayan universities slightly outnumbered Malays and Indians combined. By 1977 three-quarters of all students admitted to universities were Malay, and only one-fifth were Chinese. More than half the Chinese applicants for university places are turned down.[48] The overall results achieved by Malay students were said to be poor. Far too many of them continued to opt for subjects such as Islam, Malay Studies, Malay language, and too few for the scientific and technical courses. It was foreseen that unless this trend was reversed, there would be an unemployable surplus of graduates in 'arts subjects' in the 1980s. Among positive measures to redress the balance a number of residential 'science schools' were opened in rural areas to equip Malay students for entry to technical courses at universities.

The Malay community is disposed to treat this policy and its results as belated justice to themselves. The Chinese resent it bitterly as unfair discrimination. The official response to Chinese complaints is that many Chinese families can afford to send their children to schools and above all to universities overseas. It is argued that in assessing the balance of opportunity, the Malaysian students overseas, who number about 36,000 (not all at universities), should be added to the count at Malaysian universities. A small number of the Malaysian students abroad are Malays. Indeed it is said that the ablest Malay students get scholarships to study abroad and that this factor explains the poor results of those who go to Malaysian universities. But the large majority, perhaps four-fifths of overseas students, are Chinese seeking the opportunities of higher education which are denied to them in Malaysia. The Chinese community might accept this argument more readily if they were allowed to use the wealth which is imputed to them to finance additional opportunities for their children in Malaysia. There was already a project for a Chinese Merdeka University when the riots of 1969 brought a check to all Chinese aspirations for a larger share of the cake. The legislation of the interregnum period included the University and University Colleges Act 1971, which effectually reserved to the state the exclusive right to establish universities. There are powers of derogation, but the National Front government has steadfastly refused to permit the Merdeka University project to proceed. The principal objection to it is that it would be a Chinese-language university and it is contrary to national education policy to permit the creation of such a centre of Chinese cultural nationalism. There is no doubt that the national government could, if it wished, give consent on conditions which would effectually safeguard the position and maintain satisfactory standards and policies within the proposed university. The sponsors, who are drawn from the Chinese business community, are very willing to compromise and in particular to give Malay its place as a major subject. The real Malay objection is to any university which will help young Chinese to compete with their Malay contemporaries, and polarize the conflict between Malay and Chinese education.

The Merdeka University question, which had been simmering for some time, came to the boil late in 1978. A member of the parliamentary DAP opposition obtained a debate in the lower chamber on the refusal to grant a charter or even to permit a public meeting to be held to discuss the matter. It was an unusually lively debate with considerable political repercussions.[49] As the National Front government had a massive majority, the outcome was never in doubt. Indeed the sponsors of the university were critical of the DAP for precipitating a public and final decision to turn down the project. The two Chinese parties within the National Front were placed in some difficulty. Both the MCA and Gerakan supported the government stand, though only the MCA declared its position in the debate. The cost of doing so was a loss of support among the Chinese electorate, more especially by the MCA. It was difficult for the Malay ministers to retrieve the situation for their partners, since any concession on their part would have opened them to criticism by PAS, now in opposition. There was the usual search for compromise behind closed doors and assurances were given, with which the Chinese ministers professed themselves satisfied, that there would be some retreat from the position of extreme discrimination against non-Malay students in the allocation of university places in Malaysia.[50] Meanwhile, the sponsors of the university planned to challenge the official refusal of their application by proceedings in the courts.

Language and Culture

Malay is now well established in the universities. Since 1970 it has been the sole 'official' language of the University of Malaya and most of the lectures are given in Malay. It is held that as the majority of students are Malay there should be a corresponding proportion of Malays among the academic staff. But the priority assigned to scientific and technical courses, for which English is the accepted international language, imposes some limits.

National Unity

The use of the Malay language should be distinguished from the encouragement of a sense of national identity expressed in a common culture, which it is one objective of the language policy to create (the other is to widen the career opportunities of Malays). Even before positive measures to spread the use of Malay were first taken, it was widely used *lingua franca* when English could not be used — though many non-Malays and Europeans did not speak it well. It is not difficult to learn to speak correct 'basic Malay' of a simple kind. The pronunciation, spelling (in the *Rumi* or roman script), grammar, and syntax are straightforward. At a more advanced level there are many subtleties of form and meaning and there is a worthwhile corpus of literature, ancient and modern. The measures taken to introduce a common spelling of Malay and Indonesian have obvious benefits for both in their general usage. Much work has been done in recent years to develop a technical vocabulary for use in science, commerce, and industry.[51] The general effect of the education policy described above must be to produce in time a Malaysian population which is able if it wishes to communicate adequately through the medium of Malay. In his dealings with government agencies the citizen is obliged to do so. The position is regulated by the National Language Act passed in 1967 on the expiry of the ten-year period in which English was to be a second 'official' language. The Act permits the use of English translations to supplement the Malay text in official reports and documents; it also allows the limited use of English for speeches in legislature, but this is a privilege which is not now commonly used. These concessions caused some discontent among Malay nationalists who also felt that official Malay texts should be written in the *Jawi* script, adapted from Arabic, since that is the script which Malays themselves first learn at school. But *Jawi* is much more difficult to learn and its compulsory use by non-Malays would militate against the wider use of the Malay language.

The more searching question is whether the non-Malay Malaysian citizen uses or will come to use Malay in the privacy of his home or even at his place of business. Languages other than Malay may still be taught in the schools where there is sufficient demand. In Malaysia, unlike Thailand and Indonesia, a Chinese trader may still display the auspicious name of his firm in Chinese characters above his shop. There has even been some reversion to the use of Chinese, as a means of communicating with non-English speakers in the mother-tongue, on the part of Straits Chinese who had previously abandoned Chinese for English or a sinicized variety of Malay.[52] The conflict over national culture and identity tends to strengthen the hold of the mother-tongue on each community. Whether Malay will displace English as the preferred second language, in circumstances where there is a choice between them, is likely to depend on the success or failure of Malay in business usage. People will use a language if it pays them to do so. As the

Malay community gains ground in commercial contexts, they may bring their language with them as the normal mode of communication. But it will take time.

The Malay determination to create national unity by the wider use of the Malay language (but not as yet their culture or religion) has so far been self-defeating. There is nothing new about this—Daudet exposed the problem in his short story 'La Dernière Classe', about the German policy in Alsace Lorraine after 1870. Enforced cultural change begets resistance. Malay opinion justifies the positive discrimination in favour of their language by the argument that the indigenous peoples (in effect this means the Malays since the indigenous peoples of Sabah and Sarawak do not claim any primacy for their languages) have a special position. Malaya was a Malay country before the arrival of the Chinese and the Indians, and the cultural divide should be bridged by their assimilation to Malay as the national language of all communities. But the insistence on the special position of the Malays widens the distance which its seeks to span. This is not to deny the need for unity; a nation of different cultures needs 'a new culture which can provide the psychological or spiritual basis of political unity'.[53] But unity can be achieved without cultural assimilation—the Swiss are a nation without a single national language. The resistance of the non-Malay communities to Malay assimilation policies is not just perverseness. The differences of language, culture, and religion which keep the communities apart are, within each community, the springs of their vitality and cohesion. Deprive them of those elements and their community is destroyed.

The only example to date of partial assimilation in the Malaysian context is the absorption during the colonial period of the English language and some of its associated ideas. It may be argued that this was not a voluntary process since colonial rule demanded of the subjects a proficiency in the language of the rulers; that it affected only the minority of those who were drawn into the stream of English-medium education; and that it alienated the anglicized minority from the broad mass of their communities. But it does suggest that the sharing of an experience, the working of common institutions, is as important as the use of a common language. The argument that the use of English was the product of colonial rule also raises doubts as to whether Malay can be similarly established in an independent Malaysia in which the Malays have their hands on the levers of power. Colonial rule in its heyday had a prestige and authority which cannot be reproduced by one of the Malaysian communities in their dealings with the others.

There is as yet little sign of the evolution of a common Malaysian culture. The religion and life-style of each community remains a distinctive barrier against the others.[54] Modern literature is represented in the main by journalism in various languages, and by some accomplished academic work in English on economic and social problems, history, and other subjects. There is a considerable flow of modern fiction in Malay, and also some verse and other literary work. It is difficult for the non-specialist to assess how much of this kind of work is written in the other languages. Malay academics, and some others, have begun to publish their work in the Malay language. Foreign, mainly English, writing of all sorts has been translated into Malay—mainly for teaching purposes. But it is doubtful whether many Malaysian writers of the present day read the work of their contemporaries written in another tongue. So long as each stream runs in its separate channel there can be no mingling of tradition and of thought. A minor but interesting recent development is the publication of a simple Chinese–Malay dictionary. It may mark the beginning of a change.

The shared knowledge of the Malay language will be—as is intended—a slow leaven of the mass. As the years go by, the mere process of growing up and being educated, of living in towns and working in offices and factories with other Malaysians, some of them men and women of a different community, creates a shared experience. The NEP objective of eliminating 'the identification of race with economic function' is a practical recognition of that fact. But unification by these means must be a gradual and a voluntary process. It is unlikely to be fully achieved within the twenty years of the NEP programme. If the tempo is forced meanwhile, the purpose will be defeated.

Notes

1   TMP, para 1309.
2   Gullick (1958), 53 and 140.
3   Winzeler (1974), 266 describes these local centres of Islamic teaching,
    particularly characterisitc of Kelantan, as—'students live in ones, twos,
    or threes in small individual or double huts—called *pondok*. . . .
    students occupy themselves with the lessons given by the teachers on one

or another subject or with practising reading and chanting, studying texts or commentaries, helping one another or in some cases teaching younger children'.

4 Roff (1967) and (1974), Hooker (1970) and (1976), Majid Mohamed Mackeen (1969), Majid bin Zainuddin, in Roff (ed.) (1978), provide a varied and detailed coverage of this topic.

5 Cheeseman (1955), 31: Wong and Gwee (1972), 7.

6 In tracing the development of British policy on Malay education down to 1906, I am much indebted to Stevenson's study.

7 Annual Report of District Officer Kuala Langat 1896 (the writer was W. W. Skeat, the well-known ethnologist).

8 Winstedt in Annual Report FMS 1920. Winstedt served as Assistant Director of Education (Malay) 1916-23, and as Director of Education 1924-31. Despite his immense learning and commitment to his task, his approach was unimaginative and has been criticized (Roff (1967), 139) — justly in my opinion.

9 Cheeseman (1955), 35, citing an official report.

10 Annual Report FMS 1897.

11 Roff (1967), 130-3 and elsewhere: Stevenson (1975), Chapter v, 'The New Era'. Wilkinson was among other things an outstanding scholar of Malay who will long be remembered for his dictionary (Wilkinson 1932), and as the editor of and a substantial contributor to *Papers on Malay Subjects* (Wilkinson 1906-).

12 Quoted in Roff (1967), 143. Roff, 142-57 gives a full account of the progress and achievement of the SITC.

13 Annual Report of British Resident Negri Sembilan 1910.

14 Stevenson (1975), 185 citing an official report. In 1935 the MCKK was described as dedicated more 'to developing a sense of duty and responsibility than to mere scholastic achievement' (Annual Report of British Resident Perak 1935). Hargreaves, described by a pupil as 'a sturdy, fierce-looking man. . . with a long white moustache with grey hair and he used a glass in his right eye' (Gullick 1957), was headmaster until 1918. The transition to a more democratic system in the 1920s did not pass unnoticed; Winstedt (1947), 43 mentions that a Sultan objected to the admission of boys from non-aristocratic families, pointing out that one of them was the descendant of a slave.

15 Three of the four chief ministers appointed to office in the former FMS in 1948 were MCKK old boys. In later years its most eminent *alumnus* was Tun Abdul Razak, deputy prime minister and then Prime Minister of Malaysia, who was president of the old boys' association. As a bastion of the old regime the MCKK was threatened with closure at the time of the Malayan Union, but that decision was rapidly reversed under Malay pressure.

16 Purcell (1948), Chapter XII on the general subject of Chinese schools.

17 Purcell in his memoirs (Purcell 1965), 154-9 gives a frank account of problems encountered as an inspector of Chinese schools in the 1920s. Elsewhere (Purcell 1954, 40), he opines that an opportunity was missed in the inter-war period of introducing English teaching into Chinese schools as a means of widening their horizons.

18 Annual Report Federation of Malaya 1952, 160.

19 Arasaratnam (1970), 179.

20 Barnes Report followed by the Fenn Wu Report on Chinese education. See Wong and Gwee (1972), 24.

21 The Razak Report.

22 See below on the *Universiti Kebangsaan* and Wong and Gwee (1972), 41.

23 e.g. Silcock, a long-serving professor of Economics at the University of Malaya in the immediate post-war period and an influential academic writer, said in an essay entitled 'Forces for Unity' (Silcock 1961, 41), 'A Malay language education could not *per se* unify the people; English education is the only instrument that could. But to succeed it must be a widespread education'.

24 Razak Report, 3. There was a review in 1960 (the Rahman Talib Report), but it merely endorsed its predecessor's views on this particular point.

25 This was one of the Chinese grievances which nearly split the Alliance at the time of the 1959 elections (Chapter 8).

26 286,254 at English and 128,069 at Malay schools: Education Statistics of Malaysia 1938 to 1967.

27 Tham Seong Chee (1979), 338. By 1967 the rate of wastage had been reduced to 50 per cent. In the section of this Chapter dealing with educational policy during the period since independence I am much indebted both to Tham Seong Chee's paper and to the study by Wong and Gwee.

28 Wong and Gwee (1972), 47. The joint authors are lecturers in education at the Universities of Malaya and of Singapore respectively.

29 Wong and Gwee (1972), 158.

30 On education in Sabah and Sarawak there is much in Wong and Gwee (1972). Tregonning (1965), and Milne and Ratnam (1974) also provide much useful information. See also J. C. Jackson (1968) on Sarawak.

31 TMP, para 1310.

32 TMP, para 129.

33 TMP, paras 225, 231, and 468.

34 Wong and Gwee (1972), 135. The authors have some sharp things to say on the colonial past — 'the colonial masters' conception of their education task was to produce docile clerks', etc., etc. (132). With respect I believe that the causes were more deep-seated than the attitudes (in any case exaggerated) of a few British officials. The attitude complained of would otherwise have vanished long since — and it has not.

35 TMP, para 1352.

36 Wong and Gwee (1972), 142.

37 TMP, para 492.

38 TMP, para 1320: Tham Seong Chee (1979), 339.

39 In 1970 total enrolment for 'diploma and certificate courses' was 3,347, of whom 2,865 were Malay; in 1975, 13,547 and 8,153 respectively: TMP, para 1382. Enrolment for degree courses over the same period increased by a mere 75 per cent.

40 The three successive Malay Prime Ministers have been lawyers. In the immediate post-war period (1946-56) a large number of scholarships were awarded both to students and to rather older-serving government officials to enable them to study at overseas universities and colleges, mainly in the United Kingdom and Australia, to improve their qualifications. Many of the

239

leading politicians and civil servants of the first decade of independence
were drawn from this group.

41   See Tilman (1964), Esman (1964), and also the Report of the Committee on
Malayanization of the Public Service 1956.

42   Report of the Higher Education Planning Committee. The chairman was
Encek Khir Johari, at that time Minister for Education.

43   Wong and Gwee (1972), 50. Its declared purpose was to 'show sceptics that
[university education] through the medium of Malay could be done'.

44   The Majid Ismail Report.

45   The proportion of Malay graduates out of the total for 1970 was 22 out of
493 in Science, 1 out of 71 in Engineering, 15 out of 49 in Agriculture, and
4 out of 67 in Medicine: Majid Ismail Report, 44 cited by Tham Seong Chee
(1979), 336.

46   Majid Ismail Report, 48.

47   *FEER* (23 June 1978).

48   The figures given in TMP (Table 22-8) for 1970 and 1975 for students
enrolled for courses in Malaysia are:

	1970	1975
Malays	3,237	8,153
Chinese	4,009	5,217
Indians	595	743
Others	307	141
Total	8,148	14,254

In justification of the policy it is argued that although the proportion of
non-Malay students has fallen sharply in absolute numbers, it has risen over
this period. On the general situation in 1979 see *FEER* (31 August 1979), 57.

49   *FEER* (6 October, 20 October, 3 November and 24 November 1978).

50   It appears that the non-*bumiputra* proportion of entrants to universities is
to be gradually increased by 2 per cent *per annum,* so as to raise it from 34
per cent in 1978 to 44 per cent in 1983, when—by pure coincidence—the
next federal elections are due to be held.

51   Only an expert can assess the results. Tham Seong Chee, an associate
professor of Malay Studies at the University of Singapore, refers to 'the
low functionality of the national language' (331). It is my impression,
however, that it serves well enough.

52   Tan Cheng Lock continued as an English speaker throughout his political
career. Lee Kuan Yew, Prime Minister of Singapore since 1959 and a Straits
Chinese by origin, learnt to speak Chinese in adult life partly —it is
believed—as a gesture of solidarity with the non-English-speaking proletariat
of Singapore who made up a large part of his electorate.

53   Sir Sydney Caine, former Vice-Chancellor of the University of Malaya, in
Malaya (June 1958), 22.

54   There have been disturbing signs that the religious turmoil among Muslims
in Iran and elsewhere in the Middle East may be spreading to the Malays,
who are by tradition very tolerant of other religions. The 'Kerling trial' of a
group of Hindu temple guards on charges of using violence against vandals

desecrating their temple became a *cause célèbre* in 1979: *FEER* (25 January 1980). The Lord President of the Court of Appeal, one of the architects of the Malaysia constitution and the author of the leading commentary on it (see Suffian bin Hashim 1972), on another occasion rebuked those who sought to 'exploit [religion] as a passport for getting into parliament'. His courageous statement that the majority of Muslims did not wish to see Islamic law extended since they recognized the limits imposed by the circumstances of a multi-racial community provoked a storm among the UMNO youth movement: *FEER* (23 November 1979). But legislation of this kind is the prerogative of State legislatures, more susceptible to local pressures than the federal parliament: see *FEER* (6 July 1979), 22.

13   A Changing Society

Let your child die but do not let the custom die. So runs a Malay
proverb which many Malays find out of tune with their times. It is
indeed often reversed — let the custom die but do not let our
children die.[1] The process of social change is selective. Some
habits, such as the ceremonial of a wedding or the ritual of a
harvest-home, may be preserved from generation to generation,
while the underlying structure of society and its social values
change at an accelerating pace.

A hundred years ago or more the economy of the Malay village
was based on impermanence and equality . . . . 'no one could be
certain that he would not have to fly on the morrow'. . . 'few commoners accumulated any wealth; if they did so a Raja would rob
them of it'.[2] The stability established after 1874 encouraged the
Malay peasant to improve his land with the certainty of enjoying
the fruits of his labours. The incidental consequence of plantation
development was a land system which gave to the peasant also a
permanent title to his land, and also a valuable cash crop — rubber.
Access to markets through improved communications benefited the
traditional staples of Malay agriculture — rice, coconuts, fruit, etc.
As land became a valuable and heritable fixed asset of the Malay
economy (in contrast to its previous temporary use as a natural
resource), inequality of wealth began to divide peasant society into
classes. In modern times pressure of population on the land has accelerated this process. A number of excellent modern surveys[3] present a remarkably uniform picture of economic class structure in
different Malay village communities. Much of the land is owned by
landlords, some of whom are absentee townsfolk and others
wealthy members of the village community.[4] Some village
landlords work part of their land and rent out the surplus; others
are just landlords in receipt of rents. Some working cultivators own
all the land which they occupy, but others rent additional land to
supplement what they own. There are tenants who own no land of
their own, and at the bottom of the scale are landless labourers who

work for a cash wage or a share of the crop. In one such village 14 per cent of the cultivated land was in absentee ownership, and more than half the remainder was owned by less than 10 per cent of the resident householders. At the other extreme 13 per cent owned no land at all. From these gradations of landownership emerges a village society divided into three classes — the well-to-do, the land-owning smallholders, and the landless or almost landless wage-earner whose inadequate income is 'highly variable and unpredictable'. Malay convention is against the explicit recognition of economic classes — 'We are all fellow-Muslims; how could there be any differences between us?'[5] But there is tacit, and sometimes explicit, resentment among the poor at the exploitation by the well-to-do of their economic strength.[6] Bargaining over the renting or sharecropping of land is the most frequent occasion of conflict. But it also occurs when a poor kinsman seeks a loan from a more fortunate relative; the latter cannot by convention refuse, but he resents it. The landlord class has in recent years also branched out into retail shopkeeping, taking the place of the Chinese when they were removed into New Villages in the course of the Emergency (Chapter 6). Differences of wealth are reflected in such things as the size, construction, and furnishing of houses, leadership in such social activities as prayer meetings, and the choice of marriage-partners for children.[7]

There are changes also in the village leadership. Both the village headman (*ketua kampong*) and the sub-district headman (*penghulu*) are now generally chosen by election, though the choice continues to fall on those who have traditional claims by descent (reinforced by wealth and personal merit). But these traditional offices are losing their influence. . . 'At one time the *Penghulu* was a traditional head whose post was hereditary. He personified the source of leadership and authority in the *mukim* [sub-district] community. . . . the *Penghulu* is chosen by popular election but. . . . he automatically becomes a minor cog in the general administrative machinery'.[8] Influence is passing by a process of 'politicization' (what a word!) to a new type of leader, the local party organizer, and above him the elected State assembly-man or member of the federal parliament.[9] Twenty years of rural development programmes promoted and administered to relieve his discontents have induced in the Malay villager a shrewd understanding of how the system works. The political candidate, supported by the local UMNO or PAS branch, seeks the votes of the electorate with promises that if elected he will secure funds for village welfare or improvement — or if he is the incumbent seeking re-election, he recites the record of benefits obtained in the past.

New men and new functions have so far blended with the old without much friction. The traditional leaders of the village community are the well-to-do members of the peasant class, and the much-respected Islamic worthies who are officials of the prayerhouse or mosque or religious teachers.[10] They play their part in the management of schools and mosques, of co-operative societies, and other social activities, and also in the local branches of the political parties. The village schoolmasters are required to hold aloof from active involvement in politics, but are often influential behind the scenes since they are better able to understand the issues. Their salaries are larger than the incomes of most villagers and they often invest their savings in land. For these reasons they, and other government employees resident in the villages, are placed among the well-to-do in the social scale. The teachers have usually been supporters of UMNO rather than of its opponents.[11] The organization of local political activities offers an opportunity to those villagers who are interested and adroit enough to become proficient in it. It happens only rarely in these tradition-bound communities that the rural poor take a leading part.

Since 1955 the government of Malaya and then of Malaysia has been founded on the hold of UMNO on the political allegiance of the recognized leaders of these village communities. At election time the Malay elector is reminded of UMNO's achievements, promised more of the same medicine, and assured that UMNO knows how to keep the Chinese in their place without precipitating open conflict. PAS and any other opponents of UMNO put forward a less rosy view. Progress in relieving poverty is painfully slow; the 'fat cats' of the Malay middle and upper classes have done a deal with the Chinese at the expense of the true interests of the Malay community, etc. As it becomes clear to the Malay villager that the considerable benefits of 'wider share ownership' for Malays (Chapter 10) are going to the middle class which alone has or can borrow the money to invest in securities, his distrust may increase. On the other hand, it reassures him to see that control of the world of big business is increasingly in the hands of Malays.

It has been cogently argued in a recent study of Malay rural life in Kelantan that the failure of UMNO for a period of almost twenty years (1959-78) to win control of that State reflected agrarian conflict and discontent within the Malay community, rather than a crude exploitation of Islamic sentiment by religious leaders, whose fundamentalism was outraged by Malay accommodation with the Chinese and with the Western style of life.[12] If this is so, UMNO remains politically vulnerable in those areas, especially the rice-bowl of the north-west as well as the north-east, where economic conflicts within the Malay community are especially sharp and unlikely to be relieved in full by the policies of the NEP.

There is also a substantial Malay migration both to the new areas of land settlement opened by FELDA and other agencies, and to the towns. It is too early yet to assess the social consequences of moving Malay settlers to the new settlement areas, where they must in effect make new communities on the frontier of rural life. This programme relieves rural poverty and land-hunger. It does so at the cost of imposing on the new communities the bureaucratic constraints of central management of their economy. The smallholder must, for example, collect his latex or his palm-fruit under a timetable regulated to the intake of central processing plants. In a similar way the rice-grower whose land benefits from improved irrigation is chivvied into a cycle of double-cropping according to a strict timetable and with the use of fertilizers.[13] It is of course in the Malay tradition to look for leadership and organization from above. But there is also a traditional disinclination for regimented activity. This may be one of the collective attitudes which is changing; many more Malays are now seeking employment on estates and in factories.

Malay migration to industrial employment is also a recent phenomenon. A recent survey of one of the new industrial estates in western Malaya found that most of the workers, of whom about half were Malay, were young men attracted by the opportunity of earning higher wages. The extra money was spent on buying household goods, motor cycles, electrical gadgets, etc. There was a general sense of frustration at the lack of opportunity for further progress by learning specialized skills. Few of the workers had satisfactory or permanent living accommodation. They made do with makeshift housing, in some cases mere shacks on estates, and travelled 5 miles or more to work.[14] Unless there is a massive programme of low-cost housing construction, the new industries in or near towns are likely to create as many social problems as they resolve. For that reason it is government policy to encourage industries which are labour-intensive or which use mainly local materials to find sites in established areas of settlement in the countryside.[15]

The employment statistics (Appendix 2, Table 8) show a rapid growth of jobs in government and other services and much of this employment is taken up by Malays under NEP requirements. Some of the jobs are low-paid, but others enlarge the growing salariat of middle-class office workers and service staff of various kinds. With the very rapid expansion of secondary and technical education for Malays there must come a time when white-collar and blue-collar work for Malay school-leavers is insufficient to meet demand. There is a similar imbalance foreseen for the early 1980s between the supply of jobs for Malay graduates in arts subjects. In the villages there is a continuing problem of the 'drop-out': the schoolboy who fails to complete the nine-years schooling available to him and so emerges into a more competitive world ill-equipped to compete. It is part of the price of creating opportunities for the Malay community that there must be losers as well as winners. It is no comfort for the failure that other Malays have succeeded. It is the children from the poorer section of the rural community who most often suffer these setbacks.

The cement which bonds together the increasingly heterogeneous elements of Malay society is fear of the economic strength of the Chinese. The greater the success of 'restructuring' under the NEP the weaker the bond becomes. It is well understood, however, that if the Malay vote is split, of which there were incipient signs in the 1969 elections, this could seriously weaken the Malay hold on the levers of political power. The other main uncertainty of the future is whether the world economy, on which Malaysia so much depends for its markets, will continue to sustain a rate of economic growth in Malaysia sufficient to permit the satisfaction of Malay demands for better living standards, without depriving the other communities of an acceptable share of the national income and resources.

The Chinese are a rural as well as an urban community. As immigrants the Chinese have had to build a new social structure rather than adapt an existing framework. An intensive study of a Chinese rural community in Province Wellesley found that the main social institutions were the village school and two societies established to organize religious ceremonies.[16] The school and its elected management committee had become the centre of authority for the community. In this case, unlike some other local Chinese communities, there were no important associations based on dialect or clan-groups originating in China. If there was a dispute within the village, it would be carried to the school committee and its officers for settlement. The villagers, who were of the Teochiu language group, earned their living by growing vegetables and sugar-cane for sale. In a characteristic Chinese fashion relationships were built on economic transactions. The growers preferred to sell their produce to the same buyer each time. But in return they expected him to show his commitment to them by giving them loans. A loan would be demanded, as a sort of test of the buyer's attitude, even if the borrower did not need the money. If the buyer had shown his friendliness in this way, the grower would continue to sell to him even at a lower price than he could obtain elsewhere.

Chinese religion is an essentially practical approach to establishing a mutually satisfactory working relationship with the local deities and supernatural powers. 'The Teochiu expect the gods to act in the same way as themselves. . . . a mixture of affection, subtlety and deception'.[17] In their own relationships within the village they cultivated an informal but systematic nexus of the ties of friendship (for which there was a recognized term — *gaanchyng*). In case of need the individual drew on his stock of this intangible but valuable asset. 'Surrounded by a hostile world. . . they appreciate having as many friends as possible who will support them right or wrong'.[18] With this inward-looking defensive solidarity went a noticeable detachment from the larger society outside. As farmers they rented their land from Malay landowners of a nearby village; the latter had no use for what had been wasteland, which the Malays could not cultivate since they lacked the special resources and skill in vegetable-growing of the Chinese. There was some bargaining but no rancour — 'the Malay–Teochiu individual relationship is in the nature of a game, the rules of which are perfectly well understood by both sides'. Each community went its own way and had no dealings with the other (except over the payment of rent for the land). The Chinese respected the authority of the Malay *penghulu* within whose sub-district (*mukim*) their village lay, but did not often involve him in their affairs. They had no contact with the MCA or any other Chinese political organization. Three of the villagers were members of a secret society, but the society had no effective hold on the community as a whole.

This was not one of the New Villages created by resettlement during the Emergency, but probably had something in common with them in its social and economic structure. The 400 New Villages vary a great deal in size and type. There are communities of several thousand people settled as a sort of dormitory suburb, from which the inhabitants of working age sally forth daily to earn their living in a nearby town or on an estate or a mine. At the other extreme are much smaller and more remote settlements which have an agricultural economy. In some cases the villagers have been given leases of their land, but in others their rights of tenure are precarious. There is also poverty and unemployment, especially among the younger people. These are the conditions in which the MCP was able to establish its hold during and after the war. The New Villages exist to make it difficult for such a situation to return, and the MCP has been driven away from most of them. But here lies one potential area of instability.

This brief account of Chinese rural communities may show what barriers have to be surmounted in the course of 'restructuring society' and creating 'national unity'. These are people who are content to be isolated. They ask nothing of the world outside except the minimum of necessary economic contact — and to be left alone. It is part of the immigrant tradition of self-help and collective solidarity to rely only on one's immediate neighbours, who share a common culture and language, for help in case of need. The obvious chink in the defensive perimeter is the need for education. The introduction of Malay as the universal language of instruction in government-aided schools came some years after the survey from which the description above has been taken. At that time the village school, in which Chinese was the language of instruction (though some English also was taught), received a government grant. In spite of their commitment to the school, the villagers were finding it difficult to raise the additional money needed for its support. Under the current educational policy they would have to choose between conforming to the Malay language requirement or doing without any subvention. The education policy is a powerful force for integration; but it has to overcome a resistance no less determined.

In the towns the teeming Chinese working-class population includes a large number of self-employed workers — street-hawkers and market-peddlers, trishaw-peddlers, and craftsmen — as well as employees of small businesses, lorry-drivers, etc. They live in overcrowded tenement blocks or in shacks in urban squatter areas around the towns. The urban squatter erects his pathetic contraption of wooden planks from packing-cases, flattened petrol tins, pieces of corrugated iron, palm-thatch, or even cardboard—and calls it home. Water is drawn from a standpipe (if there is one), the cooking-fires lead to conflagrations which sweep through the shacks, and everywhere there is filth. It is part of the development programme to improve these conditions—but it is uphill work. The urban squatter may have left his wife and children in slightly more salubrious surroundings in a New Village. He goes about his business in the anthill of his environment. If he works for a wage, he will have a personal but probably hard-faced relationship with a small Chinese employer who is his boss. In spite of the over-crowding of urban life the Chinese townsman is usually isolated from the non-Chinese world by barriers of language, feeding habits, culture, and spatial separation in residential areas. He may of course work in a factory where there is a mixed labour force or have dealings as a street trader with customers of other com-munities. But such contacts, where they exist, hardly suffice to bridge the gap.

A good deal has already been said of the Chinese middle-class in the context of politics and commerce.[19] There are some very suc-cessful Chinese big businessmen and a growing class of managers, technical staff, and professional men. But the typical Chinese business is still a small-scale enterprise managed by the proprietor. His small group of employees may include members of the same clan or dialect-group as the *towkay*. He associates with others of his kind through trade associations and local chambers of com-merce, guilds, committees for the management of schools, temples, and the like. It is a class which is much less isolated than the manual workers. Many of them speak either Malay or English or both and perforce they have dealings with the government officials, business associates, bank staff, etc., with whom their gainful activity brings them in contact. This is the class from which the MCA and other middle-class parties draw their support. It is increasingly troubled at the restrictions and discrimination, as they see it, to which the current policies of assisting the Malays expose them. Here there is an enforced competition between small Chinese businesses and the large ones, now under Malay control, through which PERNAS and other government agencies operate in the commercial sector.[20] A large business is not necessarily more efficient than a small one, but in some activities the former has the inherent advantage of size. It is a situation which raises interesting questions concerning the future of Malaysian business organization.

The Chinese middle class will not soon forget the bloodshed of May 1969. Many of its members are inclined to bow to pressures which they cannot resist and try to make the best of it. This is the argument of realism upon which the MCA bases its appeal to the Chinese electorate. Within the ranks of the government coalition, however much dominated by the Malays, the MCA can do more, it asserts, for its community than the outright opponents of the regime such as the DAP. The Chinese businessman seems rather disenchanted with politicians of all shades. But there is no obvious alternative to co-operation or opposition through MCA or DAP. The risk in these situations is that some Malay action, such as the rejection of the Merdeka University proposal (Chapter 12), causes the Chinese partners in the coalition to lose support among their own community. This in turn rouses Malay resentment at the failure of the Chinese to 'support' the principle of co-operation. Thus a slide into open conflict can begin.

The largest element of the Indian population is still the labour force on rubber and oil-palm estates to which their parents or grandparents migrated before the war. The Indian estate labourer is threatened on two sides. Employment on plantations is no longer an Indian preserve. These are large-scale enterprises regulated in the conditions which they offer to their employees, and subject to inspection by the Labour Department. Valuable improvements have been obtained by the trade unions which are stronger among Indian estate workers than in most other industries. A growing proportion of the estate labour force is Chinese or Malay. Hence there is competition for jobs and it is somewhat more difficult for husband and wife to secure employment as was the practice in the past. It is among families which have only one wage-earner that poverty is found in the estate labour forces.[21] The other threat to the placid existence of the Indian estate labourer is the possibility of a sale of the estate to buyers who then break it up for resale as smallholdings. There is less of this fragmentation than there used to be. But when it happens, the estate labourer finds himself without either a job or a home.

It is partly on this account that the Indians on estates have demanded — with some success — that they should be able to purchase the dwellings in which they spend their working lives. The plantation companies have been encouraged to build houses at the edge of their properties which can be sold to the labourers who occupy them without creating an enclave in the estate itself. The stabilization of estate labour forces so that they become permanent and continuing communities has produced some interesting changes in the pattern of leadership and social activity on the estates. It is much more of a normal family life and the Indian talent for cultural and social activity (and occasionally for a feud) finds more scope.[22]

In Sabah and Sarawak there is a continuing search for identity even within the recognized ethnic groups. When these peoples were in 1963 'rushed into some adventure of whose outcome they are uncertain',[23] they hardly knew each other. Difficult communications kept them apart. This situation was reflected in the first attempts at concerted political action. In Sarawak the Iban of the Second Division formed a political party (SNAP), but their Iban neighbours a few miles up the coast in the Third Division also formed a party (PESAKA). In Sabah the leaders of the Dusun community established a party — UMKO — in which the letter 'K' stands for 'Kadazan', which in the ears of the party founders sounded better than 'Dusun', which they thought disparaging. But elsewhere the Dusun community regarded this as an attempt by a Kadazan minority in their group to pre-empt the leadership.[24] When electioneering took community leaders into parts of the territory with which they were previously unfamiliar, they became better acquainted with their own ethnic kindred of those foreign parts.[25] Although political parties in Sabah and Sarawak draw their main support from identification with one or other community, they are not generally organized as explicitly communal parties. A predominantly Iban party may include some Malays or vice-versa. It does not make for total harmony, but it sets an example of flexibility to the major Malayan parties.

For a generation at least, the peoples of Sabah and Sarawak are likely to be preoccupied with trying to catch up the social and economic progress of Malaya. It is a simple and attractive objective which may give a sense of purpose and identity to the local communities. There are no deep animosities such as lie beneath the surface in Malaya. Understandably, however, every group wishes to have its share of shaping the future and of the immediate benefits which are at hand. This has so far made of Bornean politics a sort of game of musical chairs, organized by the national leaders in Kuala Lumpur, in which those who will not accommodate themselves to Malayan policies are likely to be left standing outside in the cold.

In every community and every part of Malaysia the immediate decisions rest with the minority who man the machinery of government, including its considerable ramifications into the business world. Theirs is the partially Westernized life-style of the town-dweller. They are committed to policies, especially in the field of education, which will be slow to produce their effects. So far the Malaysians have been able to manage their affairs with considerable success. One can only wish them the continued skill, good fortune—and patience—which seems necessary. It takes a long time to build a mountain.[26]

Notes

1   *Biar mati anak, jangan mati 'adat.* Husin Ali (1964), 102 has an instance of a village conservative invoking the adage. It was, I believe, Datuk Onn who first publicized the reverse form. The authors of TMP, paras 305 and 1310 have their own words for the same need to change a way of life.
2   Gullick (1958), 29-30. The quotations are from Annual Report of British Resident Negri Sembilan 1892 and Straits Settlements Despatch to the Colonial Office dated 16 October 1875.
3   Husin Ali (1964) and (1975), Swift (1965), Wilson (1967), Kessler (1978), and Rogers (1976).
4   Husin Ali (1964), 19, 21, and 36.
5   Husin Ali (1964), 15.
6   Swift (1965), 151-5, Firth (1966), 315-18, Husin Ali (1964), Chapters v and vi, Kessler (1978), Chapter 6.
7   Husin Ali (1964), 82, 91-2.
8   Husin Ali (1964), 21-2.
9   Rogers (1976), Chapter iii, Musolf and Springer (1979), Chapter 4.
10   A prayer-house (*surau*) has an *imam* who leads the prayers, and a *bilal,* who makes the call to prayer, and also an elected supervising committee. It is the local centre of prayer for 20 or 30 households nearest to it. The Friday prayers are held at the nearest mosque, which is a larger building with a more substantial organization. Those members of the community who can save enough are likely to make the pilgrimage to Mecca, thereby acquiring much prestige and the title of 'Haji'. Religious instruction both in schools and privately is given by teachers who have attended a centre of learning either in Malaya (on the *pondok* schools of Kelantan—see Chapter 12), or possibly at one of the Middle Eastern centres.
11   Kessler (1978), has a good deal of material on the role of the Malay teachers. See also Husin Ali (1975), Chapter vi ('The New Leaders').
12   Kessler (1978), passim. I do not know Kelantan well, but am inclined to think that Kessler's analysis relates better to the socio-economic conditions of Kelantan than elsewhere. On Kelantan see Roff (1974).
13   In 1951 the Commonwealth Development Corporation (CDC) proposed to RIDA joint schemes on these lines. There was considerable Malay opposition

(partly because CDC was a foreign, British, body) to the imposition on Malay smallholders of the degree of control inherent in such schemes. But times have changed.

14 The Shah Alam Industrial Estate near Kuala Lumpur described in EconRep (1979-80), 172 ff..

15 TMP, paras 1029 and 1034.

16 Newell (1962). Although both are over twenty years old, the surveys by Newell and Freedman (1957) are two of the best accounts of Chinese rural and urban society in Malayan conditions.

17 Newell (1962), 117.

18 Newell (1962), 169 and 40 (Sino-Malay relations).

19 Freedman (1957) deals fully with the world of small Chinese business.

20 Milne (1976), 252 — a very interesting analysis.

21 TMP, para 502.

22 Limited space precludes the introduction here of material from Jain's (1970) very interesting final chapters.

23 Cobbold Report, para 178 above (Chapter 7).

24 Milne and Ratnam (1974), 97-8 and 124.

25 Milne and Ratnam (1974), 178.

26 *Lama-lama jadi bukit* — another Malay saying.

APPENDICES
1 The Territories of Malaysia

Malaya is a geographical concept which, until Singapore was hived off in 1946, usually included the island of Singapore as well as the island of Penang, since these territories were subject to a common system of British administration. In this book 'Malaya' is generally used to denote the Malay Peninsula and Penang (for which the current official term is 'Peninsular Malaysia'). In some historical contexts, however, where the distinction is not material, 'Malaya' and 'Malayan' are used to comprehend Singapore with the other territories.

Until 1945 the territories under British rule or protection from which Malaysia has evolved were:

1 The British colony of the *Straits Settlements* (known colloquially as the 'ss'), which comprised the island seaports of Singapore and Penang (together with the mainland territory of Province Wellesley opposite to Penang island ceded in 1800 by the Malay State of Kedah) and the mainland enclave of Malacca, also an historic port. Each of these three territories was individually called a 'Settlement'. They were first united as the ss in 1826, and the capital was moved from Penang to Singapore in 1832. The ss reflected the British preoccupation with safeguarding the sea-route to China during the first half of the nineteenth century. In addition the island of Labuan near Brunei was ceded to Britain in 1846 and administered as part of the ss from 1907 to 1945; the ss also included the distant Christmas and Cocos-Keeling islands.

2 The *Federated Malay States* ('FMS') of central Malaya were the Malay States of Perak, Selangor, Negri Sembilan, and Pahang, which came under British protection during the period 1874-89 in connection with the development of tin-mining in west central Malaya. They were federated as the FMS in 1896 with Kuala Lumpur as the federal capital.

3 The *Unfederated Malay States* ('UMS') of Johor, Kedah, Perlis, Kelantan, and Trengganu, came under British protection in the period 1909-14 in the course of extending British rule to the natural limits of Malaya.

4 In northern Borneo *British North Borneo* ('BNB') was administered by the Chartered Company from 1881, and *Sarawak* was a principality ruled by the Brooke family from 1841. Both were carved out of the territory of the Malay State of Brunei, and Sabah also absorbed territory

from the Malay State of Sulu (now part of the Philippines — hence the Philippine claim to Sabah in the 1960s).

In the post-war reorganization of 1945-46, the former FMS and UMS plus the Settlements of Penang and Malacca became the *Malayan Union,* which in turn was reorganized in 1948 as the *Federation of Malaya,* comprising eleven States: nine Malay States and two former Settlements. Singapore was left as a separate British colony. BNB and Sarawak also became British colonies in 1946, and Labuan reverted to become part of BNB territory. Brunei continued as a protected Malay State.

When *Malaysia* was formed in 1963, it originally comprised the eleven States of the former Federation Malaya plus three new States: *Sabah* (the new title of the former BNB), Sarawak, and Singapore. Singapore, however, withdrew from Malaysia in 1965. Brunei declined the invitation to join Malaysia and continued as a separate State.

2   Selected Statistics

Table 1 Area and Population of Malaysia

Territory	Area (sq. miles)	Population (1979 est.)
Malaya	50,806	11,050,000
Sarawak	48,050	1,220,000
Sabah	28,725	980,000
Malaysia	**127,581**	**13,250,000**

MALAYA

Year	Population ('000)			
	Malays and Indonesians	Chinese	Indians	Total
1947	2,428	1,885	531	4,908
1968	4,221	3,076	982	8,465
1973	5,066	3,362	1,000	9,502
1979	5,975	3,850	1,144	11,050
	(54%)	(35%)	(10%)	(100%)

SABAH AND SARAWAK

Group	Sabah	Sarawak
Muslim: Malay, Melanau, Bajau, etc.	38%	26%
Non-Muslim Native: Kadazan, Murut, Iban, etc.	42%	46%
Chinese	20%	28%
	100%	100%

Sources: EconRep 1979-80; Census Reports

Table 2 Agriculture and Mining Production
('000 tonnes unless otherwise stated)

Commodity	1970	1980 (est)
Rubber	1,269	1,680
Palm-oil	431	2,300
Saw logs ('000 cu m.)	17,698	24,300
Sawn timber ('000 cu m.)	2,780	5,400
Tin	74	65
Rice		1,531
Pepper		40
Petroleum ('000 barrels p.d.)	18	317
Copra		865
Fresh pineapple		200
Cocoa	4	33

Source: EconRep 1979-80

Table 3 Rubber

PLANTED AREA ('000 ha)	1970	1978
Estates (40 ha and above)	647	588
Smallholdings	1,360	1,448
	2,007	2,036
Malaya		1,733
Sabah		106
Sarawak		197
		2,036
PRODUCTION ('000 tonnes)	1970	1978
Estates	621	666
Smallholdings	649	939
YIELD (kg/mature ha)		1978
Estates		1,380
Smallholdings		844

Source: ARBNM 1978

Table 4 Palm-Oil

PLANTED AREA ('000 ha)	1970	1975	1979
Malaya			
Estates (40 ha and above)	194	331	
Smallholdings	87	250	
	281	581	758
Sabah	38	58	64
Sarawak	1	15	31
Malaysia	**320**	**654**	**855**
PRODUCTION ('000 tonnes)	*1970*	*1975*	*1979*
Malaysia	**390**	**1,255**	**2,090**
Malaya			1,880
Sabah			177
Sarawak			31

Table 5 Malayan Tin Production

	1928	1937	1961	1978
PRODUCTION ('000 long tons)	65	75	56	63
METHOD (per cent of total)				
Dredging	30	48	53	32
Gravel-pump	45	38	34	54
Lode-mining	6	4	4	} 14
Other methods	19	10	9	
	100	100	100	100

Table 6 Malaysian Imports

($ million)

Category	1970 Value ($ m)	Per cent	1978 Value ($ m)	Per cent
Food, beverages, and tobacco	880	21	2,167	16
Raw materials	322	8	722	5
Mineral fuel	518	12	1,470	11
Animal and vegetable oils and fats	24	1	26	1
Chemicals	313	7	1,228	9
Manufactured goods	770	18	2,264	16
Machinery and transport equipment	1,197	28	4,946	36
Manufactured articles	200	5	724	5
Miscellaneous	66	2	142	1
	4,288	100	13,690	100

Source: EconRep 1979-80

Table 7 Malaysian Exports

($ million)

Category	1970 Value ($ m)	Per cent	1978 Value ($ m)	Per cent
Food, beverages, and tobacco	306	6	903	5
Raw materials	2,778	54	6,324	37
Mineral fuel	366	7	2,343	14
Animal and vegetable oils and fats	310	6	2,106	12
Chemicals	36	1	103	1
Manufactured goods	1,183	23	2,821	17
Machinery and transport equipment	84	2	1,820	11
Manufactured articles	43	1	496	3
Miscellaneous	58	1	138	1
	5,163	100	17,094	100

Source: EconRep 1979-80

Table 8 Employment

('000 persons)

Category	1970 Number ('000)	Per cent	1978 Number ('000)	Per cent
Agriculture, forestry, and fishing	1,776	53	1,973	44
Mining and quarrying	87	3	90	2
Manufacturing	301	9	587	13
Construction	91	3	197	4
Finance, insurance, and commerce	411	12	603	14
Transport, storage, and communication	133	4	208	5
Government services	398	12	622	14
Other services	143	4	214	5
	3,340	100	4,494	100

Source: EconRep 1979-80

Table 9 Education

SCHOOLS

Age Group	Numbers in age group in 1980 ('000 persons)	Estimated Enrolment in 1980 ('000 persons)
Primary (6 to 11)	1,748	1,683
Lower secondary (12 to 14)	888	604
Upper secondary (15 to 16)	558	181
Post-secondary (17 to 18)	474	33

UNIVERSITY AND OTHER TERTIARY EDUCATION

Type	1970		1975	
	Numbers	Malay per cent	Numbers	Malay per cent
Diploma and Certificate courses	3,457	83	13,547	85
Degree courses	8,148	40	14,254	57
Preliminary and pre-university courses	1,719	30	3,728	22
	13,324	50	31,529	65

Selected Bibliography

Special Official Reports (in date order)

Report of the Committee appointed by H. E. the High Commissioner to investigate the Squatter Problem (Federal Council Paper No 14/1950) ('the Squatter Committee').

Report of the Committee on Malay Education 1951 ('the Barnes Report').

Report of a Mission invited by the Federation Government to study the problem of the Education of Chinese in Malaya 1951 ('the Fenn Wu Report').

Report of the Constituency Delineation Commission 1954 ('the Merthyr Commission').

The Economic Development of Malaya: Report of a Mission organized by the International Bank for Reconstruction and Development 1955 ('the World Bank Report').

Final Report of the Rice Committee 1956.

Report of the Education Committee 1956 ('the Razak Report').

Report of the Committee on Malayanization of the Public Service 1956.

Report of the Federation of Malaya Constitutional Commission 1957 ('the Reid Report').

Report of the Education Review Committee 1960 ('the Rahman Talib Report').

Report on the Economic Aspects of Malaysia by a Mission of the Bank for International Reconstruction and Development 1965 ('the Rueff Report').

The May 13th Tragedy: National Operations Council 1969.

Report of the Higher Education Planning Committee 1967.

The Second Malaysia Plan (SMP) 1971.

Report of the Committee appointed by the National Operations Council to study campus life of students of the University of Malaya 1971 ('the Majid Ismail Report').

Economic Co-operation for ASEAN ('the Robinson Report') 1973.

The Third Malaysia Plan (TMP) 1976.

See also official reports by individuals listed under Del Tufo, Fermor, Mudie, Sastri, Vlieland, and Watson and Caine in the section on 'Books and Articles' below.

263

Annual and Other Periodic Reports and Official Correspondence and Papers

Annual Reports of British Residents, District Officers, and Heads of Departments.
Economic Reports of the Ministry of Finance Malaysia ('EconRep').
Annual Reports of the Bank Negara Malaysia (ARBNM).
Census Reports.
Proceedings of FMS Federal Council.
Despatches from the Governor SS to Secretary of State for the Colonies (PRO ref CO 273 etc.).

Newspapers and Journals

Contemporary Southeast Asia.
Far Eastern Economic Review (FEER).
Journal of the Malaysian Branch Royal Asiatic Society (JMBRAS).
Journal of Southeast Asian History (JSEAH) (1960-69).
Journal of Southeast Asian Studies (JSEAS).
Malaya (monthly magazine of British Association of Malaya).
Malayan Economic Journal (MEJ).
Malayan Historical Journal (MHJ).
Malayan Journal of Tropical Geography.
Sari Berita (official newssheet).
Selangor Journal (1892-97).
Straits Budget (weekly issue of *Straits Times*).
Straits Times.

Books and Articles

Abdullah Al-Qari bin Haji Salleh, 'To' Kenali; His Life and Influence' (in Roff (ed.) 1974).
Akashi, Y., 'Japanese Policy towards the Malayan Chinese 1941-1945' (*JSEAS* Vol. 1, No. 2, 1970).
Alatas, Syed Hussein, *The Sociology of Corruption* (1968).
_____ , *Modernization and Social Change in South-east Asia* (1972).
_____ , *The Myth of the Lazy Native* (1977).
Allen, G. C. and Donnithorne, A. G., *Western Enterprise in Indonesia and Malaya* (1957).
Allen, J. de V., 'The Colonial Office and the Malay States 1867-73' (*JMBRAS* XXXV, Pt 1, 1963).
_____ , 'Two Imperialists: a study of Sir Frank Swettenham and Sir Hugh Clifford' (*JMBRAS* XXXVII, Pt 1, 1964).
_____ , *The Malayan Union* (1967).
Allen, L., *Singapore 1941-42* (1977).

Andaya, B., 'The Indian *Saudagar Raja* in Traditional Malay Courts' (*JMBRAS,* LI, Pt 1, 1978).

———— , *Perak: The Abode of Grace: a Study of an Eighteenth Century Malay State* (1979).

Andaya, L. Y., *The Kingdom of Johor 1641-1728* (1975).

Arasaratnam, S., *The Indians in Malaysia and Singapore* (1970).

Barlow, C., *The Natural Rubber Industry: its Development, Technology and Economy in Malaysia* (1978).

Barr, P., *Taming the Jungle: the Men who made British Malaya* (1977).

Bastin, J. and Winks, R. W. (ed.), *Malaysia: Selected Historical Readings* (1966).

Bauer, P. T. 'The Economics of Planting Density in Rubber-Growing' (*Economica* 1946 and Silcock (ed.) 1961).

———— , *The Rubber Industry: a Study in Competition and Monopoly* (1948a).

———— , *A Report on a Visit to Rubber Growing Smallholdings in Malaya* (1948b).

———— , 'Malayan Rubber Policy' (*Political Science Quarterly* 1957 and Silcock (ed.) 1961).

Bedlington, S. S., *Malaysia and Singapore: the Building of New States* (1978).

Benham, F. C., 'The Rubber Industry' (*Economica* 1949 and Silcock (ed.) 1961).

Bird, I., *The Golden Chersonese and the Way Thither* (1883).

Blythe, W. L., 'Historical Sketch of Chinese Labour in Malaya' (*JMBRAS,* XX, Pt 1, 1947).

———— , *The Impact of Chinese Secret Societies in Malaya* (1969).

Bonney, R., *Kedah 1771-1821: the Search for Security and Independence* (1971).

Boyce, J. L., 'The British Eastern Exchange Banks: an Outline of the Main Factors affecting their Business up to 1914' (Cowan (ed.) 1964).

Brimmell, J. H., *Communism in Southeast Asia: a Political Analysis* (1959).

Brown, C. C. (trans.), '*Sejarah Melayu* or Malay Annals' (*JMBRAS* XXV, Pts 2-3, 1952).

Burgess, A., *The Malayan Trilogy: Time for a Tiger, The Enemy in the Blanket, Beds in the East* (1972).

Burns, P. L. (ed.), *Papers on Malay Subjects* (reprinted 1971).

Caine, S., 'Monetary Systems of the Colonies' (The *Banker,* 1950, and Silcock (ed.) 1961).

Chai Hon-Chan, *The Development of British Malaya 1896-1909* (1964).

Chapman, F. S., *The Jungle is Neutral* (1949).

Cheeseman, H. R., 'Education in Malaya 1900-1914' (*MJH,* Vol. 2, No. 1, 1955).

_____ , *Bibliography of Malaya* (1959).

Cheng Siok Hwa, 'The Rice Industry of Malaya: a Historical Survey' (*JMBRAS,* XLII, Pt 2, 1969).

Chew, E., 'British Intervention in Malaya: a Reconsideration' (*JSEAH,* Vol. 6, No. 1, 1965).

Chin Kee Onn, *Malaya Upside Down* (1946).

Chou, K. R., *Saving and Investment in Malaya* (1966).

Clodd, H. P., *Malaya's First British Pioneer: the Life of Francis Light* (1948).

Clutterbuck, R., *The Long, Long War: the Emergency in Malaya 1948-1960* (1967).

_____ , *Riot and Revolution in Singapore and Malaya 1945-63* (1973).

Coedes, C., *The Making of South East Asia* (trans. H. R. Wright) (1966).

Comber, L., *Chinese Secret Societies in Malaya: a Survey of the Triad Society from 1800 to 1900* (1959).

Cowan, C. D., *Nineteenth Century Malaya: the Origins of British Political Control* (1961).

Cowan, C. D. (ed.), *The Economic Development of South East Asia: Studies in Economic History and Political Economy* (1964).

Cowan, C. D. and Wolters, O. W. (ed.), *Southeast Asian History and Historiography: Essays presented to D.G.E. Hall* (1976).

Cunyngham-Brown, S., *The Traders: a Story of Britain's South East Asian Commercial Adventure* (1971).

Del Tufo, M. V., *Malaya: a Report on the 1947 Census of Population* (1949).

Djamour, J., *Malay Kinship and Marriage in Singapore* (1959).

Dobby, E.H.G., *Southeast Asia* (1950).

Drabble, J. H., *Rubber in Malaya 1876-1922: the Genesis of the Industry* (1973).

Eastham, J. U., 'Rationalization in the Tin Industry' (*Review of Economic Studies,* 1936, and Silcock (ed.), 1961).

Edwards, C. T., *Public Finances in Malaya and Singapore* (1970).

Emerson, R., *Malaysia: a Study in Direct and Indirect Rule* (1937, reprinted 1964).

Esman, M. J., *Administration and Development in Malaysia* (1964).

Evers, H. D. (ed.), *Modernization in Southeast Asia* (1973).

Fauconnier, H., *The Soul of Malaya* (trans. E. Sutton) (1931).

Fermor, L., *Report on the Mining Industry of Malaya* (1939).

Firth, R. W., *Malay Fishermen: their Peasant Economy* (1946: 2nd ed. (revised) 1966).

Fisher, C. A., *South-East Asia: a Social, Economic and Political Geography* (2nd ed. 1966).

Fitzgerald, C. P., *History of East Asia* (1966).

Freedman, M., *Chinese Family and Marriage in Singapore* (1957).

———— , *The Study of Chinese Society: Essays by Maurice Freedman* (ed. G. W. Skinner 1979).

Fryer, D. W., *Emerging Southeast Asia: a Study of Growth and Stagnation* (1970).

Fryer, D. W. and Jackson, J. C., *Indonesia* (1977).

Geoghegan, J., *Note on Emigration from India* (1973).

Ginsburg, H. and Roberts, C. F., *Malaya* (1958).

Goh Cheng Teik, *The May Thirteenth Incident and Democracy in Malaysia* (1971).

Goldman, M. F., 'Franco-British Rivalry over Siam 1896-1904' (*JSEAS* Vol. 3, No. 2, 1972).

Gould, J. W., *The United States and Malaysia* (1969).

Gullick, J. M., 'The Malay Administrator' (*Merdeka Outlook* Vol. 1, No. 1, 1957).

———— , *Indigenous Political Systems of Western Malaya* (1958).

———— , *Malaysia and its Neighbours* (1967).

———— , 'Syers and the Selangor Police Force 1875-1897' (*JMBRAS* LI, Pt 2, 1978).

———— , 'Isabella Bird's Visit to Malaya' (*JMBRAS* LI, Pt 2, 1979).

Gullick, J. M. and Hawkins, G., *Malayan Pioneers* (1958).

Hall, D.G.E., *A History of South-East Asia* (3rd ed. 1968).

Han Suyin, *And the Rain my Drink* (1956).

Hanrahan, G. Z., *The Communist Struggle in Malaya* (1971).

Harrisson, T., 'The Peoples of North and West Borneo' (Wang Gangwu (ed.) 1964).

Hodder, B. W., *Man in Malaya* (1959).

Hooker, M. B., *'Adat' Laws in Modern Malaya: Land Tenure, Traditional Government and Religion* (1972).

———— , *The Personal Laws of Malaysia: an Introduction* (1976).

Hooker, M. B. (ed.), *Readings in Malay 'Adat' Laws* (1970).

Husin Ali, S., *Social Stratification in 'Kampong' Bagan: a Study of Class, Status, Conflict, and Mobility in a Rural Malay Community* (1964).

———— , *Malay Peasant Society and Leadership* (1975).

Hyde, F. E., 'British Shipping Companies and South-East Asia 1860-1939' (Cowan (ed.) 1964).

———— , *Far-Eastern Trade 1860-1914* (1973).

Ibrahim Nik Mahmood, 'The To' Janggut Rebellion of 1915' (Roff (ed.) 1974).

Innes, E., *The Chersonese with the Gilding Off* (1885).

Irwin, G., *Nineteenth-Century Borneo: a Study of Diplomatic Rivalry* (1955).

Itagaki, Y., 'The Japanese Policy for Malaya under the Occupation' (Tregonning (ed.) 1962).

Jackson, J. C., *Planters and Speculators: Chinese and European Agricultural Enterprise in Malaya 1786-1921* (1968).

———— , *Sarawak: a Geographical Survey of a Developing State* (1968).

———— , 'Rice Cultivation in West Malaysia: Relationships between Culture History, Customary Practices, and Recent Developments' (*JMBRAS* XLV, Pt 2, 1972).

Jackson, R. N., *Immigrant Labour and the Development of Malaya 1786-1920* (1961).

———— , *Pickering: Protector of Chinese* (1965).

Jain, R. K., *South Indians on the Plantation Frontier in Malaya* (1970).

Jones, S. W., *Public Administration in Malaya* (1953).

Kanapathy, V., *The Malaysian Economy — Problems and Prospects* (1970).

Keith, A. N., *Land below the Wind* (1939).

Kessler, C. S., *Islam and Politics in a Malay State: Kelantan 1838-1969* (1978).

Khera, H. S., *The Oil-Palm Industry of Malaysia: an Economic Study* (1976).

Khoo Kay Kim, 'The Origin of British Administration in Malaya' (*JMBRAS* XXXIX, Pt 1, 1966).

———— , *The Western Malay States 1850-1873: the Effects of Development on Malay Politics* (1972).

———— , 'Malay Society 1874–1920s' (*JSEAS* Vol. 5, No. 2, 1974).

King, V. T. (ed.), *Essays on Borneo Societies* (1978).

Lee Kuan Yew, *The Battle for Merger* (1962).

Leifer, M., *The Philippine Claim to Sabah* (1968).

Lim Chong-Yah, *Economic Development of Modern Malaya* (1967).

Lim Teck Ghee, *Peasants: their Agricultural Economy in Colonial Malaya 1874-1941* (1977).

Loh Fook Seng, P., *The Malay States 1877–1895: Political Change and Social Policy* (1969).

McFadyean, A., *The History of Rubber Regulation 1934-43* (1944).

McGee, T. G., *The Urbanization Process in the Third World: Explorations in search of a theory* (1971).

McIntyre, D., 'British Intervention in Malaya' (*JSEAH* Vol. 2, No. 3, 1961).

Mackenzie, C., *Realms of Silver* (1954).

McNair, J.F.A., *Perak and the Malays 1878* (reprinted 1972).

———— , *Prisoners their own Warders* (1899).

Mahathir bin Mohamed, *The Malay Dilemma* (1970).

Majeed Mohamed Mackeen, *Contemporary Islamic Legal Organization in Malaya* (1969).

Majid bin Zainuddin, Haji A., *The Wandering Thoughts of a Dying Man: The Life and Times of Haji Abdul Majid bin Zainuddin* (ed. Roff) 1978.

Means, G. P., *Malaysian Politics* (1970).

Meilink-Roelofsz, M.A.P., *Asian Trade and European Influence in the Indonesian Archipelago between 1500 and about 1630* (1962).

Middlebrook, S. M., 'Yap Ah Loy' (*JMBRAS,* XXIV, Pt 2, 1951).

Miller, H., *Menace in Malaya* (1954).

———— , *Prince and Premier* (1959).

Mills, L. A., 'British Malaya 1824-1867' (*JMBRAS* III, Pt 2, 1925).

———— , *British Rule in Eastern Asia* (1942).

———— , *Malaya: a Political and Economic Appraisal* (1958).

Milne, R. S., *Government and Politics in Malaysia* (1967).

———— , 'The Politics of Malaysia's New Economic Policy' (*Pacific Affairs* Vol. 49, No. 2, 1976).

Milne, R. S. and Ratnam, K. J., 'Politics and Finance in Malaya' (*Journal of Commonwealth Studies* III, No. 3, 1965).

———— , *Malaysia — New States in a New Nation: Political Development of Sarawak and Sabah in Malaysia* (1974).

(See also Ratnam, K. J. and Milne, R. S.).

Mudie, R. F., Raeburn, J. R. and Marsh, B., *Report of the Mission of Inquiry into the Rubber Industry of Malaya* (1954).

Musolf, L. D. and Springer, J. F., *Malaysia's Parliamentary System: Representative Politics and Policy-Making in a Divided Society* (1979).

Ness, G. D., *Bureaucracy and Rural Development in Malaysia* (1967).

Newell, W. H., *Treacherous River: a Study of rural Chinese in north Malaya* (1962).

Ooi Jin Bee, 'Mining Landscapes of Kinta' (*Malayan Journal of Tropical Geography*, 1955, and Silcock (ed.) 1961).

Parkinson, C. N., *British Intervention in Malaya 1867-1877* (1960).

Parmer, J. N., *Colonial Labor Policy and Administration: History of Labor in the Rubber Plantation Industry c. 1910-1941* (1960).

Parry, M. L., 'The Fishing Methods of Kelantan and Trengganu' (*JMBRAS* XXVII, Pt 2, 1954).

Pringle, R., *Rajahs and Rebels: the Ibans of Sarawak under Brooke Rule 1841-1941* (1971).

Purcell, V., *The Chinese in Malaya* (1948).

———— , *China* (1962).

———— , *Malaya, Communist or Free?* (1954).

———— , *the Chinese in Southeast Asia* (2nd ed. 1965).

———— , *The Memoirs of a Malayan Official* (1965).

Puthucheary, J. J., *Ownership and Control in the Malayan Economy* (1960).

———— , James Puthucheary's Statement of Political Belief (in Lee Kuan Yew, 1962).

Rahman, Tunku Abdul, *May 13th — Before and After* (1969).

Ratnam, K. J., *Communalism and the Political Process in Malaya* (1965).

Ratnam, K. J. and Milne, R. S., *The Malayan Parliamentary Election of 1964* (1967).

Roff, W. R., *The Origins of Malay Nationalism* (1967).

———— , 'The Persatuan Melayu Selangor: an early Malay Political

Association' (*JSEAH* IX, No. 1, 1968).

———, 'The Origin and Early Years of the Majlis Ugama' (Roff (ed.) 1974).

Roff, W. R. (ed.), *Kelantan: Religion, Society and Politics in a Malay State* (1974).

(See also Majid bin Zainuddin.)

Rogers, M. L., *Sungai Raya: a socio-political study of a Malay rural community* (1976).

Rudner, M., 'The Draft Development Plan of the Federation of Malaya 1950-55' (*JSEAS* III, No. 1, 1972).

Runciman, S., *The White Rajahs* (1960).

Sadka, E., 'The State Councils of Perak and Selangor 1877-1895' (Tregonning (ed.) 1962).

———, *The Protected Malay States 1874-1895* (1968).

Sadka, E. (ed.), 'The Journal of Sir Hugh Low Perak 1877' (*JMBRAS* XXVII, Pt 4, 1954).

Sandhu, K. S., 'The Saga of the Malayan Squatter' (*JSEAH* Vol. 5, No. 1, 1964).

———, *Indians in Malaya: Immigration and Settlement 1786-1957* (1969).

Sastri, V.S.S., *Report on Conditions of Indian Labour in Malaya* (1937).

Shaharil Talib, Robert, 'The Trengganu Ruling Class in the Late Nineteenth Century' (*JMBRAS* L, Pt 2, 1977).

Sharom Ahmat, 'The Structure of the Economy of Kedah 1879-1905' (*JMBRAS* XLIII, Pt 2, 1977).

Sheppard, M. C. ff, 'A Short History of Trengganu' (*JMBRAS* XXII, Pt 3, 1949).

Shinohara, M., 'Japan's Strategies towards New Developments in the Economies of East and Southeast Asia' (*Contemporary Southeast Asia,* Vol. 1, No. 1, 1979).

Short, A., *The Communist Insurrection in Malaya 1948-1960* (1975).

Short, D. E. and Jackson, J. C., 'The Origins of an Irrigation Policy in Malaya: a review of development prior to the establishment of the Drainage and Irrigation Department' (*JMBRAS* XLIV, Pt 1, 1971).

Siew Nim Chee, 'The Federation Central Bank' (Silcock (ed.) 1961).

Silcock, T. H., *The Commonwealth Economy in Southeast Asia* (1959).

———, *Towards a Malayan Nation* (1961a).

———, '*Merdeka* in the Money Market' (in Silcock (ed.) 1961) (1961b).

Silcock, T. H. (ed.), *Readings in Malayan Economics* (1961).

Silcock, T. H. and Fisk, E. K. (ed.), *The Political Economy of Independent Malaya* (1963).

Silcock, T. H. and Ungku Aziz, *Nationalism in Malaya* (1950).

Simandjuntak, B., *Malayan Federalism 1945-1963* (1969).

Slimming, J., *Malaysia: Death of a Democracy* (1969).

Smith, T. E., *Population Growth in Malaya: a Survey of Recent Trends* (1952).

Soenarno, R., 'Malay Nationalism 1900-1945' (*JSEAH* Vol. 1, No. 1, 1960).

Soh Eng Lim, 'Tan Cheng Lock' (*JSEAH,* Vol. 1, No. 1, 1960).

Stenson, M. R., *Industrial Conflict in Malaya: Prelude to the Communist Revolt of 1948* (1970).

Stevenson, R., *Cultivators and Administrators: British Educational Policy towards the Malays 1875-1906* (1975).

Suffian bin Hashim, Tan Sri, *An Introduction to the Constitution of Malaysia* (1972).

Swettenham, F. A., *British Malaya* (1948) (revised).

Swift, M. G., 'The Accumulation of Capital in a Peasant Economy' (Silcock (ed.) 1961).

_____ , *Malay Peasant Society in Jelebu* (1965).

Tan Ee Leong, 'The Chinese Banks incorporated in Singapore and the Federation of Malaya' (*JMBRAS* XXVI, Pt 1, 1953 and Silcock (ed.) 1961).

Tham Seong Chee, 'Issues in Malaysian Education — Past, Present and Future' (*JSEAS* X, No. 2, 1979).

Thio, E., *British Policy in the Malay Peninsula 1880-1910* (1969).

T'ien Ju-K'ang, *The Chinese of Sarawak: a Study of Social Structure* 1953).

Tilman, R. O., *Bureaucratic Transition in Malaya* (1964).

Tregonning, K. G., *A History of Modern Sabah 1881-1963* (1965).

_____ , 'Tan Cheng Lock: A Malayan Nationalist' (*JSEAS* X, No. 1, 1979).

Tregonning, K. G. (ed.), *Papers on Malayan Subjects* (1962).

Turnbull, C. M., *The Straits Settlements 1826-67: Indian Presidency to Crown Colony* (1972).

Vasil, R. K., *Politics in a Plural Society* (1971).

Vlieland, C. A., *British Malaya: a Report on the 1931 Census* (1932).

Wales, H.G.Q., *The Malay Peninsula in Hindu Times* (1976).

Wang Gungwu, 'The Limits of Nanyang Chinese Nationalism 1912-1937' (Cowan and Wolters (ed.) 1976).

_____ , *The Chinese Minority in Southeast Asia* (1978).

_____ , 'China and the Region in relation to Chinese Minorities' (*Contemporary Southeast Asia* Vol. 1, No. 1, 1979).

Wang Gungwu (ed.), *Malaysia: a Survey* (1964).

Ward, A. B., *Rajah's Servant* (1966).

Watson, G. M. and Caine, S., *Report on the establishment of a Central Bank in Malaya* (1956).

Wilkinson, R. J., *Papers on Malay Subjects 1906-1924* (reprinted 1971).

_____ , *Malay-English Dictionary* (2nd ed. 1932).

_____ , 'The Malacca Sultanate' (*JMBRAS* XIII, Pt 2, 1935).

Wilson, P. J., *A Malay Village and Malaysia* (1967).

Winstedt, R. O., *Malaya and its History* (n.d.).

_____ , 'A History of Malaya' (*JMBRAS* XIII, Pt 1, 1935).

_____ , *The Malays: a Cultural History* (1947).

_____ , *Start from Alif, Count from One: an autobiographical Memoir* (1969).

Winzeler, R. L., 'The Social Organization of Islam in Kelantan' (Roff (ed.) 1974).

Wolters, O. W., *The Fall of Sri Vijaya in Malay History* (1970).

Wong, D.S.Y., *Tenure and Land Dealings in the Malay States* (1975).

Wong Hoy Kee and Gwee Yee Hean, *Perspectives: the Development of Education in Malaysia and Singapore* (1972).

Wong Lin Ken, *The Malayan Tin Industry to 1914* (1965).

Wright, A., *Twentieth Century Impressions of Malaya* (1908).

Wright, A. and Reid, T. H., *The Malay Peninsula* (1912).

Wurzburg, C. E., *Raffles of the Eastern Seas* (1954).

Yip Yat Hoong, *The Development of the Tin-Mining Industry of Malaya* (1969).

Yuen Choy Leng, 'The Japanese Community in Malaya before the Pacific War: its Genesis and Growth' (*JSEAS* IX, No. 2, 1978).

Zaharah binti Hj Mahmud, 'The Period and Nature of "Traditional" Settlement in the Malay Peninsula' (*JMBRAS* XLIII, Pt 2, 1970).

Abbreviations

ANRPC	Association of Natural Rubber-Producing Countries
ASA	Association of South Asian States
ASEAN	Association of South-East Asian Nations
BMA	British Military Administration
CDC	Commonwealth Development Corporation
CIAM	Central Indian Association of Malaya
DAP	Democratic Action Party
EMR	Extract of *Mukim* Register
EPF	Employees' Provident Fund
FAMA	Federal Agricultural Marketing Authority
FELCRA	National Land Consolidation and Rehabilitation Authority
FELDA	Federal Land Development Authority
FIDA	Federal Industrial Development Authority
FMS	Federated Malay States
FOA	Farmers' Organization Authority
GRM	*Gerakan Rakyat Malaysia* (Malaysian Peoples' Movement)
ICA	Industrial Co-ordination Act
IIL	Indian Independence League
IMP	Independence of Malaya Party
INA	Indian National Army
KMM	*Kesatuan Melayu Muda*
KMT	Kuo Min Tang
KRIS	*Kesatuan Ra'ayat Indonesia Semenanjong*
LPN	National *Padi* and Rice Authority (*Lembaga Padi Negara*)
MAJUIKAN	Fisheries Development Authority
MAJUTERNAK	Livestock Development Authority
MARA	*Majlis Amanah Rakyat* (Council of Peoples' Trust) formerly RIDA
MARDEC	Malaysian Rubber Development Corporation
MAS	Malaysian Airline System
MCA	Malaysian Chinese Association
MCP	Malayan Communist Party
MDU	Malayan Democratic Union
MIC	Malayan Indian Congress
MIDF	Malaysian Industrial Development Finance Berhad
MISC	Malaysian International Shipping Corporation
MNP	Malay Nationalist Party

MPAJA	Malayan Peoples' Anti-Japanese Army
MPU	Malayan Planning Unit
MRLA	Malayan Races' Liberation Army
NEP	New Economic Policy
NF	National Front
NOC	National Operations Council
OPEC	Organization of Petroleum Exporting Countries
PAP	Peoples' Action Party
PAS	*Partai Islam SeMalaysia* (see also PMIP)
PERNAS	*Perbadan Nasional Berhad*
PETRONAS	*Petroliam Nasional Berhad*
PKI	*Partai Kommunis Indonesia*
PMCJA	Pan-Malayan Council of Joint Action
PMIP	Pan-Malayan Islamic Party (see also PAS)
PN	*Partai Negara*
RIDA	Rural and Industrial Development Authority (now MARA)
RISDA	Rubber Industry Smallholders' Development Authority
RRI	Rubber Research Institute of Malaysia (also RRIM)
RSS	Ribbed Smoked Sheet (standard form of rubber)
SCBA	Straits Chinese British Association
SDC	Smallholders Development Centre
SEATO	South-East Asia Treaty Organization
SEDC	State Economic Development Corporation
SF	Socialist Front
SMP	Second Malaysia Plan 1971-75
SMR	Standard Malaysian Rubber (classified by technical properties)
SNAP	Sarawak National Party
SS	Straits Settlements
SUPP	Sarawak United Peoples' Party
TMP	Third Malaysia Plan 1976-80
UDA	Urban Development Authority
UMNO	United Malays' National Organization
UMS	Unfederated Malay States
VOC	Dutch East India Company (*Verenigde Oost-Indische Compagnie*)
$	Malaysian *ringgit* (or the dollar currency previously in use at the time referred to)

Glossary

'Adat. custom, tradition

Bendahara. chief minister (pre-colonial)

Berhad. limited (applied to companies with limited liability)

Bilal. mosque official (caller to prayer)

Bumiputra. son of the soil, indigenous

Dewan Negara. upper house of the federal parliament (Senate)

Dewan Rakyat. lower house of the federal parliament

Haji. title of a returned pilgrim to Mecca

Imam. mosque official (leader in prayer)

Istiadat. ceremonial (at court, etc.)

Kampung. village, hamlet

Keris. Malay dagger

Ketua kampung. village headman

Kongsi. Chinese association, society, or firm

Laksamana. admiral (pre-colonial)

Majlis. council

Mentri. minister

Mentri besar. chief minister (of a State government)

Merdeka. independence

Mukim. parish, sub-district

Nakhoda. master of a trading-ship

Negri (also *Negara*). State, country

Orang laut. seafarer (applied to certain Malay communities in pre-colonial period)

Penghulu. sub-district headman

Pondok. hut (applied to Islamic rural schools especially in Kelantan)

Rakyat (also *Ra'ayat*). person or people of the subject class in contrast to those of the upper or ruling class.

Shahbandar. harbourmaster (pre-colonial)

Temenggong. chief of police or military commander (pre-colonial)

Towkay (or *Tauke*). Chinese employer

Ugama. religion

Yam Tuan Muda. Under-king (applied to *Bugis* in eighteenth century)

Yang dipertuan Agong. Paramount Ruler, i.e., head of state of Malaysia

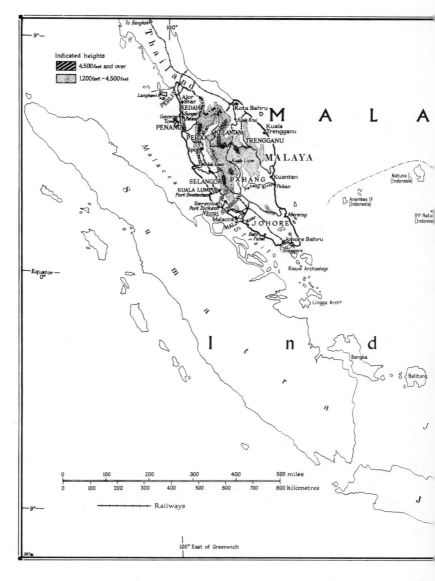

Indicated heights
4,500 feet and over
1,200 feet – 4,500 feet

100°

9°

Thailand

Langkawi I.

PERLIS

Alor
Star
KEDAH
Sungei
Patani
George
Town
PENANG
PERAK
Ipoh
Telok Anson

Kota Bahru

KELANTAN

Kuala
Krai

Kuala
Trengganu

TRENGGANU

M A L A

Kuala Lipis

MALAYA

SELANGOR
KUALA LUMPUR
Port Swettenham
Seremban
Port Dickson
NEGRI
Malacca
MAL

PAHANG
Pahang River

Kuantan

Pekan

Natuna I.
(Indonesia)

Anambas Is.
(Indonesia)

Sth Natu
(Indones

Malacca

S u m

JOHORE

Kuala
Batu
Pahat

Mersing

Johore Bahru
Singapore

Riouw Archipelago

Strait

Equator
0°

a t r a

Lingga Arch°

I   n   d

Bangka

Belitung

Bangka

r

a

J

9°

0   100   200   300   400   500 miles
0   100   200   300   400   500   600   700   800 kilometres

Railways

J

100° East of Greenwich

Malaysia and Its Neighbours

Palawan
(Philippine Is)

120° Philippine
Islands

Mindanao 9°

Balabac Strait

Sulu Sea

Kudat

S I A

A

Kota Kinabalu
(Jesselton)

Mt.
Kinabalu
13,455 Ft.

Sandakan

Brunei

S A B A H

Beaufort

Sulu Archipelago

Miri   Seria

Tawau

Sulu

S A R A W A

Celebes Sea

tuk   Sibu

Rajang River

ching

S

B   o   r   n   e   o

Equator
0°

Strait of Makasar

n   e   s   i   a

C e l e b e s

S e a

Flores   Sea

9°

v   a

120°

Index

Index

Index